FLYING BOAT PILOT IN WAR AND PEACE

Dedication

I met Edna Watson when I was a young boy, on a visit to Bermuda with my family. At the time, I knew that this lady had been an important figure in my father's life – but many years were to pass before I truly understood. On a bitter windswept night in January 1939, the Imperial Airways flying boat RMA *Cavalier,* of which my father was captain, came down in the empty wastes of the North Atlantic Ocean – and it was there that Edna had saved my father's life. I therefore owe her my life also. I know my father would have agreed that this book should be dedicated to her.

FLYING BOAT PILOT IN WAR AND PEACE

Disaster and Survival: The Extraordinary Life of
Captain M.J.R. 'Roly' Alderson

Aviation Pioneer in the Golden Age of Commercial Flight

'A Very Private Man'

Mark Alderson

AIR WORLD

AIR WORLD

FLYING BOAT PILOT IN WAR AND PEACE
Disaster and Survival: The Extraordinary Life of
Captain M.J.R. 'Roly' Alderson

First published in Great Britain in 2024 by
Air World
An imprint of
Pen & Sword Books Ltd
Yorkshire – Philadelphia

ISBN 978 1 03611 204 2

Typeset by SJmagic DESIGN SERVICES, India.

Printed and bound in the UK by CPI Group (UK) Ltd.

Pen & Sword Books Limited incorporates the imprints of After the Battle, Atlas, Archaeology, Aviation, Discovery, Family History, Fiction, History, Maritime, Military, Military Classics, Politics, Select, Transport, True Crime, Air World, Frontline Publishing, Leo Cooper, Remember When, Seaforth Publishing, The Praetorian Press, Wharncliffe Local History, Wharncliffe Transport, Wharncliffe True Crime and White Owl.

For a complete list of Pen & Sword titles please contact

PEN & SWORD BOOKS LIMITED
George House, Units 12 & 13, Beevor Street, Off Pontefract Road,
Barnsley, South Yorkshire, S71 1HN, England
E-mail: enquiries@pen-and-sword.co.uk
Website: www.pen-and-sword.co.uk

or

PEN AND SWORD BOOKS
1950 Lawrence Rd, Havertown, PA 19083, USA
E-mail: uspen-and-sword@casematepublishers.com
Website: www.penandswordbooks.com

MIX
Paper | Supporting
responsible forestry
FSC® C013604

Contents

Author's Note

For as long as I could remember, I was aware that my father had 'flown boats'. To a young boy, this was as mysterious as it was fascinating – but he revealed little of his aviating past, either to his family or, for that matter, to anyone else. Until the very last years of his life my father was a closed book.

I did not intend to write this story. The more I delved, the more irresistible became the tale – and then, one evening over a bottle of wine, I had my arm twisted. So now, exactly three decades after my dad took off on his very last journey, the layers of mystery have been peeled away, revealing the extraordinary story of this very private man.

Acknowledgements

I owe a debt of thanks to those who have been part of this journey, and most especially to members of the Alderson family who have been a mine of invaluable information – notably my dear mother Jo (now sadly deceased) and my brother Kit. I have had the privilege of unfettered access to my father's enduring legacy of letters, papers, photographs, voice recordings and ephemera, and in particular his fascinating and punctilious pilot's flight logbooks dating back to 1927.

I would also like to thank Tom Burgis and Garry Thompson, who let the genie (and the wine) out of the bottle; Tim Godfray, erstwhile CEO of The Booksellers Association, my trusted friend for sixty years, who kindly agreed to review the first draft and offered unwavering support throughout; Liz Godfray, Tim's wife, for her professional editing skills; and finally, my wife Debbie and daughters Harriet, Alice and Izzy for their encouragement and support during the gestation of this book.

Mark Alderson
2024

Prologue

23:00 hours, 21 January 1939 – Atlantic Ocean, 285 miles south-east of New York City, USA.

Searchlights slice through the black night, scanning the ragged waves, as the great ship ploughs through the angry winter seas of the North Atlantic.

Ten hours earlier, Captain Frank H. Spurr, Master of the American tanker *Esso Baytown*, had responded to an SOS relayed by the US Coastguard. An Imperial Airways flying boat, en route from New York to Bermuda, had ditched in the sea due to engine failure. The last message, at 13:13, had simply stated 'Sinking' – nothing more had been heard. The vessel is now closing in on the last known position of the aircraft, when another message comes through the R/T on the bridge: 'We think you have just passed their estimated position. Retrace your route.'

The great ship turns slowly through 180 degrees, back onto a reciprocal course. Just minutes later, to the astonishment of the deck crew, faint sounds of shouting are heard through the cacophony of wind and spray. The searchlights swing round, and through the darkness their shafts of light pick out two, then four waving arms – and then a small group of bobbing heads between the waves.

Miraculously, after nearly eleven hours in the water, ten survivors from the doomed flying boat are plucked from the wild North Atlantic seas. The RMA *Cavalier* had flown her last journey – and thus entered the history books as the first scheduled passenger airliner to come down in mid-ocean. Three souls lost, ten souls saved….

But more of this later. We have gone ahead of our story, and Roly would have hated that … so here follows the true account of the life of Captain M.J.R. 'Roly' Alderson, commander of the *Cavalier*.

Introduction

Some of what you are about to read may sound improbable, some even perhaps downright unbelievable – but this is the true life journey of a quiet, retiring young man who had no formal education after the age of 11, and yet who, parentless by 18, gained entry to the hallowed halls of Cambridge University, and went on to become one of the unsung pioneers of the Golden Age of Aviation.

There are echoes of Biggles and Finch-Hatton, of Douglas Bader and Beryl Markham. One can almost smell the leather and fabric of the early biplanes, the stench of castor oil from the thrumming radial engines. One is transported back in time, to the elegance and opulent luxury of the huge silver Imperial Airways flying boats, and to the dangers faced by these transatlantic pilots during the Second World War.

This is a tale not simply of the extraordinary life of one of the true pioneers of modern commercial air travel – it is also a yarn of romance, of personal tragedy borne with stoicism, and of one man's dogged devotion to his chosen profession.

Unlike many pilots of the 1930s who revelled in their hero status amid the adulation of the public, Roly Alderson shunned the limelight, and was loath to talk about his work. In January 1939, as commander of the doomed C-Class Imperial Airways flying boat *Cavalier* – which plunged into the North Atlantic between New York and Bermuda with the loss of three lives – he found himself in front of the world's media amid vituperative accusations of incompetence and the threat of litigation. When the full truth was revealed by the official enquiry, Alderson was more than merely exonerated – he was praised for his professionalism and courage. Overnight, the lawsuits were consigned to history, and he was hailed a hero, becoming the darling of Bermudian society, with his name inscribed on the State of New York's Chamber of Commerce Roll of Honour.

The story propels one through the war years – there is adventure off North Africa, intrigue in Lisbon, personal tragedy at home – and romance. More drama follows as Comets fall from the sky…

This is not simply the chronicle of a fascinating life – it is an important piece of social history, part of the jigsaw that defines the dying years of the British Empire, and the beginnings of globalisation. From the frail aircraft of the 1920s, through the glamour and glitz of the flying boat era, to the coming of age of commercial jet travel in the 1960s, and the pinnacle of technical achievement that was Concorde – this story of one man's journey spans it all.

How this early aviator survived while so many of his colleagues perished may sometimes defy belief, and yet often he made his own luck. So full of action and high adventure is the narrative, the reader could be forgiven for imagining this to be a work of fiction, from the pen, perhaps, of Saint-Exupéry, Shute or Monsarrat.

But no – this is the Real McCoy. This is an epic tale; it is where fact trumps fiction – and it is a story that was very nearly never told, because Roly Alderson was, after all, 'A Very Private Man'.

Chapter 1

Early Days (1907–1926)

From his very first day on this earth, the life of Marmaduke Jonathan Rowland Alderson was destined to be unconventional, weird even. He was born – or so he was led to believe – in St Leonard's-on-Sea, on either 12 or 18 August 1907. No one seemed quite sure, so they simply gave him a birthweek. As for his given name, it was quickly abandoned – they just called him Roly.

R.A. with elder sister
Dorothy, Ceylon c.1912.
(*Author's collection*)

His father owned tea and rubber estates in Ceylon (now Sri Lanka); he was also a major in the Ceylon Mounted Rifles. He had shipped over with his brother from Ceylon to South Africa to fight in the Boer War, returning unscathed in 1902 – but his brother didn't make it; he lost his life at Trenanfontein. When little more than a toddler, Roly made the long sea voyage out with his mother and siblings, to join the major in Ceylon.

In 1912 a little sister was born, but she failed to thrive and died at the age of just 6 months. The family led a typical planter's life until the outbreak of the First World War, when they returned to England to answer the Call to Arms. The major went to the Western Front, leaving the family at home at Tickhill, near Doncaster.

As soon as his brother Guy (christened Marmaduke Guy, but just called Guy), had finished his education at Wellington College – where he had designed and built a timber-framed four-wheeled 'cyclecar' – Guy was sent straight out to Ceylon to attend to the family interests, in place of his father who was still away fighting in France.

Meanwhile, it was not long before Roly was packed off to boarding school in Sussex – and it was while he was here that he was bludgeoned by the first of many family tragedies. His brother Dixwell

R.A.'s elder brother Guy (aged 15) scribbled this design for a 'cyclecar' while still at school…. (*Author's collection*)

…and the finished article: R.A.'s brother's 'cyclecar', in the grounds of Wellington College, c.1915. (*Author's collection*)

Ian (but predictably called Ian), had been to Dartmouth Royal Naval College and, on 1 January 1916, was posted to HMS *Conqueror* as a midshipman – not yet 16 years old. He very soon saw action with the Grand Fleet at the Battle of Jutland. On 15 December the following year, he apparently sustained a grave head injury in a gun turret accident, and official records state that he died a few hours later, at the age of 17, on the fleet hospital ship HMS *China*. His father received a telegram of condolence direct from Buckingham Palace: 'The King and Queen deeply regret the loss of your son in the service of his country. Their Majesties truly sympathise with you in your sorrow.' (Why Their Majesties should concern themselves with the death of a midshipman – the lowest officer rank in the Royal Navy – is very strange.)[1]

Some eighteen months later, while still at boarding school, Roly developed a tumour beneath his jawline; he underwent radical surgery and was forced to return home to Tickhill.

It was during this period at home that Roly's interest in aviation was first piqued. It was on the frosty morning of Wednesday, 12 November

Ross Smith's Vickers Vimy Bomber preparing to depart Hounslow, Britain, for Australia on their record-breaking flight, 12 November 1919. (*Author's collection*)

Ross Smith's Vickers Vimy Bomber *G-EAOU* (fondly known by the crew as *'God 'Elp All Of Us'*) with engines running, preparing to depart for Australia, 12 November 1919. (*Author's collection*)

1919 that the huge First World War Vickers Vimy Rolls Bombing Aeroplane, piloted by Captain Ross Smith, took off from Hounslow on its record-breaking flight from Great Britain to Australia. This was an event that received worldwide publicity at the time, and it was a 'lightbulb moment' for young Roly – he decided there and then that he was going to fly.

Meanwhile, the health of Roly's mother, Ethel, was declining. She had always been of a somewhat delicate constitution, and her health had not fared well in the sultry climate of Ceylon. Her condition became more serious, and she passed away on 28 February 1920, at the age of just 48. Roly was still only 12 years old.

Shortly after the death of his mother, his father George (christened Marmaduke Jonathan George) decided to move the family away from Tickhill, and they settled near the village of Welsh Frankton in Shropshire.

Gannow Hill was a rambling, spooky-looking Victorian pile in the Gothic manner, with a substantial courtyard and complete – as Roly's luck would have it – with a blacksmith's forge. His father owned a Hansa-Lloyd motor car, which he had brought back with him from Ceylon and,

Gannow Hill, Welsh Frankton, Shropshire: R.A.'s home 1920–1926, where he restored the Bradbury and then built the *Bentbeam*. (*Author's collection*)

on account of his ill-health (he had been suffering from recurring bouts of malaria for years) Roly was put in charge of both maintenance and chauffeuring – at just 12 years old. Fortunately, his logical brain took to this responsibility: it was the beginning of a love affair with all things mechanical, which remained with him throughout his life.

Roly made the move to Gannow with his two remaining siblings – a sister Dorothy (really Augusta Dorothy Josephine Grace), now aged 14, and younger brother Gerald, just 10. (By the time he had come along, they had apparently run out of absurdly long family names, so he was christened Gerald Aubrey.)

Young Roly, like his brother Guy, was now developing a taste for engineering, and as soon as he arrived at Gannow he embarked on the restoration of an abandoned belt-driven Bradbury motorcycle of the Edwardian era.

This project was duly completed, whereupon – under the watchful eye of Gannow's resident blacksmith – he started work on constructing a three-wheeled motor vehicle from scratch.

Due to Roly's medical issues he remained at home, his father employing a part-time governess in an attempt to plug the educational gap. The regime suited young Roly well, allowing him sufficient freedom

A 3.5hp Bradbury belt-driven motorcycle c.1909 – similar to the one restored by R.A. 1920–1921.

to develop his interest in metalwork and motors. The three-wheeler made steady progress, and by 1923 it was sporting bright aluminium bodywork and a direct-drive chain-driven 10hp twin-cylinder J.A.P. engine. Unofficially, the little car could be seen in the narrow lanes around Welsh Frankton over the next few months – for testing purposes only, of course. The *Bentbeam* – so called because it shared features of both Sunbeam and Bentley – was first road-registered on 31 July 1924 as NT 4830, in time for Roly's seventeenth birth-week.

On 20 July 1925 – just three weeks (or maybe four, depending on his actual birthday) before Roly turned 18 – tragedy struck yet again. His father George, at just 60 years old, died suddenly. This was a huge hammer blow to the children, now left orphaned at Gannow. As the oldest at 25, Guy was immediately recalled from Ceylon in order to take control of the situation – and, indeed, to step up *in loco parentis* to his three younger siblings.

Probate was granted in September, and under the terms of George Alderson's will, the bulk of his estate was left to his eldest son Guy, daughter Dorothy and his deceased wife's brother. Strangely, no provision had been made for Roly and Gerald, so it fell to Guy to handle their immediate needs.

The *Bentbeam*'s first 'Licence for a Mechanically Propelled Vehicle', 31 July 1924. (*Author's collection*)

Over the following months, Guy wrestled with future planning for his younger siblings. Dorothy had married the previous year, but Roly and Gerald would be homeless, as Gannow Hill was to be sold. Gerald was given into the care of an uncle living on the Isle of Man but Roly, having just turned 18, was altogether another matter.

The penniless Roly's unconventional upbringing and limited education – academically at least – had ill-prepared him for life in the outside world. Guy, in a masterstroke of compassionate and level-headed wisdom, decided that Roly should complete his education by studying engineering at Cambridge University. There was, however, one major stumbling block: Roly had no academic qualifications with which to support his application to one of the oldest and finest universities in the world.

Guy was undaunted: he arranged for his little brother to be privately tutored at Cambridge in order to reach the academic standard necessary for admission. Guy also found some modest lodgings for his young brother.

So, on a sunny day in June 1926 – it had to be sunny, as the Bentbeam was completely open to the elements – Roly packed a bag with some clothes and one or two treasured belongings and stowed them in the passenger seat of the aluminium three-wheeler. On top of the bag, he carefully placed a single memento from his childhood home: an ornate enamelled carriage clock.[2] Young Roly started the little vehicle and (we surmise) with a brief valedictory wave to his brother, drove out of Gannow's cobbled courtyard for the last time, and turned to the southeast on the 160-mile journey to Cambridge, and a new life.

Chapter 2

Catz, Bentleys, Biplanes (1926–1930)

June 1926 – And so it was that young Rowland – Roly to close family and friends – drove through the gates of the historic city of Cambridge, where the famous university had been established for over 700 years, in his little home-built Bentbeam. One can only imagine what effect such a daunting new world must have had on this callow youth, still only 18 years old.

It was not long before Alderson had his head buried in books, under the gimlet eye of his private tutor. His fees were being paid for by Guy, as were his lodgings, which were close to the university.

By September, student Alderson was ready to take the Cambridge entrance examinations, and on 22 October 1926 he formally matriculated, having been admitted to Saint Catherine's College – fondly known as *Catz* by the undergraduates – to study engineering. Alderson proved to be a natural at his chosen subject; he took to it like a duck takes to water. His logical and mathematical brain, together with an inborn aptitude for precision and detail, lent itself ideally to this area of study. His lack of any formal secondary education, however, proved to be a considerable handicap, and Roly was very aware that he must work hard over the next three years if he was to emerge with a degree.

R.A., Cambridge University undergraduate, c.1926/1927. (*Author's collection*)

R.A. at the helm, c.1929. Seamanship skills would prove useful later as a flying boat pilot. (*Author's collection*)

As was common practice in those days, Alderson resided in college accommodation, at Number 70, Trumpington Street, throughout his time at Cambridge. When not studying, much of his spare time was taken up in employing his already keenly developed skills in maintaining the automobiles of several wealthier students, who were more than happy to pay him handsomely for his services.

It was not long before Alderson discovered another passion – flying. In the closing weeks of 1927, having satisfactorily completed his first year of Engineering Class 1 studies, he joined the select band of university students who were proud to form the ranks of the Cambridge University Air Squadron. Indeed, as Roly recalled many years later, 'it became something which was very much coveted'.[1]

Oxford and Cambridge University air squadrons were constituted in 1925 – the first two university squadrons in the country. By 1928 the CUAS had a nominal membership of some seventy-five, although the small cohort of regular flyers consisted of barely a third of that number.

Roly took to the air on his first training flight at Duxford Aerodrome on Tuesday, 8 November 1927 – less than six months after Charles Lindberg had made history by completing the very first non-stop solo flight across the Atlantic in the one-off Ryan NYP monoplane, the *Spirit of St Louis*.

The keen new recruit took to the skies in a wood and canvas Avro Lynx biplane training aircraft,[2] registered *J8527*, under the tutelage of Flight Lieutenant French. This brief experience in the air was a turning point in Roly's life: he had discovered his true métier. As it transpired, these were to be the first 35 minutes of over 10,000 hours in the air for this fledgling aviator.

This was an age of amazing pioneering feats in private aviation. On 22 February 1928, the young student pilot was in the air on his eighth trip aloft, in Lynx *J8713,* with instructor Flight Officer Hordman. On that very day, thousands of miles away in Darwin, Herbert John Louis 'Bert' Hinkler, had just arrived in Australia in his Avro 581 Avian *G-EBOV*, achieving the first solo flight between England and Australia in just over fifteen days.

Avro Lynx biplane trainer *F.8713*, in which R.A. first flew solo, 4 July 1928. (*Aeroplane Monthly*)

Hinkler was an extraordinary aviator – he even competed in the Schneider Trophy race, as well as notching up numerous other flying firsts. Sadly, like many of these early pioneers of the skies, he did not grow old. He was killed on 7 January 1933 when his de Havilland Puss Moth crashed into the mountains of Tuscany, on yet another Australia record attempt.

Young Alderson flew regularly over the next six months out of Duxford Aerodrome, a few miles from Cambridge – a short trip in his little home-built Bentbeam. This airfield, constructed in 1917 with the help of German prisoners of war, had been the base of the Royal Flying Corps, and was home to a squadron of First World War Bristol Fighters – exciting stuff to a budding airman. On Sunday, 24 June, now with some seven hours under instruction in his logbook, he arrived with a handful of other student pilots at the wartime airfield of Old Sarum, just a couple of miles from Salisbury in Wiltshire. This airbase was home to 16 Squadron, which was also equipped with Bristol Fighters. The summer term at Cambridge had just finished, and this fortunate contingent were to spend the next two weeks at RAF Old Sarum, going through the rigmarole of a concentrated regime of instruction, both in the classroom and in the air. This suited young Alderson well, and he was able to fly almost daily – and sometimes fitting in three flights in a single day. On the Monday, and again on Tuesday, he flew with instructor Flying Officer Hitchins in two different Lynx biplanes, and in yet another on his first flight of the day on Wednesday.

His second flight out of Old Sarum on Wednesday, 27 June 1928 – exactly ten days after Amelia Earhart became the first woman to fly across the Atlantic – was a special one: he found himself in the cockpit of a Bristol F2B Fighter, No. *7650*.

The F2B was a two-seater biplane fighter and reconnaissance aircraft and was, without doubt, one of the most important and successful British designs to serve during the First World War. It was equipped with a 12-cylinder 275hp Rolls-Royce engine and was capable of 125mph – much faster and more powerful than the Lynx. On this occasion, at the controls in the rear seat was Flight Lieutenant Goddard,[3] and it seems that Roly was in good hands: Goddard was already a seasoned pilot when, at the age of 28, he was appointed adjutant to CUAS on its inception in 1925.

Goddard and Alderson flew out from Old Sarum on a south-easterly course, down to the coast and out across the Solent to the Isle of Wight.

R.A. in Bristol F2B Fighter No. *7650*, 27 June 1928. (*Author's collection*)

They took photographs, and it was an opportunity for young Alderson to get to grips with the intricacies of cross-country flying. They landed back at Old Sarum after sixty-five minutes in the air – his longest flight so far. The following day he was in the air again – twice, this time with

Flying Officer Kennedy in Lynx *J8561*. After a local flight of forty minutes, they took off for Worthy Down, another First World War RAF Station, 3 miles north of Winchester, on a seventy-minute round trip.

Then, on their tenth day at the airfield, with a total of just fourteen hours and fifty-five minutes in Alderson's logbook, Flight Lieutenant French deemed that this young aviator – still just 20 years old – was ready to go solo. Alderson took to the air, alone in the cockpit for the first time, on 4 July 1928 in Lynx *J8713*; the flight lasted fifteen minutes. (It appears to have gone without a hitch, as there were no notes in the 'Remarks' column of his logbook entry!)

It would seem that Flight Lieutenant French was now sufficiently confident in Alderson's piloting skills, for the day after that first solo flight, French settled himself into the passenger seat of *J8738*, en route for Netheravon, the home of No. 1 Training School. They landed safely back at Old Sarum after a fifty-minute flight – the first time Alderson had flown as pilot-in-command with a passenger. Flight Lieutenant French

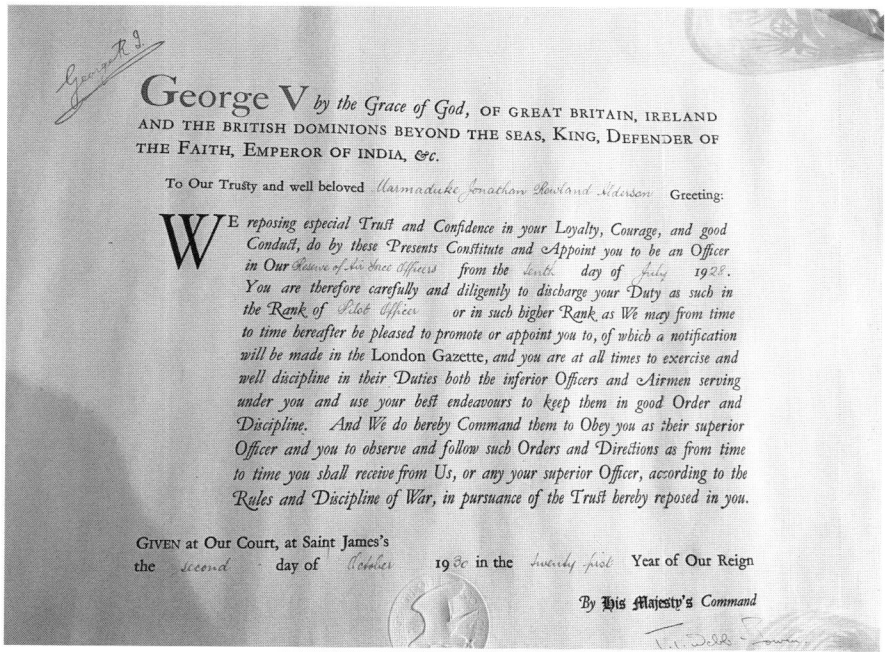

R.A.'s official appointment as a pilot officer in the Reserve of Air Force Officers from 10 July 1928 (2 October 1930). (*Author's collection*)

did not know it, of course, but he would be the first of many thousands of passengers that Alderson was to carry over the following decades.

Five days later, the young pilot was appointed – by the Command of His Majesty George V – as an 'Officer in the Reserve of Air Force Officers'.

It happened that the *Flight*[4] magazine correspondent, Major F.A. de V. Robertson, visited Cambridge UAS during their annual camp at Old Sarum that year – and in the article he wrote following his visit he described the training conducted at Cambridge:

> There is a ground-training centre at Fen causeway, near the engineering laboratories. There instruction is given in aircraft, engines, wireless, photography, navigation, armament, and instruments. A small wind tunnel is installed, and there is also a research laboratory. In this matter the squadron is giving active help to the University, for the Chair of Aeronautics is not equipped with a laboratory, and Professor Melville Jones uses that of the squadron of which he is an honorary member. A lecture room is also provided, which is fitted up as a reading room and aeronautical library, and members can get light refreshments there. Outside authorities give lectures there usually once a fortnight, and members are expected to attend these. Flying training is carried out at Duxford, about nine miles away, on four afternoons a week during term time. The usual attendance of members is about 10 a day. During term time, no member of the University who is in statu pupillari is allowed to fly solo unless he is a qualified pilot. Quite a number of members have, however, earned their 'tickets', and one, at least, is the owner of a DH 53.

Praise indeed for the quality of the pilot training afforded to the CUAS members.

On one of these occasions while with the University Air Squadron, the young pilot officer was honoured to be introduced to Sir Hugh Trenchard, Chief of the Air Staff. Trenchard had conceived the idea of a university air officer training corps, a sort of Territorial Army for the RAF, and was involved in the creation of the university air squadrons at Cambridge and then at Oxford in October 1925. Young Alderson evidently made an impression on Trenchard, as in August 1928 he received a gift in the post – direct from Trenchard at the Air Ministry Office in London – a file on the Vickers Vimy Bomber, *G-EAOU* (known affectionately by the crew as 'God 'Elp All Of Us'), which had won the £10,000 prize for the fastest flight from England to Australia in 1919 – the very same aircraft which had fired young Roly's imagination when just a boy of 12. The file contained a collection of first-proof Vickers photographs of the machine at Hounslow just prior to departure, and the original 'flimsies' of the telegrams sent back by Ross Smith as they progressed across Europe.

Meanwhile, back at Cambridge, Roly's student life continued on its designated trajectory. He applied himself to his engineering coursework – which fortunately included aeronautics – and continued to fly when he could, while saving every penny from his car servicing exploits.

The faithful old direct-drive Bentbeam was always kept in trim and roadworthy condition, and was subject to steady technical improvement – including the designing and fitting of a clutch, which Roly had fashioned from two frying pans converted for the purpose by removing the handles and lining them with cork.

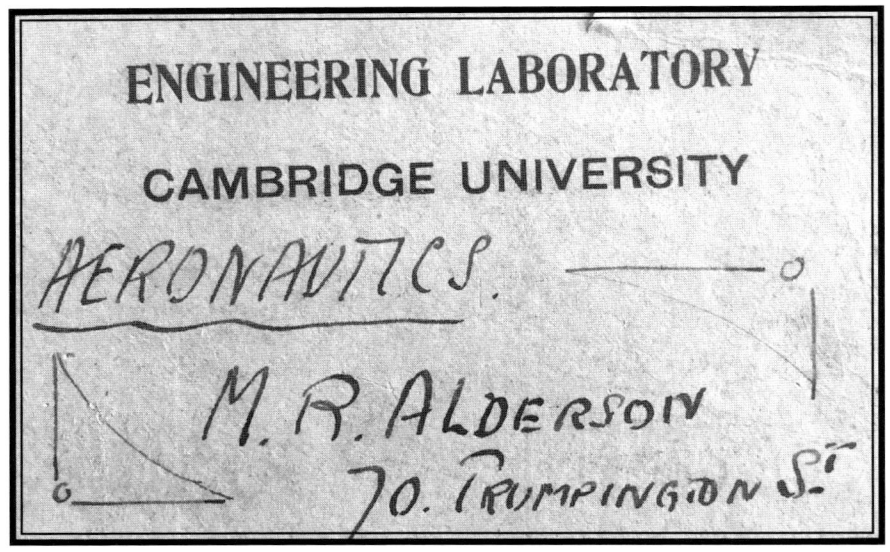

One of student Roly Alderson's *Aeronautics* notebooks. (*Author's collection*)

Young Roly, however, had an engineer's natural hankering for more performance, and by the spring of 1928 he was able to purchase his heart's desire: nothing less than a 1923 3-litre Bentley. He was still only 20. He was young, he was single, and he was single-minded – and, of course, he wanted to race his Bentley. His first competition with *CD 8335* was at Shelsey Walsh, and then at the Cambridge University Hill Climb at Branches Park. The following season he competed at Skegness Motor Races, held on the beach, where he won several trophies.

He was assisted in the preparation of the Bentley's engine at these events by Senior Proctor Frederick Dykes, who had long held a lectureship in engineering at the university. Alongside being an academic, Dykes was past president and now secretary of the University Automobile Club, hence the practical expertise. Dykes must have recognised in Alderson a like-minded and very determined young man and, judging from the results, it seems to have been a mutually enjoyable and successful partnership.

Roly was delighted when, on 2 November 1928, his younger brother Gerald gained a place at Cambridge, joining him at *Catz*. Gerald was

R.A. competing at Shelsey Walsh in his 3-litre Bentley *CD 8335*, 1928. (*Author's collection*)

At the Cambridge University Hill Climb, Branches Park. (Author's collection, Bentley Drivers' Club Archives)

Skegness Motor Races 1929 (R.A.'s Bentley in second place). (*Author's collection*)

academically less focused than his brother – first studying French and then English, and finally graduating in law – but he shared Roly's interest in flying.

Back once more at Duxford Airfield, Roly continued to build steadily upon his flying experience on both the Lynx and the Bristol Fighter – two hours ten minutes in the Michaelmas term of 1928, three hours fifteen minutes in the Lent term of 1929, five hours forty minutes in the summer term.

Although the training was intense, and a serious endeavour not to be undertaken lightly, there were inevitably some amusing incidents. One of Roly's colleagues in the University Air Squadron took a little detour on one of his early solo cross-country flights. He flew low over his family home at Inkpen, near Hungerford, throwing out a message inside a cigarette packet (perhaps requesting a large gin-and-pink on his return?) which landed on the lawn as he roared by just above the treetops – or so he thought. He duly returned to Duxford, believing he had got away with his detour undetected. Unfortunately for him, however, he was unaware that the top of a fir tree from the curtilage of the family garden was now firmly lodged in his undercarriage. On landing, it was clear to the adjutant that he had not adhered to his flight plan, and the unfortunate young would-be aviator – a certain Henry Usborne Esquire – was summarily dismissed from the squadron.

On 15 June 1929 Marmaduke Jonathan Rowland Alderson graduated with a BA in Engineering. He had successfully completed his degree, and thus his days at Cambridge drew to a close. Roly had a nice new degree in one pocket, and a private pilot's licence in the other.

A month after his graduation, he was once more back at Old Sarum for the CUAS Annual Attachment. Between Monday, 15 and Friday, 26 July, he logged some twenty hours, almost exclusively on Bristol Fighters. In these two weeks, he ventured to Yeovil, Farnborough, and as far as Filton (Bristol), where the Bristol Aircraft Company ran a Reserve Flying School. Almost all of these flights were undertaken solo. The Annual Attachment total was signed off in Roly's logbook in the usual way: 'Flight Lieutenant French, Chief Flying Instructor, C.U.A.S. Old Sarum', and he was officially awarded his Pilot's Wings on 6 August 1929.

This was an exciting era to be entering the world of aviation, and often it was women who were leading the way. Just four days earlier

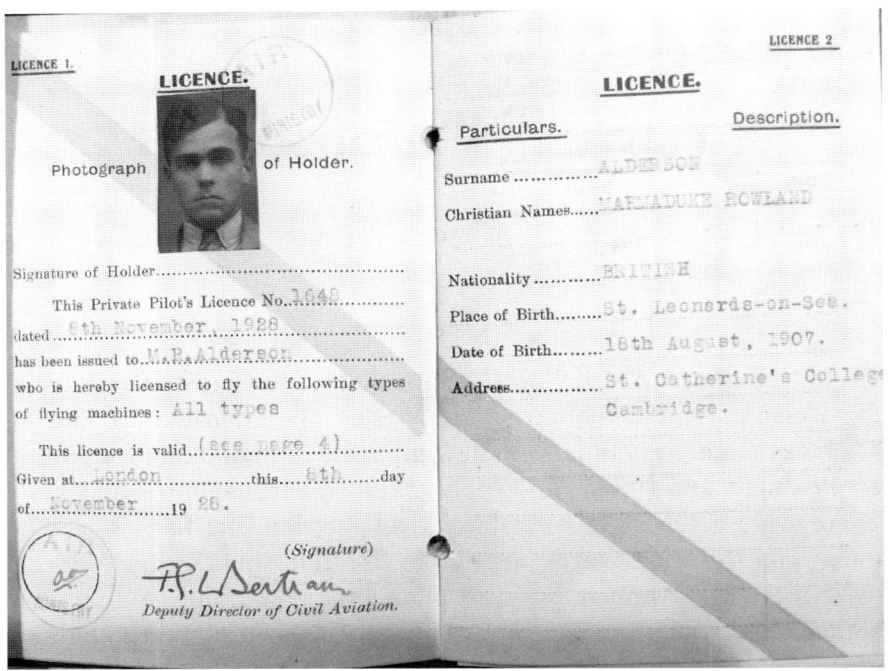

R.A.'s first Private Pilot's Licence, dated 8 November 1928 (aged 21). (*Author's collection*)

the English aviator Mary Russell, Duchess of Bedford, accompanied by her personal pilot and her mechanic, had taken off from Lympne, in Kent, bound for Karachi in her Fokker F.VII *Spider G-EBTS*. They completed the 10,000-mile round trip in just eight days, touching down again on UK soil on 10 August.

Having left Cambridge University – and therefore the University Air Squadron – Roly Alderson was now a member of the Reserve of Air Force Officers. In this way, he was able to continue to hone his skills as an aviator and gain experience on a variety of different machines. These included the Bristol Type 83 Lucifer PTM (Primary Training Machine), the Bristol Fighter, the de Havilland DH.9J, and the ageing – but very powerful – Armstrong Whitworth Wolf, which was fitted with a 350hp 14-cylinder radial engine. Roly logged another fifty-five hours with the Reserve between 1928 and 1930, of which fifty hours were solo flights.

His student days were behind him – so what now for Alderson?

Chapter 3

Fairey Tale (1930–1933)

The dying embers of 1929 heralded the start of the Great Depression – the worst economic meltdown the Western World had ever known. This was not a good time for a new graduate to be looking for gainful employment, and at first Alderson was, like many, unable to find a job. There were a few apprenticeships available, but one had to pay for these, and Roly was not in a position to afford this. Young Alderson wanted to fly – but there were precious few opportunities for pilots in commercial aviation in 1929, compounded by a surfeit of much older, more experienced ex-First World War flyers in the jobs market. It was clear to him that he would have to bide his time, and meanwhile put his engineering and mathematical skills to good use in order to earn a living. Finally, Roly managed to secure a position as a draughtsman in the design office of the Fairey Aviation Company based in Hayes, Middlesex – not far from the Great West Aerodrome (now better known as Heathrow Airport). It was not flying, but it was as close as he could get, and it was an opportunity to advance his knowledge in the science of aeronautics.

Roly was 22 years old when he joined Faireys. He kept his head down and worked hard. As with his skill in engineering, his draughtsmanship was meticulous, and he was engaged in a variety of aircraft design projects. At this time Fairey Aviation was involved in manufacturing aircraft for the RAF and was in the process of developing the first all-metal long-range bomber, known as the *Fleetwing*, as well as the Fairey *Hendon* and the better-known *Swordfish* torpedo bomber.

These were the depression years, and Roly acknowledged that he was fortunate to be employed – even though his pay was only £2 a week (about £100 today) and his shared room consumed three-quarters of this. However, there was no doubt in Roly's mind that this was not his destiny. He found that (in his own words) 'studying the more exotic use of mathematics for the stressing of structures was extremely boring', and he was 'not prepared to be stuck with just being a slide rule pusher'.[1] He had to fly, and he kept the dream alive by getting up in the air at every opportunity; he also kept in close contact with the RAF Reserve. In the spring of 1930, an old friend from Cambridge days, Bobby Anderson, bought himself a de Havilland DH.60 Cirrus Moth which they agreed to share.

The arrangement was that Bobby would put up the purchase monies, while Roly would carry out all the maintenance and servicing – as well as doing most of the flying. This plan suited Roly admirably. Bobby had not been a member of the University Air Squadron but had learned to fly privately (and according to Roly he was 'not a very capable pilot'!). This particular 80hp Moth was first purchased in August 1927 by a well-known pioneer aviator from New Zealand, Douglas Mill. Mill became the New Zealand distributor for de Havilland aircraft, so the company supplied him with a new DH.60X at a discount. Mill was a friend of

R.A.'s first 'shared' aircraft, the 1927 DH.60 Cirrus Moth *G-EBTI* (*Auckland Libraries Heritage Collections*)

Leonard Isitt – later Sir Leonard Isitt, Chief of the Air Staff of the Royal New Zealand Air Force – and they flew together to witness the famous Schneider Trophy Air Race.

On Saturday, 10 May, Roly and Bobby drove out to Woodley Aerodrome (today the home of the Museum of Berkshire Aviation), spending the day familiarising themselves with *G-EBTI*. They would certainly have been aware that just five days earlier, the remarkable 27-year-old English aviator Amy Johnson had set off from Croydon on her epic solo flight to Australia in her de Havilland Gipsy Moth, *G-AAAH Jason.* (She made it, landing at Darwin on 24 May after a journey of 11,000 miles.)

A week later, the two young men were once again over at Woodley. The following day, Sunday, 18 May, they departed to the east, landing at Cambridge for the night and flying back the next day. A few days later Bobby took the controls for the first time, under Roly's instruction, and they flew across to Brooklands Aerodrome in Surrey, where the aircraft was initially to be hangared.

For these two young airmen, adventure beckoned. After just two more local familiarisation flights, they fuelled up, stowed their bags, and on the morning of 5 June, with Roly at the controls, they roared off from Brooklands, bound for … Europe!

The first leg of their adventure took them to Ostend in Belgium, a flight of two hours forty-five minutes. Early next morning, they flew up to Rotterdam – a short leg of an hour and twenty-five minutes. They then embarked on the long trip to Berlin – seven hours twenty minutes in the air – stopping en route at the First World War airfields at Osnabrück and Hanover. After a three-night stop-over in Berlin – where they were invited to dine in the Luftwaffe Officer's Mess (fortunately their pre-flight planning had included the packing of black-tie attire) – off they went again, this time to Vienna, calling at Dresden and Prague on the way. Two days of sightseeing in the Austrian capital, and the two intrepid young airmen headed back into Germany, landing at Munich, where they stayed over. An early start on the morning of 12 June saw Bobby and Roly heading for home. They stopped first at Frankfurt, then Brussels, and from there the little biplane crossed the French coast between Calais and Dunkirk, overflew Hythe on the Kent coast, stopped briefly at Lympne Airfield, then Croydon – and finally, after just over eight hours in the air, tired and oil-streaked, the young aviators touched down back at Brooklands. Over the eight days they were away, Bobby and Roly had spent twenty-seven hours in their little open-cockpit Moth, covering over 2,000 miles, and visiting eleven European cities in five different countries. Roly was pilot-in-command and chief navigator throughout the trip.

Roly was never out of the cockpit for long. The next Friday he and Bobby flew down to Eastbourne and back, and the following day they were off up to Liverpool. Why Liverpool remains a mystery – but the Cirrus Moth was not flown back to base at Brooklands until 11 July.

On the very day that he and Bobby buzzed down to Eastbourne – it was Friday, 20 June 1930 – a young man by the name of Eric Hook, together with his mechanic, Jim Matthews, lifted off from Lympne Aerodrome in Kent, bound for Australia, in an attempt to break Bert Hinkler's fifteen-day record set two years earlier. Their Gipsy Moth, *G-AAWV*, crashed in the Burmese jungle two weeks later. It took Matthews a harrowing ten days to walk out, but he was unable to save the badly injured Hook.

Monday, 14 July 1930, was a 'Red Letter Day' for Roly: for the very first time, he was able to take his elder brother Guy flying. To be able to do this must have given Roly great satisfaction, as Guy had been so instrumental in the success of his younger brother at Cambridge. This flight was to relocate the aircraft to Hanworth, which was nearer to Roly's workplace with Fairey's at Hayes. Guy evidently thoroughly enjoyed himself – he was up again on three more occasions before the month was out.

Another brief sortie to Europe followed in early August – this time over to Le Bourget aerodrome near Paris, via Heston and Saint-Inglevert.[2] This was a four-hour flight, with Roly's log noting 'Head Wind', no doubt due to summer high pressure. Roly and his passenger returned to England after three days, stopping at Lympne and Croydon before landing back at Brooklands. It seems that, shortly afterwards, Bobby Anderson made the decision to sell *TI* – although he did continue to accompany Roly quite regularly thereafter. On 26 August they flew together over to Reading, to demonstrate the aircraft to a prospective buyer. A deal was done, and four days later Roly flew the Cirrus Moth for the last time, delivering it to its new owner. The logbook entry reads: '30.08.30/Pilot Self/G-EBTI/ Solo/Time 20 mins/Brooklands–Reading/ To sell G-EBTI'.

Summer had ended; *TI* had gone; autumn turned into winter, with no flying. By November, Alderson was suffering severe withdrawal symptoms. He went down the road to Hanworth and hired a DH.60X for a quick 'fix', then two weeks later took an Avro 594 Avian IV, again hired from National Flying Services at Hanworth, on a two-day trip down to Ford (Yapton) Airfield in West Sussex. This airfield had recently been reopened for civil use and was close to his current bachelor home at Emsworth. He dropped in at Croydon Airfield on the way down, and again on the return flight to Hanworth.

The 'flying bug' could evidently not be denied, for on 5 December 1930, Roly treated himself to an early Christmas present. Three days later he made the journey from Emsworth to Stag Lane Airfield,[3] the de Havilland Aircraft Company base, to collect *G-AALN*, a DH.60G Gipsy Moth biplane, sporting a 100hp Gipsy 1 engine and capable of 100mph. He was still only 23 years old. The famous aviator Amy Johnson had worked in the hangar at the DH Stag Lane HQ and had prepared *Jason* there for her Australia flight; meanwhile, HRH The Prince of Wales had also recently 'discovered' aviation, and had purchased *G-AALG*, a similar Gipsy Moth, from de Havilland.

Young Alderson's new acquisition had just had a brand-new Certificate of Airworthiness (No. 2945) issued on 13 November, so she was 'flight-ready'. This Gipsy Moth was originally purchased from de Havilland in August 1929 by the Comte Amédée Costa de Beauregard, of Villeneuve-Orly in France; he returned the machine to DH in November 1930, shortly before Roly bought her.

Roly took the plane straight down to Reading, and four days later embarked on a three-hour twenty-minute solo familiarisation and proving circuit, stopping at Croydon, Lympne, and Hamble, and finally back to Croydon. On arrival at Croydon, Alderson was asked if he would do a short delivery flight down to Tunbridge Wells for a Mr Charles Robinson, the founder/owner of Home Counties Aircraft Services. It would be a night flight in the DH.60M but, nothing daunted, young Roly took off, and thirty-five minutes later landed at Penshurst Airfield as requested. The following morning, he was back at Croydon, taking his old flying buddy Bobby Anderson as passenger in the new Gipsy Moth on the return hop to Reading.

In the eighteen months that Roly owned his first machine, he clocked up over 200 hours in the air, both in his own aircraft as well as in a

R.A. in his DH.60G Gipsy Moth, *G-AALN*. (*Author's collection*)

variety of others – the DH.9J, Armstrong Whitworth Atlas and Siskin, and a Comper Swift *G-ABJR*.[4]

He also continued to keep his hand in with the RAF Reserve. On 1 April 1931, the Reserve Flying School at Hamble ('Air Service Training Ltd') was formed, and Roly wasted no time in getting down there, recording his first flight at the new base on 29 April in a DH.9J, *G-AARS*,[5] under the tutelage of Flying Officer Maynard Cecil Dudding.

Between 25 May and 1 June, he also logged over ten hours there in a Siskin Mk III (DC) *G-ABHT* (No. 651), practising 'reconnaissance, map-reading, x-country and pinpointing'. Just seven days later, Flying Officer O'Brien, a skilled and experienced RAF pilot of 35, took off from the airfield and was involved in a tragic accident in the same aircraft while attempting a loop; it was written off and Flying Officer O'Brien was killed. This machine had only been officially registered to Air Service Training Ltd on 27 May (The AW Siskin was the first all-metal fighter to be operated by the RAF).

Comper Swift *G-ABJR*. (*Author's collection*)

Comper Swift *G-ABUU* (similar aircraft to *G-ABJR*). (*Author's collection*)

de Havilland DH.9J *G-AARS*. (*Air Service Training Ltd*)

Armstrong Whitworth Siskin Mk III (DC) *G-ABHT,* owned by Air Service Training Ltd, at the Reserve Flying School, Hamble, May 1931. (*Author's collection*)

In those early days of recreational flying, accidents were a regular occurrence. On 12 May, Roly took himself from Hanworth to Tangmere in the Gipsy Moth. This was an airfield he knew well – an RAF Reserve Training aerodrome located near Chichester on the Sussex coast. He stayed for a couple of days and was still there when the news came through that, 4,000 miles away to the south-southeast in Africa, a chap called Finch-Hatton had been killed in an identical Gipsy Moth, *G-ABAK*.

'F-H', darling of the Kenyan 'Happy Valley Set'[6] – and incidentally the principal character in the 1986 Sydney Pollack film *Out of Africa* – had taken off from Voi airfield, 100 miles west-northwest of Mombasa, bound for Nairobi. His Kĩkũyũ manservant Kamau was in the front passenger seat. According to the accident report, 'They circled the airfield twice before the plane stalled and dived to the ground and caught fire. The two occupants, Finch-Hatton and his Kĩkũyũ servant Kamau were killed instantly.' The Hon. Denys G. Finch-Hatton – professional British big game hunter and boyfriend of the Danish Baroness Karen van Blixen – had been a well-known and popular figure in Africa, and this incident would have been sobering news indeed, not only to his many friends both in Africa and the UK, but also to fellow pilots of DH Gipsy Moths, which included his Nairobi-based protégé, Beryl Markham[7].

Later in the year – on the day when Roly was flying *LN* from Tollerton in Yorkshire back home to Hanworth but had to divert to Hooton ('Detour on account of weather' noted in his log) – a sister

G-EBOT, de Havilland Gipsy Moth (Watercolour painting by Stanley Orton Bradshaw 1927). (*Author's collection*)

29

aircraft, *G-EBOT*, was involved in a fatal accident. The report stated: 'The pilot George G. Tomlin was performing a local training flight out from Broxbourne Airport. While descending to the airfield, at a height of 1,000ft, the aircraft entered an uncontrolled descent and crashed, bursting into flames. The pilot was killed.'

Aviators must aviate, however, and Alderson flew his Moth back to Hanworth. Yet again, adventure was in the air, and on 16 May 1931, Roly and Bobby set off into a 'strong S.wind', on a seven-and-a-half-hour flight, across the English Channel – destination Lyons, stopping briefly at Heston and Paris en route. On the 17 May, they continued to Nice via Avignon, and the following day pressed on to Pisa and Rome. After two days in Rome, they were off back to France, stopping at Pisa again, then Fréjus. On 21 May, Roly and Bobby took off from Fréjus in poor conditions – 'Mistral blowing' according to Roly's flight log – on a seven-hour flight to Paris, calling briefly at Montélimar (for nougat, perhaps?) and then Dijon (maybe for mustard?) on the way. The next morning, with Bobby at the controls for the first time, the intrepid couple flew from Paris to Saint-Inglevert, and later that day – having swapped seats once more – they took off into a headwind, homeward bound. They made a final stop at Heston before landing back at Brooklands on 22 May. On this week-long journey across France and down to the toe of Italy, they had been in the air for over thirty-two hours and had flown a distance of some 2,500 miles.

Roly Alderson took great pleasure in taking his two brothers, Guy and Gerald for regular spins in his Gipsy Moth. Guy – the elder brother who had helped Roly – had developed into an inventor of aeronautical instruments, so flying was in his DNA. Gerald was equally keen, having qualified as a pilot with Marshall's Flying School at Cambridge on 8 March, also on a Gipsy Moth – so to fly with his brothers would have been a huge thrill. Roly's other regular passengers were mostly former Cambridge University undergraduate colleagues, and included his old friend John Marshall, as well as a certain Tommy Usborne and Tommy's brother Henry – of the 'conifer in the undercarriage' incident. On his return from the trip to Rome, it was straight back to a week of RAF Reserve Flying at Hamble. Completing this on 1 June, he collected his Moth from Hanworth and took it down to Hamble, stopping at RAF Tangmere en route.

On 6 June, he presented himself and his beautifully repainted machine at the Brooklands Aerial *Concours d'Elegance* hosted by The College of Aeronautical Engineers (Brooklands and Chelsea). He won third prize, and at the end of the day he flew away with a fine silver aeroplane trophy. On 19 June, he was off again – this time to Whitley Abbey and Old Sarum and back; the next day to Old Sarum (again) and across to Bristol; the day after, it was over to Reading – to a 'fly-in' at the Berks, Bucks and Oxon Aero Club, where he added yet another silver trophy to his collection for the turn-out of his aircraft – before dropping in briefly at Brooklands and flying back to Hanworth.

Over the next few months – through the autumn and into winter – Roly continued to clock up the hours, both in his own aircraft and those of the RAF Reserve, ranging far and wide: Tangmere, Cardiff, Blackpool, Doncaster, Winchester, the Isle of Wight, and multiple other destinations.

In August 1931, Roly and one of his regular passengers, the aforementioned John Marshall, roared off up to North Wales for a weekend house party at the family home of his friend Betty Woodville.[8] No doubt to the surprise of the locals, Roly landed the Gipsy Moth on Abersoch beach, whereupon John disembarked, to be collected and taken by road

R.A.'s repainted Gipsy Moth *G-AALN*, as displayed at the Brooklands and Chelsea *'Aerial Concours d'Elegance'* and the Berks, Bucks and Oxon Aero Club 'Fly-in', June 1931. (*Author's collection*)

to the Woodville home, where they met up with, among others, Roly's old flying pal Bobby Anderson. Roly promptly roared off again down the beach, landing in a field close to the Woodville house. This process was reversed when they departed again, as the field was too short for the Moth to take off fully laden. This was evidently a month for beach landings, for just the previous week, at 13:30 on 6 August, a certain Scot by the name of Jim Mollison coolly put down on a beach on the Sussex coast, having just arrived from Australia in his Gipsy Moth. He had been heading for Lympne in Kent, but became disorientated in cloud over the English Channel, and thought he should perhaps land and get some directions.

Little did Roly know it, but when he took his elder brother Guy up in *G-AALN* on 13 September 1931, this would be the last time for them both. In the early weeks of 1932, Guy contracted lobar pneumonia; he died on 24 February at the age of just 32. This was another major blow to Roly, who had already endured the deaths of his baby sister in Ceylon, his older brother Ian, and both of his parents. Roly did his best to bury his emotions and threw himself even more fervently – if that were possible – into his work and his flying. He cleared the decks, sold the Bentbeam and moved into his younger brother Gerald's flat in Gloucester Court, Kew. This was much more convenient than Emsworth – closer to his work at Fairey's in Hanworth, and less expensive. For the time being, at least, he still had the 3-litre Bentley as his main means of transport – and, of course, the Gipsy Moth.

Exactly a month after Guy's death, Roly and John flew up once more to the Woodvilles' in North Wales for the long Easter break, arriving on Thursday, 24 March 1932. On this occasion, he decided that Llandudno beach was a more suitable airstrip – otherwise the passenger transfer process was the same as before, and after a jolly weekend they departed on Bank Holiday Monday back to Hanworth.

As the two young men were in the air, on their way up to Llandudno, the same indefatigable Mr Mollison took off from London in his de Havilland Puss Moth *G-ABXY*, bound for South Africa. He took four days, seventeen hours and thirty minutes, breaking the existing world record by some seventeen hours. He arrived in Cape Town just as they were heading home after their sojourn in North Wales. (Mollison was now married to Amy Johnson; they vied furiously for flying records.)

By May, the keen young aviator was hankering for more. In September 1929, Geoffrey de Havilland had first flown his new creation, the

DH.80A Puss Moth. This was a considerable advance on the biplanes, being a high-wing monoplane with an enclosed cockpit, capable of carrying three people. The fuselage was now of fabric-covered tubular steel construction, and it was powered by a 120hp Gipsy II 4-cylnder in-line air-cooled engine which was inverted, offering unimpeded vision across the nose without the protruding cylinder heads of the earlier Gipsy units. The Puss Moth was also considerably faster than the Gipsy Moth, with a top speed of 128mph, and a cruise of 108mph. Alderson decided on an upgrade.

On 7 May, Roly took a final overseas daytrip in *LN*, this time across to Antwerp and back. Five days later, he flew his trusty Gipsy Moth up to Skegness – a place he knew well from his Bentley racing days – to show the machine to a prospective purchaser. He went over again on 16 May, and agreed a sale for the grand sum of £300 to one Alexander Adolphus Dumfries Henshaw, of Mablethorpe, Lincs.

As it happened, the day after Roly had sold *LN*, Beryl Markham – friend and protégé of the late Denys G. Finch-Hatton – casually landed at Heston after a 6,000-mile solo flight from Nairobi in her Avro Avian IV. Perhaps even more incredibly, less than seventy-two hours later Amelia Earhart roared off from Newfoundland in her bright red supercharged Lockheed Vega 5B; when she landed near Londonderry in Northern Ireland some fifteen hours later, she became the first woman to have achieved a solo transatlantic flight (and indeed was only preceded by Charles Lindbergh's crossing in 1927). These were certainly pioneering days.

By mid-June, in joint ownership this time with his pilot brother Gerald, Alderson had taken possession of a Puss Moth, *G-ABTD*.

As usual, his passenger on the first flight in *TD* was his old flying buddy Bobby Anderson, for a quick half-hour flip out of Hanworth. The first couple of months with *TD* were busy. It was high summer, and Roly flew as often as work would allow. In those two months, he logged twenty-two flights, often with a passenger, sometimes two, including his co-owner brother Gerald, his old Cambridge friend Henry Usborne, and of course Bobby. Somehow, he also managed to fit in seventeen hours solo with the RAF Reserve Flying Training during August and September.

The DH.80A Puss Moth was a popular choice for many amateur aviators at this time – 259 were built by de Havilland. In fact, in July

R.A.'s friend Betty Woodville, with the Puss Moth *G-ABTD* in the background. (*Author's collection*)

of that year Amy Johnson took the solo record for flying from London to Cape Town in *Desert Cloud*, her DH.80A, *G-ACAB*. The following month her husband Jim Mollison made the first solo east-to-west crossing of the Atlantic in his own Puss Moth, named *The Heart's Content*. He flew from Portmarnock Strand near Dublin to New

Brunswick, Canada – taking the same machine that he had used for the Cape Town flight in March. Mollison followed this up with the first east-to-west crossing of the South Atlantic from Lympne Aerodrome to Natal, Brazil, in February 1933.

The DH Gipsy engines were renowned for their reliability – but they were not totally infallible. On 1 September, Roly took off from Hanworth in *TD* with Bobby in the passenger seat. Shortly after take-off, the Gipsy II engine stopped. Evidently the forced landing which followed was carried out without drama – the log states simply 'Engine failure – landing OK'. Others were not so lucky: just a few weeks earlier, on 27 July, a Puss Moth *G-ABDH*, owned by Brian Lewis and Company and piloted by Bruce Bossom, son of the politician Alfred Bossom, encountered thundery weather and turbulence en route from Heston to Hamble. The plane broke up in mid-air and crashed near Hindhead, killing all three occupants.

In Roly's case, the mechanical issue was soon resolved, for Roly took her down to Hamble and back five days later and continued to rack up the flying hours through the autumn and into winter, as often as time and weather would permit. On Sunday, 20 November, he slipped over to Hanworth for a forty-minute spin in the Puss Moth. News had come through that just forty-eight hours before, on Friday, 18 November, the indomitable Amy Johnson had touched down in Cape Town in *Desert Cloud* – no doubt much to the annoyance of her husband Jim, whose previous speed record she had succeeded in breaking by eleven hours.

As 1932 drew to a close, it was clearer than ever to Alderson that there was more to life than a seat in front of a drawing board. A seat in the front of an aeroplane was much to be preferred.

It might take patience, but he had a plan – in fact he had always had a plan…

Chapter 4

Golden Years 1 – Imperial Airways O.D.3 (1933–1936)

> It is a romance, all this, such as the world has never known before – a romance of speed, of human ingenuity, of immense technical achievement; a romance also of tremendous courage and personal skill … We have seen this great movement of the air go forward irresistibly. Nothing has been able to stop it. And today it has a future before it which will bring benefits and advantages to the entire world.
>
> G.P. Olley, *A Million Miles in the Air*, 1934[1]

On 28 December 1932, Roly flew *TD* over to Croydon to demonstrate her to a certain Mr Harris, a prospective purchaser. He called in briefly at his old haunt, Brooklands Aerodrome, on the way back to Hanworth. He had evidently come to a suitable arrangement with Mr Harris, because his log for 2 January 1933 records his last flight in *TD*, stating simply: 'Croydon delivery'.[2]

At the start of 1933, the stars were beginning to align for 25-year-old Alderson. He had been keeping his ear to the ground, and through his ongoing training with the RAF Reserve, he had heard on the grapevine that the fledgling Imperial Airways might be hiring. Imperial Airways was in those days the embryonic British airline which later became BOAC and ultimately British Airways. The company had been formed on 31 March 1924, under the chairmanship of Sir Eric Geddes, and had been loaned a million pounds by the government to expand the air routes across the British Empire. Effectively, Imperial Airways had been granted a monopoly.

The Managing Director, George Woods Humphrey, was keen to recruit the cream of qualified pilots to join Imperial, in order to crew the fast-growing fleet of aircraft serving the far-flung dominions of the realm. However, Britain was only just beginning to emerge from the gloom of the Great Depression; there were plenty of ex-RAF/RFC pilots in the market, so the chances of employment for a young amateur flyer were slim indeed.

Undaunted, Alderson immediately applied. From the handful of pilots that Woods Humphrey selected, just one was a civilian applicant. Roly could scarcely believe it: he was actually going to be paid to fly!

Alderson worked his notice with Fairey Aviation, and promptly threw himself into his induction with Imperial; by late February 1933 he was deemed ready for service. Roly was duly issued with his Imperial Airways 'Q' Code book.

Roly was ferried out to Cairo on a scheduled Imperial flight, and on 16 March took the right-hand seat as first officer on board an Avro 618 X named *Achilles*, registered *G-AASP*,[3] under Captain Samuel Wheeler.

'Q' Code book issued to R.A. on his appointment to Imperial Airways, February 1933. (*Author's collection*)

'Q' Code book (inside cover). (*Author's collection*)

Avro 618 X *Achilles G-AASP,* the first Imperial Airways aircraft flown by R.A. as a commercial pilot, in the role of first officer, Cairo, March 1933. (*National Aerospace Library/ Royal Aeronautical Society*)

R.A. (right) with colleagues, on arrival in Cairo, March 1933. (*Author's collection*)

Wheeler was an old hand, having joined the RFC in 1915 at the age of 17; he had been with Imperial for six years. Alderson by now not only held a 'B' (commercial) pilot's licence, but also a second-class navigator's licence, a ground engineer's licence, and a radio-telephony licence. This was First Officer Alderson's first commercial flight – his career as a professional pilot had begun.

The Avro departed Cairo, levelling off at 3,000ft, and three hours and thirty-five minutes later landed at Galilee. Wheeler had handed Alderson full control of the aircraft for an hour and fifteen minutes – a show of confidence in the new recruit. After a two-night stop, they took to the air on a six-and-a-half-hour flight to Baghdad – this time at an altitude of 5,000ft. On this leg Alderson took the Avro for a little over two hours.

This was a six-week posting, so the newly fledged first officer remained on the Middle East routes until early May 1933, routinely calling at Haifa, Rutbah Wells, Mafraq (Jordan), Abadan, Kowcet, Ahwaz and Teheran (Iran), Khaniquin and Haditha (Iraq). The second part of this posting turned out to be a fascinating episode for Alderson – and, as it happened, one of vital importance to British interests in the Middle East…

On Monday, 3 April the *Achilles*, with Captain Roger Mollard in the left-hand seat and First Officer Alderson in the right, departed from Baghdad on a private charter flight and, in Alderson's own words, they 'flogged through the desert to Teheran'.[4] On board was the chairman of the Anglo-Persian Oil Company, Sir John Cadman, and several of his advisors. For nearly ten years, a dispute had raged between APOC (which became BP in 1954) and the Persian government over the terms of the firm's oil concession, and Iran was now talking of withdrawing unconditionally. At this time, virtually all of Britain's oil supply came from Persia, so the implications of this were potentially catastrophic. This visit was a last-ditch attempt to resolve the issue.

The aircraft waited at Teheran for three weeks while negotiations continued. On 24 April, when it seemed that no further progress could be made, Cadman decided to call their bluff. He secretly planned with Captain Mollard for the *Achilles* to make a low pass over the Shah's palace at an exact pre-arranged time. Cadman returned for final talks in a private audience with Reza Shah; precisely on cue, there was a roar as the machine flew low over the palace, whereupon Cadman told the Shah that, 'as the noise overhead has just borne witness', the aircraft crew had been requested to carry out flight testing in preparation for departure, as the talks were now at an end. The ruse worked: Reza Shah capitulated, and an agreement was reached. The entry in Alderson's flight log is characteristically terse: 'Teheran (Local); 00:10 mins'. The crew remained on the ground in Teheran for another week, enjoying the hospitality of the Shah and the luxuries of his magnificent palace while the details of the new deal were concluded. On Monday, 1 May, Cadman and the APOC team roared off once more into the desert sky aboard *G-AASP*, homeward bound with smiles on their faces and a shiny new 60-year contract in Sir John's briefcase.

At the end of this tour Alderson returned to the UK on an Imperial flight, and after two weeks' leave, he was sent on his next posting. This time he would be flying the European routes from Imperial's UK hub at Croydon – then known as the 'Air Port of London' – to Paris, Basle, Zurich – where he happened to meet up again with Betty Woodville – and on to Brussels.

They were using the Armstrong Whitworth 15 Atalanta, a new type for Imperial. IAL had ordered eight Atalantas in 1932 and began operations

Atalanta *VT-AEG Aurora* at Zurich Airport, 1933. (*Author's collection*)

with them in September of that year. This was an advanced machine, being a high-wing monoplane fitted with four 340hp supercharged 10-cylinder radial engines which were faired into the wing for increased aerodynamic efficiency. It was significantly faster than its predecessors, cruising at 130mph, and was hailed as 'the fastest and most luxurious aircraft designed and produced for the tropics, with ample room for passengers to walk about and chat and to enjoy refreshments'. The four-engine configuration had initially been chosen for the African routes, for safety reasons.

Over the next six weeks Alderson flew as first officer in *G-ABTK Athena* and *G-ABTM Aurora* – they were all given names from Greek mythology – under the command of several of Imperial's ex-Royal Flying Corps pilots, colourful characters such as captains Walter 'Cockney' Rogers, Frederick Travers, Herbert Perry and Gordon 'GPO' Olley; these men were all legends of their time.

In mid-June, Alderson was transferred to the big Handley Page HP.42s on the much-vaunted Silver Wing Croydon–Paris service. When it was first introduced in 1931, the HP.42 held the enviable title of the largest airliner in regular use anywhere in the world. It was a sesquiplane – in other words, a biplane with unequal-sized wings – with two 490hp 9-cylinder Bristol Jupiter radial engines mounted on each wing.

HP.42 *G-AAUD Hanno*, in the Middle East 1933–1934. (*Author's collection*)

Supreme comfort: a little snooze aboard one of the HP.42 Hannibals. (*Author's collection*)

The HP.42 was slow, cruising at 100mph, but it was very safe and reliable, and was renowned for its spacious and comfortable passenger accommodation. The type ended its commercial career in 1939 with an unblemished record – although one amusing incident concerning the very first Hannibal, *G-AAUC Horsa,* is worth recounting. The story goes that, late one night in 1935, the captain of the *Horsa* departed Basrah without advising Bahrain of his impending arrival.

> As a result, Bahrain did not light up for him and he missed it and came down in the desert 100 miles to the south. When the rescue party got there next day they found that a crowd of Bedouin had ordered the passengers and crew off, hitched a team of camels to the plane and were towing it away for scrap metal.[5]

History does not relate the name of the pilot!

Roly's commanders on these large aeroplanes again included some of the 'giants' of Imperial Airways – Captain Arthur Wilcockson,[6] Alan 'Jimmy' Youell, and the larger-than-life Oscar 'O.P.' Jones – all of whom figured among the original sixteen founder pilots who joined the airline on its inception in 1924.

After a week's leave at the end of June, First Officer Alderson again reported for duty at the Air Port of London. Commanding the Atalanta *Aurora* on this occasion was Captain Mollard,[7] with whom Roly had flown on the *Achilles* charter with Sir John Cadman. Mollard was another pair of safe hands and a well-known face at Imperial. Together the two aviators spent 3–4 July on local flights to test the wireless apparatus; the next day they departed for the Middle East. Roly would have probably been unaware at the time that he would not set foot on UK soil again for nearly three years.

First stop was Lyons, then Rome, Malta, Bengasi (Libya) and Mersa Matruh (Egypt), arriving at Cairo on 9 July – then straight on, via Gaza and Rutbah Wells to Baghdad. Rutbah Wells was Imperial's first custom-built fort, located about three-quarters of the way along the route from Cairo to Baghdad. It had been created in response to the constant pillaging of Imperial's emergency dump supplies by the desert nomads. The nomads were not interested in the fuel – they just wanted the tins, from which they fashioned all manner of objects, from spoons to mirrors, knives to water bottles. 'The fort was guarded by armed sentries and administered by an English manager and his wife. They had access to an unlimited supply of cold, sweet artesian water but they were obliged to truck in all their food, fuel and supplies from Baghdad – 240 miles away.'[8]

After an overnight stop in Baghdad, they pressed on to Basrah, Bahrein, and then Sharjah. Another night stop was followed by a four-hour flight to Gwadar in Balochistan province, finally arriving at Karachi later that day. As usual, on each of the fourteen legs from the UK, Alderson was handed full control for part of the flight – usually for about an hour.

The lack of facilities in these far-flung corners of the globe is illustrated by the fact that the first vehicle ever to be seen in Gwadar was for the use of the Imperial station manager there. According to Imperial's *Gazette* in 1933:

> Its appearance created wild excitement among the inhabitants of the village who had never previously seen a motor car. After unloading from the ship, as the van

was being pushed from the beach to Imperial Airways' headquarters, it was surrounded by a delirious crowd of men, women and children. Imperial Airways' Station Superintendent reported that when he first saw the crowd he thought it was a fanatical movement and he had a few anxious moments, until he saw the cause of the excitement.[9]

On 22 July, while First Officer Alderson was enjoying his last day of a twelve-day break in Karachi before preparing to head off to Delhi via Jodhpur aboard *VT-AEG,* the British flying couple Amy Johnson and Jim Mollison had for once decided to join forces – lifting off from Pendine Sands in South Wales in a de Havilland DH.84 Dragon, in an attempt to be the first to fly non-stop across the Atlantic from the UK to the USA. They achieved their goal, albeit ending the flight in dramatic fashion by crash-landing close to Long Island Sound, Connecticut.

Over the coming months, Alderson continued to fly with Captain Mollard, and also captains Egglesfield and Prendergast.[10] The route covered stretched from Karachi, known as 'The Gateway to India', all the way to Singapore in Southeast Asia, with stops at countless exotic-sounding places – Jodhpur, Allahabad, Cawnpore, Akyab – and of course the larger cities of Delhi, Calcutta and Kuala Lumpur. This route, started in July 1933, was the first scheduled Imperial service to stretch this far east. Imperial had three Atalantas on the route, with Karachi at the western end and Singapore at the eastern. Depending on the requirements of the day, the crews would often spend two or three days between journeys. Young Alderson enjoyed his posting out here. At Karachi, he had a comfortable room at his disposal at the exclusive Sind Club. Being a keen shot, he had the foresight to bring his shotgun with him from England. They would routinely head out from Karachi by train for some sport, and the steam engine would be stopped for them at any point they deemed suitable for a bit of action.

Some particular events stood out in the months which followed: on 26 September 1933, Mollard and Alderson took the Atalanta *VT-AEG Aurora* – her registration had been changed from *G-ABTM* in July, the aircraft in effect being seconded to Indian National Airways – on the three-hour run across from Delhi to Jodhpur.

On arrival, they were advised that His Highness the Maharaja of Jodhpur, Hanwant Singh, would rather enjoy a short trip up in the

Atalanta *VT-AEG Aurora* in India, 1933; R.A. in solar topee, left foreground. (*Author's collection*)

machine as he was a mad-keen flyer. The pair duly obliged, but on this occasion kept the flight brief – they had him back on the ground in sixteen minutes.

Two weeks later – it was lunchtime on Sunday, 8 October – Captain Mollard and First Officer Alderson were on the ground at Calcutta – in fact delayed, changing a recalcitrant engine on their Atalanta *G-ABTL* – when Sir Charles Kingsford Smith dropped in for fuel, en route from England to Australia – solo – in his Percival Gull. Now topped up, he clambered aboard and promptly took off again for Akyab, and after an overnight stop, headed off east. The Imperial crew aboard the repaired *TL* followed on, arriving in Akyab later that day – by which time Kingsford Smith had taken off once more on his epic record-breaking trip. 'Smithy' had broken many aviation records: in 1931, with G.U. Allan as co-pilot, he had flown the *Southern Cross* from Sydney to Koepang on 21–24 April to pick up the mail and take it to Darwin where he arrived on 25 April. The return flight left Melbourne on the 23rd; it was flown by Australian National Airways to Brisbane, then onwards by Qantas to

Darwin on the 26th. Kingsford Smith – who had just arrived in Darwin from Koepang the previous day, then flew the mail from Darwin to Akyab in Burma, where it was picked up by Imperial Airways on 3 May and carried to London, finally arriving on 14 May – a pretty complex operation. Sadly, Smithy was lost over the Bay of Bengal in 1935 while attempting yet another England to Australia record flight.

Three days before the maharaja's 'jolly', the first Imperial service from London to Rangoon had departed; Mollard and Alderson were on the Karachi to Rangoon leg as soon as this service began. They were also on the new route through to Singapore which started in December. These Imperial pilots of the early days were fondly remembered by the station staff. Harold Foley was the chief air traffic controller at Penang in the late 1930s, and later reminisced: 'Ah, the Atalanta pilots …. Well, there was Captain Alderson, a nice chap who always liked a chat. And Captain Mollard, who knew this part of the world so well he could have flown over it blindfolded.'[11]

At this time in early 1934 it happened that Roly's brother-in-law, Commander Arthur Hamilton Morris, was based in Singapore aboard his submarine, HMS *H.52*. Roly's sister Dorothy had recently arrived from

HMS *H.52* – R.A.'s one and only trip aboard a submarine, Singapore 1934. (*Author's collection*)

England, having undertaken the long sea voyage to join her husband. It was a serendipitous opportunity to meet up and spend a couple of precious days in each other's company, and Roly enjoyed his first – and last – trip aboard a submarine. The next one he saw was a German one, off Africa in 1941 – but that is a yarn for a little later.

On 6 May 1934, Captain Prendergast and First Officer Alderson – who by now had been issued with his Indian 'B' licence, permitting him to fly Indian-registered aircraft – took off from Singapore on a round-trip to Calcutta and back, once again aboard *Astraea*. They achieved a record-breaking time, arriving back in Singapore on 8 May. The route had taken them via Alor Setar (or Alorstar), Bangkok, Rangoon, Akyab and Calcutta – then the same trip in reverse. Alderson's log simply states: 'Relief Service in record time'.

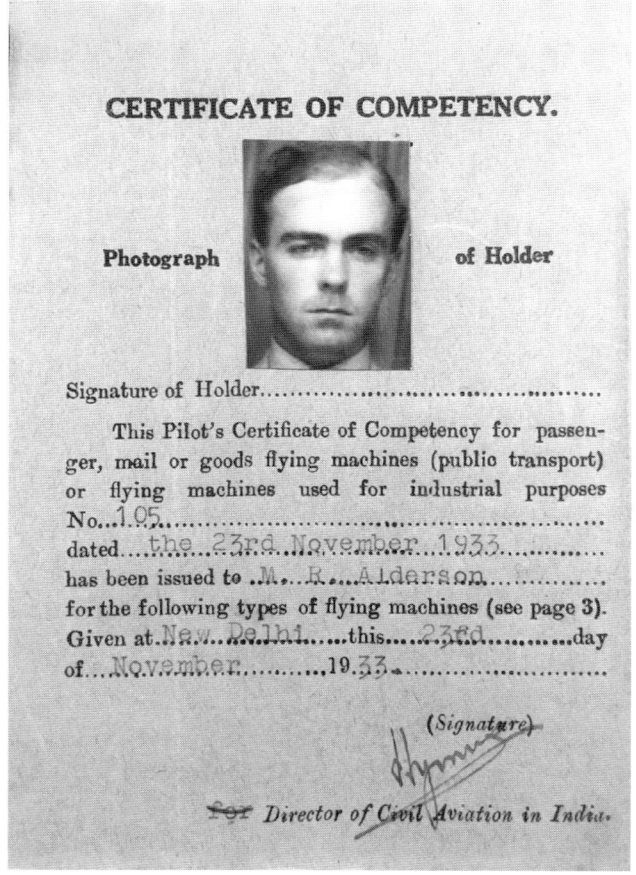

R.A.'s 'B' (commercial) licence for India, No. 105, issued on 23 November 1933. (*Author's collection*)

This particular aircraft, *Astraea*, had been the first of Imperial's fleet to reach Australia a few months earlier, in the hands of Imperial's Air Superintendent Major H.C. Brackley,[12] who wanted to show the world that the service was feasible and practicable. The attempt was not without incident: in spite of the extra fuel tanks which had been specially fitted, the contrary winds over the Timor Sea had confounded their calculations. The *Astraea* was literally running on fumes when 'Brackles' and the flight crew managed to touch down on a (very fortunately) newly cleared landing strip on Bathurst Island. It was two days before a supply of petrol could be delivered to the island to enable them to complete their flight, in the typical pioneering spirit of the era.

The following week, again in *TL* with Prendergast in the left-hand seat, they transported His Excellency the Viceroy of India, The Marquess of Willingdon, on the seven-hour flight from Delhi to Karachi, via Jodhpur.

In August, Captain Vernon Wilson was allotted Alderson as his first officer. Wilson was only five years older than Alderson – a relative youngster in the ranks of Imperial's captains – and they flew together exclusively aboard the Atalanta *VT-AEG* until the end of the year.

Atalanta *VT-AEG Aurora* taxiing, with HP.42 *G-AAUD* in foreground. (*Author's collection*)

On 22 November, a certain Mr George Flynn, a telephone engineer who worked for GEC in Coventry, arrived in Karachi from Alexandria aboard *G-AAUE Hadrian*, one of Imperial's HP.42 Hannibals. He had started his journey at Croydon Airport, Imperial's UK headquarters, and at over 4,000 miles from London, Karachi was the final stop for eastbound HP.42s; the Atalantas took over from here. Flynn sent letters to his wife and family on the 7,500-mile week-long outbound trip. He was bound for Bangkok, where GEC were hoping to secure a lucrative contract, and he boarded *Aurora VT-AEG* at Karachi. On this flight, Wilson and Alderson were in the cockpit. Flynn's letters home are both insightful and entertaining and give one an excellent impression of air travel in this era, as seen from the passenger's perspective:[13]

> The *Hadrian*, which brought us all the way from Alexandria does not fly on the course beyond Karachi, for which route they use these big four-engined monoplanes of the Atalanta type. They are built in Coventry, being Armstrong Whitworth aeroplanes with Armstrong Siddeley engines, and it is interesting to be travelling out here in a machine made, as it, were, right on our doorstep.

> At Karachi there was a fairly long wait during which they took us to the club for tea …. only seven of the original bunch remained. The cabin seats 10 in comfort and with heaps of space, so we are not crowded.

> Took off from Karachi at 4.26, but owing to a very heavy mail load, a full supply of fuel could not be carried. Therefore, we came down at Hyderabad on the Indus an hour afterwards to replace the fuel so far used [First Officer Alderson's flight log confirms this].

> Then we headed north-east on the 300-mile stretch to Jodhpur which was done in the dark with another landing in the dark, faultlessly carried out by these amazing pilots. We arrived just before nine and cars took us to our hotel, the State Hotel and the most beautiful hotel we have stayed at yet. Each of us had a suite of rooms, a large bedroom with the bed in the middle of the floor, a dressing room, and a private bathroom…

Left Jodhpur this morning at 4.54, it being pitch-dark. An hour or so later the dawn heralded a most beautiful sunrise with gorgeous orange sky for hundreds of miles along the far horizon. Was quite light when we reached Delhi at 7.37 (two hours forty-three minutes for the 300 miles). [Alderson's log records a flight time of two hours forty-one minutes.] Had a beautiful view over New Delhi in landing on the Delhi air club's ground. Here we had a good breakfast excellently served and were in the air again at 8.25 on the hop to Cawnpore (245 miles).

While writing this letter we have made two stops, one at Cawnpore for taking off mails (10.25–10.48) and another at Allahabad (11.42–2.30) for taking on fuel for passengers as well as engines! We are now just up again and passing over the confluence of the Ganges and its tributary, the Jumma, which is just now, at any rate, easily the bigger of the two. It is the river that runs down through Delhi, and we saw it earlier this morning.

12.50pm. We have been climbing steadily in the 20 minutes since resuming after our lunch in the air club building and the needle is now indicating 7,000ft – the highest we have yet been. The panorama is immense, but the haze blots out the very distant views. This is the way to study the geography of a country. It is just like looking down on a map of India. The whole of the northern plains seems to be spread out below us.

Now we are at 8,000ft and still rising. It is beautifully cool up here and if the temperature kept like this all the time, it would be ideal. I discarded my waistcoat way back at Baghdad and I thank my lucky stars I left my overcoat at home. Now 9,000ft. We are just passing Chunar, a biggish town on the south bank and Benares should soon be in view, though it is some way to the north of our path as the river takes a bend in the direction.

Up here the aeroplane moves faster and while at lunch, the pilot, Capt Wilson, was studying the meteorological charts which indicated strong following winds at this altitude. I think he hopes to make a record run on this journey as conditions are so favourable. This is a 465-mile hop (Allahabad–Calcutta) and it normally takes four to four-and-a-quarter hours. Now we are at 10,000ft and may be doing 150mph with reference to the ground, though there is no means of judging. There is no air speed indicator in the cabin as there was in the flying boat. I am afraid Benares is not visible owing to the haze but we can see just where it lies. Several big rivers are on our right – the Son and some of its tributaries.

1.30 and the pilot has just come in to tell us that our present altitude is to be our ceiling. His First Officer is at the controls. We are 10,500ft up. The pilot is staying with us for a while to get a warm-up as he says it is coolish in the cockpit. (Our compartment is ventilated with heated air, which makes it just right at this altitude.) The Ganges is now lost to view on our left and we are striking across some hilly country in a beeline for Calcutta.

Three of our seven passengers left us at Jodhpur (two American polo players and the wife of one of them, Mrs Guest – I think she is one of the Woolworth heiresses, a young girl and fairly pretty). One of the lady passengers we had in the party (joined the run at Paris) was a Miss Richardson, a Boer lady and the private secretary to General Smuts…

The number is gradually thinning out. We are now three men and a lady, a Mrs Somebody Morgan[14] who will be the only one of the original group in the Croydon aeroplane to stay the whole route. One gent leaves at Calcutta, another I believe at Rangoon and I at Bangkok.

1.45 and we have just crossed the Son River. The horizon is lost in haze which the land to the north fades into and looks exactly like a distant sea. Beyond that we can see the cloud formation which marks the line of the Himalayas, here 300 miles distant. In fact, a dim line below the clouds and above the ground haze is discernible and is probably the foothills where these abruptly meet the plain. The pilot tells me you can easily see Mount Everest from here when weather conditions are exceptionally favourable...

Well, this is a great trip and I am feeling fine up here in this cool aeroplane. It is a wonderful and fast way of covering distances and the Imperial Airways staff and organisation are very fine indeed. They look after one very well all along the line and the feeding and sleeping arrangements are very good indeed, except at some of those desert posts where conditions are very difficult for the company...

Great Eastern Hotel, Calcutta Arrived in Calcutta at 4.30. Just four hours for the 465 miles from Allahabad – the second best run ever made!

Oriental Hotel, Bangkok Now let me tell you about the rest of my journey. By the way, I was wrong in mentioning four hours in my letter from Calcutta as the time of our fast flight down from Allahabad. I forgot the time had been pushed on. The time of arrival, not counting the moving-on of watches, was four o'clock which makes it just three-and-a-half hours for the 473-mile hop, i.e. over 135mph. [Alderson's log records three hours twenty-three minutes.]

Forty winks and then the dear little alarm watch tinkled out 3.30! Dressed hurriedly and packed the cases which were collected at 3.45, then the passengers themselves were collected at 4 am and driven out to the aerodrome which we reached at 4.40. Got back in the aeroplane (still the *Aurora* which goes the whole way to Singapore), and we took off exactly at 5 am in the pitch dark as on all these early morning flights. Flew diagonally across a corner of the great delta of the Ganges – a deserted and useless waste of vast waterways, miles and miles wide with hundreds of interconnecting rivers, all flooded over in the rainy season – then across more 150 miles of open sea, getting again out of sight of land; onward over the coastal islands of Burma (very lovely indeed as seen from above) to Akyab where we were driven out to a settler's tropical bungalow, some miles away for breakfast.

Resumed flight at 9.20, this on a 300-mile stretch down the coast then inland across the mountains to Rangoon where we had lunch at the aerodrome, only seeing the city as we flew over – quite an attractive-looking place at the confluence of two great rivers (part of the Irrawaddy delta). Up again at 1.20 on the final leg of my wonderful run, the 370-mile hop to this city consisting of another long flight over the open sea, then nearly 200 miles over the absolutely impenetrable and inaccessible jungle-covered mountains of northern Siam, teeming with elephants, tigers and wild animals, but nobody can get there to shoot them.

After that, the final 100 or so miles over the flat and water-logged paddy fields of southern Siam leading right down to this city, this end of the country easily out-Venicing Venice for waterways. Landed at the aerodrome which is actually 16 miles north of Bangkok (owing, evidently, to there not being a large enough patch of dry land nearer the city) at 4.42 on Saturday, the great flight now being over and as safe as houses throughout.

Was met at the aerodrome by Mr E.R. Davy, Barrow Brown & Co's engineer, and after customs examination, passport inspection and the filling-in of various forms and papers relative to immigration, etc, which took considerable time, we caught the special motor rail coach on the railway up to Bangkok. On this was Mr Davy and myself, Mrs Mitchell (the one and only passenger left who is going through to the bitter end), the pilot Capt Wilson, his First Officer Mr Alderson, and the local Imperial Airways representative, Mr Jackson.

It is believed that Mr Flynn was awarded the contract he flew over 7,000 miles to secure.

Just a fortnight after Mr Flynn completed his adventure to the Orient, Alderson's final flight as first officer took place, on 5 December, on the leg from Jodhpur to Karachi. He had new completed 42 hours on HP.42s, 55 on Avro Xs, and 1071 on AW 15s – a total of 1,168 hours. Promotion beckoned: henceforth, he would be known as Captain Alderson.

After seven days' leave, on 13 December 1934, Captain Roly Alderson took the left-hand seat for the first time, aboard *VT-AEG*, the *Aurora*; she was now under Roly's command. With First Officer Douglas in the right-hand seat, they left Karachi on the three-and-a-half-hour night-flight to Jodhpur. The following day, they took off – again in the dark – bound for Calcutta. It took all day to cross India. They landed en route at Delhi, then Allahabad, finally arriving at Calcutta after nine hours and fifty-seven minutes airborne – a long day's flying. According to Alderson's log, they were delayed at Calcutta due to engine trouble and a tyre issue.

They managed to get away the next day to Akyab, stayed overnight and left early, bound for Bangkok, with a stop at Rangoon on the way. They

Atalanta *VT-AEG* with blown-out tyre on landing at Calcutta, 14 December 1934. Note size of wheel compared to engineer standing behind. (*Author's collection*)

flew the return trip over the next two days, having been aloft for fourteen hours on day two between Calcutta and Karachi. Jodhpur was regularly used as a stop-over, and this interlude was invariably enjoyed by both passengers and crew alike: they were accommodated in the recently built opulent Umaid Bhawan Palace Hotel belonging to Maharaja Hanwant Singh, who was mad keen on aviation in all its forms and was known at the time as 'The Flying Maharaja'. He and Roly had of course met before, and evidently got on famously. Alderson later commented: 'He was a very friendly chap who spoke excellent English.'[15]

The flying on this route was relentless. The new captain completed a total of thirty-eight legs in the eighteen days between 13 and 30 December, logging over 121 hours airborne. By June 1935 Alderson was on the full route, from Karachi right through to Singapore. Other than an occasional change of first officer or onto one of the other Atalantas, there was little to differentiate the flights. On a rare occasion, there would be a brief comment in the flight log:

> Returned – Engine Tr; Struck vulture. Minor damage. (No mention of the fate of the vulture, but for further insight into this understatement see Tributes & Memories).

An example of the busy days of flying that Roly was engaged in during this period is recorded in his characteristically precise pilot's flying log entry for 16 June:

AW 15 (G -ABTK); Pilot: Self;
   Passengers: 2;   Time: 3hrs 10; Ht: 9000;
                                           Course: Rangoon–Bangkok
         ---   Time: 1hr 52; Ht: 5000;
                                           Course: Bangkok–Kohlak
         ---   Time: 3hrs 33; Ht: 5000;
                                         Course: Kohlak–Alorstar
         ---   Time: 4hrs 05; Ht: 2200;
                                         Course: Alorstar–Singapore.

Total flying time for this day was twelve hours forty minutes – a long day's work by anyone's standards. It is perhaps not surprising that by now Captain Alderson had clocked up some half a million miles.

Atalanta *VT-AEF Arethusa*, India, January 1935. (*Author's collection*)

Atalanta *VT-AEF Arethusa*, late 1934/early 1935 (R.A. escorting unidentified young lady). (*Author's collection*)

Atalanta *G-ABTK Athena*, refuelling in India, February/March 1935. (*Author's collection*)

While Alderson was carrying out his pre-flight checks at Rangoon Aerodrome on this particular day, Beryl Markham was already in the air 4,000 miles away in Africa in her little Avro Avian biplane, *VP-KAN*, on a 350-mile solo mercy dash from Nairobi to Nungwe in the swamplands of Victoria Nyanza; her only passenger was a tank of oxygen strapped into the front seat. By the end of that day, Markham had flown direct from Nungwe to the Serengetti Plain in Masai country towards Lake Natron, to continue her near-hopeless search for a missing fellow pilot whose aircraft had disappeared nearly three days before. Short on daylight, food and fuel, Beryl not only found 'Woody', but managed to bundle the sick and dehydrated pilot into the Avian and fly him back to the East African Aero Club at Nairobi – one of the most remarkable rescue missions ever carried out by a small aircraft.[16]

The following year this intrepid aviatrix went on to become the first female to fly solo non-stop east-to-west across the Atlantic Ocean in her Percival Vega Gull *Messenger*, crash-landing on Cape Breton in Nova Scotia after a flight of over twenty hours.[17]

During the latter months of 1935, Roly occasionally records some interesting detail which lends insight into day-to-day commercial piloting in the Far East during this era. On one occasion their landing at Kohlak was delayed '10 minutes for cattle'; on another, departure from Delhi was held up as 'mail train derailed'; and en route between Jodhpur and Karachi, 'returned Hyderabad owing fog Karachi'.

In February the following year, Imperial Airways was requested by the British government on behalf of Indian National Airways to release their best available pilot on secondment to Indian National Airways for some important work: the Viceroy of India, Lord Willingdon, had been in post for five years and was about to return to the United Kingdom at the end of his duties in that role. He wished to visit a number of important Indian personages on a final farewell tour, but his regular ex-RAF pilot had failed his medical assessment: Imperial put forward Captain Alderson as his replacement.

Accordingly, on the first of the month he reported at Delhi and spent an hour on the Dutch-built Avro 642, *VT-AFM*, the Viceroy's personal aircraft, for his 'B' licence endorsement on the type. For the rest of the month, he flew an Avro X, *VT-ACT*, initially between Delhi and Agra, then spent five days in and out of Delhi on demonstration flights which, according to his log, were 'In connection with opening of Delhi Airport' (the airport was in fact opened by the Viceroy, and officially named *Willingdon*).

This was to be a busy time with VIPs for Captain Roly, for ten days later he took the Viceroy's Avro – named *The Star of India*[18] – to Jammu, on the India-Pakistan border, in order to ferry His Highness the Maharaja of Kashmir across to Lahore. The maharaja was evidently delighted with this new experience, lavishing gifts on both pilots: a gold ring for the first officer, a ceremonial sword for the captain.

Over the next two weeks, Roly ferried the Vicereine, The Countess of Willingdon, with her entourage of four, from Delhi to Jaipur and back; His Excellency the Viceroy to Jodhpur and back, with three of his staff; and His Highness the Maharaja of Jaipur on a visit to his home city, then back to Delhi (where he presented Alderson with a silver cigarette case embellished with the royal cypher). According to strict safety protocol, Captain Alderson was required to conduct a test flight on every occasion before transporting either the viceroy or the vicereine (but not, it seems, before flying the maharajas).

The Viceroy of India's personal aircraft, Avro 642 *VT-AFM*, christened *The Star of India*. (*Ed Coates Collection via AirHistory.net*)

These important duties having been discharged, Captain Alderson was soon back on the Atalantas; this continued through until the end of April 1936. On landing for the final time in Karachi on 22 April, and having now logged over 3,300 hours in total, Roly's thirty-four-month stint with Imperial Airways' new Far East Overseas Division had come to an end. His pilot's flying log reads simply:

LEFT No 3 O.D. 25.4.36 FOR ENGLAND

Chapter 5

Golden Years 2 – Imperial Airways Air Boats (1936–1938)

Alderson arrived back in England at the end of April 1936 on a scheduled Imperial flight into Croydon Airport.

It had been nearly three years since Roly had left home, and he was now able to enjoy six weeks of accumulated leave, visiting a few old friends from his Cambridge days and catching up with his younger sister and brother – the only two members of his immediate family still living.

R.A. skiing in
Switzerland,
early 1936.
(*Author's collection*)

R.A.'s brother Gerald beside their Lagonda, with empty beer bottles. (*Author's collection*)

He and his brother Gerald were keen skiers, and they managed to get away to Switzerland for a few days on the slopes.

He moved back into the flat in Kew that he had shared with Gerald. Although the aeroplane they had formerly owned together had been sold when Roly joined Imperial, they clubbed together and acquired a 4.5 litre 6-cylinder drophead Lagonda – a bit of fun for these two young bachelors.

All too soon it was time for Captain Alderson to get serious again. Ever since joining Imperial, what Roly had really wanted to do was to pilot flying boats – or 'air boats' as they were originally called. Now 28 years old and having accumulated over 3,000 hours as a commercial pilot, he was ready to realise his dream.

In the second week of June, Alderson presented himself at Air Service Training Ltd's base on the Hamble River at Southampton to begin his flying boat conversion course. He later wrote:

> This began with a seamanship course in a 30-foot yacht on So'ton Water and the Solent; having sailed small boats quite a lot I greatly enjoyed that! It was vital training, generally, but could not include, say, picking up a mooring on the

Nile, with a buoy almost submerged in a 10-knot stream, and the usual contrary wind.

After several days' sailing and theory instruction, on the morning of Tuesday, 16 June, it was time to take to the water – and to the air. With Flight Lieutenant Pascoe in command, and Captain Alderson in the right-hand seat, the Saunders-Roe (Saro) Cutty Sark A17/11 training aircraft *G-ACDR* taxied out into the Hamble River and took off on a one-hour introductory training flight.

As they lifted off from the Hamble River on that morning, Beryl Markham – who had flown herself back solo from Kenya after the 'Woody' rescue – had already been in the air for several hours, having taken off from Abingdon Airfield before dawn, and was well on her way across the Atlantic in her Percival Vega Gull. Within the next few hours, she was to become the first woman to fly the Atlantic solo from east to west.

Roly's second flight took place in the afternoon, under Flight Lieutenant Middleton. The following day, Alderson took the little *DR* solo.

R.A.'s first flying boat training, aboard *G-ACDR*, Saunders-Roe Cutty Sark A17/11. (*Flight*)

Left: R.A. in left-hand seat of Saunders-Roe Cutty Sark A17/11, *G-ACDR*. (*Author's collection*)

Below: R.A.'s second training flying boat, the 1928 Short S.8 Calcutta, *G-EBVG*. (*Toronto Star via AirHistory.net*)

After another eight flights, they progressed to the ageing open-cockpit Short S.8 Calcutta flying boat, *G-EBVG*,[1] a much larger machine of a type already in service with Imperial and which was powered by three Bristol Jupiter 9-cylinder radial engines.

After three weeks of concentrated flying, Captain Alderson completed the flying boat conversion course, and was signed off on 10 July, having logged a total of thirty-two hours on the two types – of which just over nineteen hours had been solo. Alderson was ready to 'fly boats'…

…alas, not *quite* yet. Pilots were badly needed on the increasingly popular European routes, and Alderson was returned to duties at Imperial's Croydon hub. His first flight, on 4 August, was in a Westland Wessex, *G-ACHI* – a somewhat antiquated Imperial monoplane equipped with three 120hp Genet radials – before heading off two days later in a de Havilland DH.86 direct to Budapest, acting as supernumerary to Captain Holmes.

He flew another thirty hours in the right-hand seat, and within just ten days found himself in command of his own DH.86A. Initially, Roly was rostered onto the North European circuit, to Budapest, Brussels, Zurich, Basel, Leipzig, Vienna, Prague and Cologne, and then onto the south-bound route via Paris, down to Marseilles, Rome, and Brindisi. He bided his time and continued to ply these routes for the next nine months, all the while piloting these most elegant of four-engine de Havilland biplanes, the DH.86A Express.

Imperial Airways Westland Wessex, *G-ACHI*. (*UK Airfield Guide*)

de Havilland DH.86A Express, Brindisi 1936/1937. (*Author's collection*)

Then Roly's chance came. In July 1937, Imperial formally introduced the Southampton to Durban flying boat service, twice weekly in each direction, together with a once weekly return service to Kisumu. Having already completed his flying boat conversion course the previous year, Roly was in pole position and ready to go.

On 30 July 1937, Captain Alderson – still not quite 30 – boarded the Short S.23 Empire C-Class boat *Centaurus*, *G-ADUT*,[2] at the Hythe flying boat base at Southampton.[3] Of the S.23, he wrote 'The Empire boat was indeed a beautiful aeroplane, and a great advance on anything we had, and from every point of view.'

In his pocket he carried a small booklet marked 'Strictly Confidential'. This was the *Hythe to Durban, Comparative Costs of Fuel and Oil* schedule, which was a highly sensitive document issued to all pilots on this route, in order to help the airline to mitigate fuel costs – which could be extremely high at some of the more remote stations. He was also in possession of the Imperial Airways issue map of the route from Southampton to Alexandria.

Right: Imperial Airways 'Strictly Confidential' *Comparative Costs Fuel and Oil* (cover). (*Author's collection*)

Below: Imperial Airways 'Strictly Confidential' *Comparative Fuel Costs Fuel and Oil* (inside). (*Author's collection*)

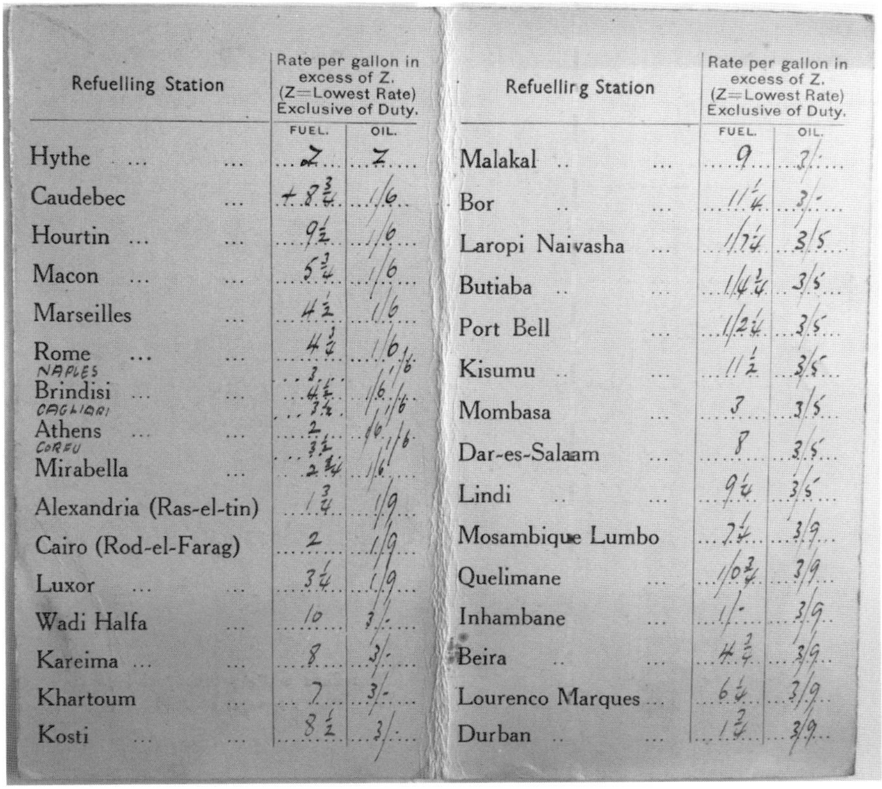

Strictly Confidential.

No. 25

HYTHE
to
DURBAN

COMPARATIVE COSTS
FUEL AND OIL.

This Card is the property of Imperial Airways, Limited

Refuelling Station	Rate per gallon in excess of Z. (Z=Lowest Rate) Exclusive of Duty.		Refuelling Station	Rate per gallon in excess of Z. (Z=Lowest Rate) Exclusive of Duty.	
	FUEL.	OIL.		FUEL.	OIL.
Hythe	Z	Z	Malakal	9	3/-
Caudebec ...	+ 8¾	1/6	Bor ..	11¼	3/-
Hourtin	9½	1/6	Laropi Naivasha ...	1/1¼	3/5
Macon	5¾	1/6	Butiaba ..	1/4¾	3/5
Marseilles	4½	1/6	Port Bell ...	1/2¼	3/5
Rome ...	4¾	1/6	Kisumu ..	11½	3/5
NAPLES		1/6			
Brindisi ...	4½	1/6	Mombasa ..	3	3/5
CAGLIARI	3½	1/6			
Athens ...	2½	1/6	Dar-es-Salaam ...	8	3/5
CORFU	3½	1/6			
Mirabella ...	2¾	1/6	Lindi ...	9½	3/5
Alexandria (Ras-el-tin)	1¾	1/9	Mosambique Lumbo	7¼	3/9
Cairo (Rod-el-Farag)	2	1/9	Quelimane ...	1/0¾	3/9
Luxor ...	3½	1/9	Inhambane ...	1/-	3/9
Wadi Halfa ...	10	3/-	Beira ..	4¾	3/9
Kareima	8	3/-	Lourenco Marques ...	6½	3/9
Khartoum ...	7	3/-	Durban ..	1¾	3/9
Kosti ...	8½	3/-			

Imperial Airways crew issue, route map Southampton–Alexandria. (*Author's collection, Imperial Airways*)

Today Captain Attwood was at the controls, with Captain Alderson acting as his supernumerary; they were bound for the South of France. From Marseilles, they headed on down to Rome, then on to Brindisi, Athens, Alexandria and Cairo, where the over-night stop was usually spent at the renowned Shepheard's Hotel. Onwards from Cairo, they headed south following the Nile, stopping at Luxor, Wadi Halfa, Khartoum, Malakal and Port Bell.

During a brief stop at Kisumu (Kenya) they met up with the Short Kent S.17 Scipio Class flying boat *Satyrus*, *G-ABFC*,[4] whose crew were busy surveying the route down to South Africa for Imperial. Attwood and Alderson then continued on to Butiaba (Uganda), and finally retraced their route back home, alighting at Hythe on 9 August.

Aboard Short C-Class S.23 in Africa – possibly *Centaurus G-ADUT* – showing port outer engine. (*Author's collection*)

Short S.17 Kent Scipio Class flying boat *Satyrus G-ABFC*, on route survey work for Imperial Airways, landing at Kisumu (Kenya), August 1937. (*Author's collection*)

Short S.17 Kent Scipio Class boat *Satyrus G-ABFC,* having just landed at Kisumu, August 1937. (*Author's collection*)

Five days on, and they were once again on their way, this time aboard *Centurion, G-ADVE*. They were bound for Kisumu, but this time they continued on, alighting on Lake Naivasha on the 18 August – keeping a weather eye open for basking hippos and semi-submerged logs as they made this first-ever landing of a flying boat on Naivasha – then on again to Mombasa, Dar es Salaam and Lindi (Tanganyika), Mozambique (four stops there, at Quelimane, Beira, Inhambane, and Lorenzo Marques), and finally arriving at Durban on 20 August.

By 18:04 two days later, they were again in the air, having swapped *VE* for *UT*, homeward bound. The two pilots duly landed back at base in England at 14:10 on 28 August. By the end of this flight, Captain Roly had already notched up over 160 hours as supernumerary captain on the C-Class boats.

Flying these Empire boats was not without risk, however. Five days after Roly arrived home, *Cambria* was damaged on landing at Lake Ontario; three weeks later *Courtier* crashed on landing in poor visibility at Athens, with the loss of two lives; and on 5 December *Cygnus*[5] came down after taking off from Brindisi, with two people killed. Among the passengers on this flight were Air Marshall Sir John Salmond,[6] Government Director of Imperial Airways, and Mr Robert Lutyens, son of the renowned architect Sir Edwin Lutyens.

Wednesday, 8 September 1937, was a day that would be forever etched in Roly's memory. Aboard *G-ADUV Cambria,* Captain Alderson took command of his own Empire boat, taking to the air at Hythe for a brief familiarisation flight of twenty minutes. The following day, 9 September, he departed Hythe on his first commercial flight as a flying boat commander, a four-hour and twenty-four-minute run down to Marignane (Marseilles) in Provence. An hour later, having taken on fuel, *G-ADUV* took off again bound for Lake Bracciano, where they landed in time for afternoon tea. Next day, an early 05:00 start took them on a two-hour flight to Brindisi, where they made a brief stop before proceeding to Athens, arriving at 11:18.

Four days later – 14 September – Alderson was aboard *UZ* bound for Alexandria, a four-hour leg. The following day was one of those marathons, starting at four in the morning. It was four-and-a-half hours back to Athens, then two-and-a-half to Brindisi, and another nearly three hours on to Bracciano – a total of nearly ten hours in the air.

R.A.'s first flying boat command, the Short S.23 C-Class boat *G-ADUV Cambria*, pictured here a few weeks earlier in July 1937 at Boucherville, Montreal. (*R.N. Smith collection, via AussieAirliners.org*)

At Bracciano they stopped overnight, going on the following morning to Marseilles – another stop-over. It was a typically early start, departing Marseilles at 05:04 and overflying France before alighting at Southampton at 09:00 – just in time, one would surmise, for a hearty breakfast in the canteen back at the Hythe base.

For the rest of the year, Captain Alderson continued to ply the Cairo to Mombasa route. One of his last flights of 1937 was down to Durban aboard *G-AETZ Circe*, reported in Southampton's *Southern Daily Echo* of Friday, 17 December:[7] 'Mail loads continue to be heavy. Three-and-a-half tons of Christmas mail were carried by the Empire flying boat *Circe* which, commanded by Captain M.J.R. Alderson, left Southampton for Durban this morning.'

1938 – A new year, a new route. The brand-new Empire C-Class boat, the *Carpentaria* had been delivered to Imperial Airways on 3 December 1937. Although ordered by Imperial, this boat had been earmarked for Qantas – hence the registration *VH-ABA* – but was temporarily retained by Imperial to help mitigate the recent Empire boat losses. *ABA* had only just completed the inaugural Southampton–Karachi–Southampton service; one of the passengers on board for this flight was Hubert Scott-Paine, Director of Imperial.

In these early days of flying boat operations, it was not just Imperial Airways who were suffering accidents. On 11 January, one of Pan American Airways' Sikorsky S-42 boats, the *Samoan Clipper*, exploded in mid-air to the west of Pago Pago in the Pacific, killing all seven crew on board. The cause of the explosion was thought to have been the result of dumped fuel igniting after the captain reported an engine oil leak and decided to return to Pago Pago.

A week after this tragedy, on 19 January, Alderson stepped aboard the shiny new *ABA* in Alexandria and set off for Karachi. They first landed on the Sea of Galilee, then Lake Habbaniyah en route to Basrah. The next day saw them departing very early – at 01:22 – continuing through to Karachi with brief stops at Bahrein (forty minutes), Dubai (twenty minutes) and Gwadar (twenty minutes); they landed at Karachi at 12:38. Roly returned through Alexandria a week later, routing on through Italy and France back to England. A few days after Roly passed through Alexandria and Athens on this trip, the *Corsair* had a close escape on the same leg: the air liner was caught in a fierce hailstorm which smashed the cockpit window: Captain Woodhouse sustained an injury to his eye and had to be replaced on arrival at Phaleron, the flying boat base for Athens.

According to the *Southern Daily Echo* of Wednesday, 23 February 1938:[8]

> Today, another milestone in the history of the flying mail was reached with the departure from Southampton of two giant Empire flying boats carrying the first loads of non-surcharge mails to be flown from England to India, Burma and Malaya. The two air liners – *Coolangatta* commanded by Captain M.J.R. Alderson and the *Centurion*, under the command of Captain F.C. Allen – took off from Southampton Water within two hours of each other, carrying between them four tons of mails.

On the return run, one of the overnight stops was at Basrah. The Imperial Airways station representative, Mr Hayhoe, as usual delivered a printed card to the captain's hotel room with the timetable for the following day:

(Capt. Alderson)
Westbound.
Station: **Basrah;**
Arrangements for: **To-morrow**
You will be called at **06-00** *and your baggage should be outside your room at* **06-30**
Tea, Rolls Butter *will be served* **In Your room**
Currency Coupons will be cashed at **Fils 250 each**
The **Launch** *will leave* **The Pontoon** *at* **06-45**
The air-liner will leave the airport at **07-00** *hours tomorrow and stops will be made at* **Habbaniyeh, Tiberias & Alexandria** *Meals on tomorrow's journey will be served as shown.*
BREAKFAST **On Board** *TEA* **Alexandria**
LUNCH **Tiberias** *DINNER* **-do -**
Mr. **Hayhoe** *the Company's representative will give to you any further information or assistance you may need during your stay at the station.*

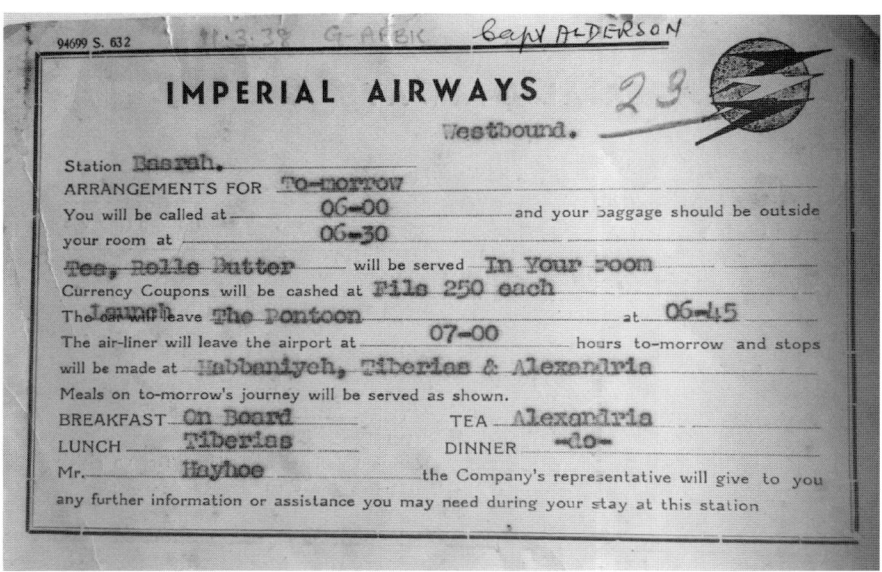

Imperial Airways card advising Captain Alderson of the following day's timetable from Basrah, 11 March 1938. (*Author's collection*)

Imperial Airways promotional card showing internal lay-out of S.23 C-Class *G-AEUA Calypso* (*Author's collection, Imperial Airways*)

Imperial Airways promotional card illustrating detail of S.23 C-Class *G-AETX Ceres* (*Author's collection, Imperial Airways*)

Alderson continued on these well-trodden paths from the UK to Alexandria for the next four months, flying a number of different C-Class boats, including *G-AEUA* and *G-AETX*, *Calypso* and *Ceres*, often continuing on, following the Nile down through Africa and terminating at Durban.

Other than the occasional note in the 'Remarks' column of Captain Alderson's flight log: 'N.T.O. 2.20hrs NF' (Night Take-Off, two hours twenty minutes Night Flying); 'Dusk L'd'g (Flares)'; 'Sun sights taken for navigation'; 'Returned – headwinds', there is little to punctuate this period. By April, Alderson had flown some 1,000 hours on 18 Empire boats – the majority of them in command. He was by now a seasoned flying boat captain, and he was ready for the next chapter.

This challenge was not long in coming. He returned to the United Kingdom, and after four weeks of 'R & R', he was on his way to Bermuda.

Chapter 6

RMA *Cavalier* (1938–1939)

The *Cavalier* was eager to depart
William Wordsworth (1770–1850)

On 24 May 1938, Captain Roly Alderson arrived by sea from the UK at Hamilton, the capital of Bermuda. For Roly, now an experienced 'boat' pilot, yet still only 30 years old, this was a new beginning, and an exciting prospect. Bermuda was exotic – a small but beautiful archipelago, a Crown Colony for 250 years, lying some 650 miles east of the USA, blessed with a sub-tropical climate and bathed by the warm waters of the Gulf Stream.

Imperial Airways promotional card depicting the RMA *Cavalier* in Bermuda. (*Author's collection, Imperial Airways*)

As one of Imperial Airways' crack young pilots, Alderson had been selected to replace Captain William 'Neville' Cumming DFC[1] on the Bermuda to New York service – known affectionately in aviation circles as 'The Golden Route'. Roly admitted that he was:

> very pleased to go to this 'remote' island, and fly our only ocean route, having become particularly interested in celestial navigation. It seems strange nowadays [recalled in a letter he wrote many years later], but there was no doubt then that a sextant – even of the somewhat primitive hand-held variety – provided quite vital insurance on our Eastbound flights. I already owned the latest American instrument, but one had to use this consistently in trying to achieve reasonable accuracy and confidence; there was often enough air-time to do so.[2]

Cumming had been with Imperial since 1931 and had decided that the time had come to move on. Also moving on was the Imperial Airways Station Manager, Captain Armstrong, and he was to be replaced by Captain Griffith 'Taffy' Powell – also a seasoned flying boat pilot – who, with his family, had accompanied Roly on the voyage over from the UK.[3]

The route was operated jointly by Imperial Airways and Pan American Airways, providing customers with a daily flight in each direction, except on Sundays. The latter operated a Sikorsky S-42 flying boat named *Bermuda Clipper*, rather smaller and slower than

R.A. in Imperial Airways' captain's uniform, 1938. (Imperial Airways captains wore three sleeve rings, whereas Royal Navy captains wore four). (*Author's collection*)

Imperial's boat, on what they proudly called their 'Clipper Service'. Imperial flew a Short C-Class S.23 Mark II flying boat named the RMA *Cavalier*[4] and registered *G-ADUU*. She was the fifth of the Empire class to be built. The range of these boats was less than 800 miles, and so it was not possible to fly the *Cavalier* across to Bermuda from England. She was therefore shipped, partially dismantled, from the UK in December 1936, in three huge wooden crates and eighteen smaller ones, aboard the RMS *Lochkatrine*. The aircraft was reassembled on arrival at IAL's new Seaplane Port at Darrell's Island in Hamilton Sound under the supervision of Imperial's Chief Engineer Len Turnhill, working with Imperial Airways' and Bermudian staff.

The reassembling of the *Cavalier* was a major undertaking. This was a big machine, weighing in at 23,500lb (empty), 88ft long, with a wingspan of 114ft and equipped with four Bristol Pegasus XC 9-cylinder radial engines of 920hp each. She was capable of a maximum speed of 200mph and cruised at 165. It took several weeks to put the flying boat back together – in itself a remarkable feat of engineering – and she first flew on 18 February 1937, with captains Armstrong and Cumming on the flight deck. On 18 May the *Cavalier* embarked on a survey flight; her first commercial flight from Bermuda to New York took place a week later, on 25 May. Captain Cumming was in the left-hand seat, with First Officer Neil Richardson acting as co-pilot; also on board were Radio Officer Patrick Chapman and Steward Robert Spence. (Richardson, Chapman and Spence remained on the crew after Captain Cumming departed the following year.) The official service began on 16 June with the Bermuda–New York runs on Mondays and Fridays, and the New York–Bermuda return flights on Tuesdays and Saturdays.

A year later, on 27 May 1938, with Captain Cumming at the controls and Captain Alderson in the right-hand seat, the *Cavalier* taxied away from the new $1 million terminal building at Darrell's Island, and at 13:34 local time she took to the clear blue Bermudian sky, bound for Port Washington on Long Island, New York.

They landed on schedule after five hours and sixteen minutes. The following day at exactly 15:30, after an overnight stop in New York – Alderson's first taste of this extraordinary city[5] – the RMA *Cavalier*, propelled by its four powerful Pegasus engines, thundered out from Port Washington flying boat base, climbing away to the south-east, bound for Bermuda, 770 miles distant.

RMA *Cavalier* docked at Imperial's flying boat base at Darrell's Island, Hamilton Harbour, Bermuda. (*Author's collection*)

RMA *Cavalier* lifting off, Darrell's Island, Bermuda. (*Author's collection*)

The same round-trip was repeated by Cumming and Alderson over 3–4 June. The Imperial Airways service was operated with clockwork precision, the Port Washington-bound flight departing at 13:30 and

RMA *Cavalier* over Bermuda. (*Author's collection*)

RMA *Cavalier* over Hamilton Sound, Bermuda. (*Author's collection*)

the Bermuda-bound service leaving at 15:30. Flight times averaged around five-and-a-half hours – sometimes a little more, sometimes less, depending on prevailing weather conditions.

On 8 June, the *Cavalier* had a new commander: Captain Roly Alderson was now occupying the left-hand seat, and First Officer Neil Richardson the right. The flight to Port Washington, and the return the following day, was completed without fuss – five hours twenty-two minutes out, five hours eighteen minutes back. Roly's first round-trip as master of RMA *Cavalier* was done and dusted.

Alderson settled into his new life in Bermuda as *Cavalier's* chief pilot for Imperial with relish. By the end of August, he had racked up 1,000 hours as pilot-in-command ('P.1') on the Empire boats – and well in excess of 5,000 hours in total flying time. Other than a brief note in Roly's log for 3 September regarding an aborted flight from Bermuda – 'Returned owing to weather' – there was nothing to suggest at this point that anything was amiss on the service.

Cockpit of RMA *Cavalier* in flight (R.A.'s shoulder on left); note whistle below instruments on left, used by the commander for instructing crew during mooring and manoeuvring. (*Author's collection*)

Behind the cockpit of a C-Class (looking aft), the radio officer's station on right. Note the four wheels on the left (aft) for controlling fuel valves and carburettor intakes. (*Short Bros*)

Life was good for young Roly. He had responsibility, he was doing a job that he loved, and indeed one at which he excelled. As with all commercial pilots of this era, he was held in high esteem by the general public; after all, these romantic figures were the celebrities of the day – men such as captains Kelly-Rogers and O.P. Jones. Roly, however, was not seduced by this new-found adulation. He was of a naturally retiring disposition, and this was not about to change.

Roly maintained a small but close circle of friends in Bermuda, among them Taffy and Marion Powell, George Wardman – Bermuda's Pan American representative – and George's wife-to-be Freda Smith, of an old-established Bermudian family; and the well-known Frith clan. Although always attractive to the opposite sex – they evidently found this quiet, brooding Englishman an exciting challenge – Roly dated only occasionally and spent any spare time when off duty keeping fit – playing tennis or golf, as well as swimming, fishing and sailing his own little dinghy, *Shiver*, in the warm turquoise waters. He had bought *Shiver* in America and had flown her over in *Cavalier*'s baggage hold.

Roly later wrote: 'Bermuda was a good place to live, but we didn't see much of it during the week; there were no flight crew reserves except Taffy Powell, who liked to fly occasionally, anyway.'[6]

R.A.'s sailing dinghy *Shiver* in RMA *Cavalier's* hold, en route from New York to Bermuda. (*Author's collection*)

The first signs that something was not quite right with the *Cavalier* in certain atmospheric conditions led Captain Alderson, with his engineering knowledge, to suspect an issue with carburettor icing. He reported on 8 October, after Flight No. 238, as follows: 'Trouble was experienced with engines fading in rain and snow conditions at a temperature of 29 degrees F. The S.I. engine[7] faded completely after all had been running on hot air for 20 minutes and had to be cleared by closing throttle for a few moments.'

Alderson was disturbed that the gravity of the situation was not more fully realised, and after another incident, he reiterated his concerns in his report (F.272) on 17 December.

It was during this period that Roly received the very sad news that Captain 'Tich' Attwood, his mentor and friend – with whom he had flown for three months the previous year as supernumerary on his first tours as a fully-fledged Empire captain aboard *Centaurus*, *Cambria* and *Centurion* – had been tragically killed while piloting the C-Class boat *Calpurnia* which crashed into Lake Ramadi on 27 November, on its approach to Habbaniyah. They had been caught in a sandstorm, and it seemed that they had descended very low in the dark in order to try fix their position by ground observation. The *Calpurnia* struck the water with the engines running at full power: four of the six-man crew – including Captain Attwood – lost their lives.

It can be seen from Alderson's flight logbook that, as November rolled into December and the North Atlantic weather became more challenging, with more frequent strong westerly winds, so the flights from Bermuda to the United States became noticeably longer.

Indeed, on 21 December, so contrary were the winds that Alderson made the unusual decision, on safety grounds, to divert to Baltimore, Maryland, even though this route was 40 nautical miles longer – at 712 rather than 672 miles. Alderson later wrote: 'Long Island, in fact, did not provide a very good terminal for Flying Boats in winter, for the sea temperature was often below zero degrees centigrade. Baltimore was our alternate.'

The flight time was just short of seven hours. He continued the following day to Port Washington with his passengers and crew, and then, after quickly refuelling and taking on his complement of Bermuda-bound charges, took off again barely forty-five minutes later. The return flight reflects the tail-wind conditions: the *Cavalier* took just four hours and twenty-three minutes from take-off to arrival at the Darrell's Island seaplane base – a very quick passage.

Captain Powell occasionally flew as relief commander on the *Cavalier* and did so on the Bermuda–New York round trip of Monday, 16 and Tuesday, 17 January 1939. The flights proceeded without incident, with Powell reporting nothing unusual on his return.

Friday, 20 January 1939 – On the morning of 20 January, shortly before he flew out once more, Alderson wrote yet again on the worrying issue of carburettor icing; this report – which was soon to prove so significant – was duly forwarded to London.

Captain Alderson   Operations Manager
Bermuda.

MRA/WR.   <u>Carburetter Icing</u>   20th January, 1939.

    In my Voyage Report on E.272, 17th December 1938, I remarked that trouble was experienced with carburetter icing.

    During the past few weeks I have been very concerned over the unsatisfactory functioning of Cavalier's engines under certain conditions on this route, and I make this separate report in the hope that the Engineering Department may give serious attention to the problem.

    The essential fact is that in atmospheric conditions frequently encountered here it is impossible to maintain the power output from any engine, and there is no doubt in my mind that the principle cause of this is ice-formation on the butterfly throttle. Its presence can be detected by sensitive use of the throttle lever, and it can be removed by manipulation .

    It is not easy to believe that this can occur when hot air is being used for the intakes, with the chokes and induction elbows already heated, but I am certain that it does so, and a supporting fact is that after collecting ice with cold intake air, a change-over to hot air will not effect a complete cure -- the ice must still be cleared mechanically.

    The carburetter heating systems on Cavalier have been checked repeatedly for correct functioning, but it seems that they fail inherently.

    It has been found that unsatisfactory running may occur, even on hot air, when the outside temperature is below 45° F; specific humidity is obviously a more important factor.

    Needless to say, the engines are run on hot air for a large proportion of the time at this season, but often require constant attention to throttle controls; on E.272, these were manipulated incessantly for $3\frac{1}{2}$ hours in order to maintain R.P.M., and this attention cannot well be spared.

    It seems likely that this inefficient carburation adds considerably to fuel consumption, but over a period of 6 hours the results are somewhat masked, and only flow-meters could give the

Letter sent by R.A. to Imperial Airways on 20 January 1939 – the day prior to the ditching of the RMA *Cavalier*. Note in particular the last but one paragraph (page 1). (*Author's collection*)

Page 2

necessary information.

It is obvious that we are having difficulties here which are not so evident on other routes, and I suggest that valuable opportunities exist for investigation, if proper equipment is used.

It is worth noting here that the system in use on the Pratt & Witney engines of the "Clipper" gives no trouble. The throttles operate wide open when cruising, control being from barometrically operated shutters at the intake, with thermostatic control of the intake air, which is maintained at 90° F. in all weather conditions.

M.R. Alderson.

Letter from R.A. to Imperial Airways, 20 January 1939 (page 2). (*Author's collection*)

This duty having been discharged, Captain Alderson met up with First Officer Richardson, who lived less than a mile away, and as usual they shared a horse-drawn carriage – the fastest transport available – to carry them to the local ferry dock, whence the Imperial Airways launch took them to the flying boat pier at Darrell's Island, out in Hamilton Sound.

There were no issues that morning: cargo and mail were stowed in orderly fashion, and the passengers were welcomed aboard. Alderson carried out his normal pre-flight routine, and the *Cavalier* taxied out from the seaplane base, becoming airborne at 09:02 Eastern Standard Time (14:02 GMT), for some reason half an hour behind schedule.

The flight to Port Washington, though apparently uneventful, was unusually long – six hours thirty-seven minutes – no doubt on account of strong winter headwinds.

On arrival at Port Washington, with the aircraft snugged down for the night on its mooring, Captain Alderson went shoreside and, as was usual in wintertime, took a train into New York City. He met up, as he often did, with Imperial's New York representative Paul Bewshea, who later recalled that Alderson seemed to be suffering from a head-cold that day, and he asked him if he was alright. Alderson replied that it was 'just a bit of a cold, nothing serious'.[8]

RMA *Cavalier* alongside the flying boat pier, Darrell's Island, Bermuda, 1938. (*Author's collection*)

RMA *Cavalier* taking off from Hamilton Sound, Bermuda, 1938–1939. (*Author's collection*)

Saturday, 21 January 1939 – The Imperial Airways Station Engineer at Port Washington superintended the refuelling and carried out his daily check of airframe and engines. He found everything in order and signed the safety flight certificate accordingly. Prior to the trip – *UU's* 290th revenue flight – Captain Alderson met with First Officer Richardson and Radio Officer Chapman in the normal way, to run through the flight plan.

Local weather conditions were light snow flurries, overcast 10/10 at 2,500ft, visibility 2.5 miles. This was well above the minimum requirements of the US Civil Air Regulations. The temperature was 32°F. Before boarding, Captain Alderson had as usual studied the meteorological reports received from Baltimore and Bermuda. These showed that:

> there would be layers of cumulus, strato-cumulus and stratus clouds up to 8,000ft for most of the way, with alto-stratus clouds 2,000 to 4,000ft above that for part of the second half of the voyage. The freezing level, which at Port Washington was at sea level, would rise gradually to 4,000ft when 250 miles out and to 12,000ft when just over halfway to Bermuda.

These conditions were to be expected at this time of year and Captain Alderson had no hesitation whatsoever about embarking on the flight at the scheduled time.

According to well-rehearsed procedures, refuelling had already taken place, and all provisions for the flight had been stowed under the watchful eye of the Chief Steward and Purser David Williams. Next came the luggage for the cargo hold – cases, trunks, and golf bags, as well as sacks of Bermuda-bound airmail. With the weight calculations completed to the captain's satisfaction and the load sheet signed off – maximum all-up load not to exceed 40,500lb, of which payload and crew not to exceed 12,489lb – and the full flight crew now on board, it was the turn of the eight fare-paying passengers to be transferred from the IAL launch and welcomed aboard the luxurious flying boat by the two stewards (Second Steward Bobby Spence had recently taken the difficult decision to give up his career in civil aviation, as he often suffered from travel sickness).

The Empire C-Class boats were beautifully fitted out, having a promenade deck with three separate cabins, providing ample space to wander about and take in the view from the windows, and equipped with deluxe seating, and dining facilities where meals were served by the white-coated stewards, employing bone china, linen napkins, crystal glassware and silver cutlery.

The meals were prepared by top hotel chefs prior to the flight – in the case of Bermuda, from the Belmont Manor Hotel – and were kept hot in steam tables in the pantry. The Ritz-style flying machines were able to accommodate between seventeen and twenty-four passengers in extreme comfort, and up to two tons of mail. Such was the attention to detail that, should a passenger wish to pen a letter during the flight for onward posting on arrival at their destination, headed writing paper printed with the aircraft's logo – a *Laughing Cavalier*, booted and spurred, with the Wordsworth quotation 'The *Cavalier* was eager to depart' below – was provided for their use. These flying hotels were regarded, in this new 'Golden Era' of commercial flight, as the height of sophistication and luxury, and were the reserve of only the wealthiest in society. A one-way ticket from New York to Bermuda would set you back $100, a return $180 – equivalent to about $4,000 today. In modern terms, this was not even business class – this was seriously first class – and these passengers certainly paid for the privilege.

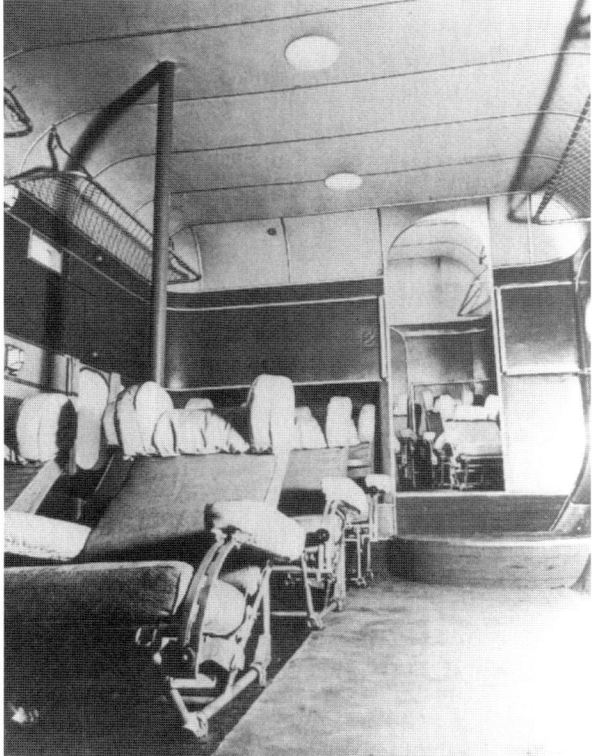

Above: *Cavalier's* promenade cabin, looking forward towards the central/ forward cabins and pantry. (*Short Bros*)

Left: The C-Class promenade deck, looking aft. (*Imperial Airways, via R.T. Jackson*)

Imperial Airways advertisement for the 'Empire Flying-Boats' illustrating the internal layout. Aircraft illustrated is one of RMA *Cavalier's* sister aircraft, the S.23 *G-ADHL Canopus*. (*Imperial Airways*)

The full list of passengers and crew aboard *G-ADUU* for this New York to Bermuda service on Saturday, 21 January 1939 would read as follows:

Passengers: (8)

Mr Donald W. Miller, of Lincoln, Nebraska – Owner of a department store (Aged 47)

Mrs Catherine Miller (Aged 48)

Mr John Noakes, of Melba, New York City – Head of a New York auction house (Aged 62)

Mrs Louise Noakes (Aged 58)

Mr Charles M. Talbot, of Brookline, Massachusetts – Harvard graduate (he had his arm in a sling due to a recent skiing accident) (Aged 24)

Mrs Edna I. Watson, of Paget, Bermuda (formerly from Canada) – Physiotherapist and guesthouse owner (Aged 34)

Mrs Catherine 'Honey' Ingham, of Pembroke, Bermuda (Aged 25)

Miss Nellie Tucker Smith, of Pembroke, Bermuda – Accountant (Aged 42)

Crew: (5)
Captain M.J.R. 'Roly' Alderson – Commander of the RMA *Cavalier* (Aged 31)

Mr Neil Richardson – First officer and co-pilot (Aged 35)

Mr H.W. Patrick Chapman – Radio officer (Aged 33)

Mr David H. Williams – Chief steward and purser (Aged 25)

Mr Robert 'Bobby' Spence – Second steward (Aged 26)

Total POB: 13[9]

10:38 (local time – 15:38 GMT, R.A. log). With Captain Alderson at the controls, the RMA *Cavalier* taxied out from the seaplane base at Port Washington, Long Island. Alderson lined up the huge aircraft for take-off and throttled up the four powerful Pegasus XC engines. The flying boat surged forward, and at 10:42 the silver behemoth lifted gracefully into the air, climbing steadily as it settled onto its south-easterly course towards Bermuda. The *Cavalier* continued its climb in order to get above the overcast predicted by the meteorological reports. As the temperature was well below freezing, icing conditions were to be expected. Accordingly, just before entering the cloud base, First Officer Richardson turned on the hot air to the carburettors. All engines were running normally, and the autopilot had been engaged.

10:45. The aircraft entered the overcast and climbed through it, eventually coming out on top at an altitude of 9,000ft. At around 11:00 they levelled off at a little over 9,000ft. The sun soon melted the ice which had formed on the wings, floats and wires, and the flight proceeded normally.

It is usual practice on these boats that one member of the flight crew shall act as navigator throughout the journey. Captain Alderson was highly skilled at this, and generally elected to act in this capacity on the Bermuda–New York route; this flight was no exception. The routine half-hourly radio messages, with position reports, went out at 11:30 and

12:00, the latter noting 'high cumulus ahead'. Captain Alderson decided to climb through this high cumulus which he anticipated would not extend to any great height. Hot air continued to be applied to the carburettors throughout. Meanwhile, the stewards began to prepare lunch.

Immediately the *Cavalier* entered the cloud, Radio Officer Chapman experienced very severe radio static on the R/T. (He later stated that it was the worst static he had ever experienced in his 5,000 hours of flying time.)

12:23. Alderson requested the radio officer to send the following message:[10] 'Running into bad weather. May have to earth'; this referred to earthing the aerial.[11] This was followed four minutes later by another message: 'Still in bad weather. Severe static.' Communication was becoming difficult due to the meteorological conditions. For the next fifteen minutes the Port Washington radio operator tried to raise the *Cavalier*, but without success.

Almost immediately, while still in cloud, and at an altitude of 11,000ft, all four engines went out of synchronisation and then started to fade. The revolutions began to rise and fall between 1,500 and 2,000rpm. Both pilots suspected carburettor icing and anticipated that – as on the previous flights – they would be able to clear it by manipulation of the throttles. However, on this occasion, despite their best efforts, the fading became more pronounced. The two inboard engines now began to falter badly, and their revs began to drop below 1,000rpm.

Now fully aware that they were facing an unusual problem, Alderson turned back in the direction of Port Washington, hoping to regain a clear patch of air in order to cruise in more favourable conditions. This proved impossible and conditions continued to deteriorate. At this point they lost the inboard engines altogether.

The *Cavalier* now steadily lost altitude at some 500ft per minute but continued to fly on the remaining two outer engines. Realising the gravity of the situation unfolding before him and accepting that it was going to be impossible to maintain sufficient altitude on two engines alone, he changed direction again – this time towards the warmer waters of the Gulf Stream. This calculated decision – cerebral rather than visceral – turned out to be a wise one , for within minutes, and while struggling to maintain altitude, the two remaining engines began to falter. Their altitude was at this point between 5,000ft and 6,000ft and still in cloud, but the snow had turned to rain. As the air temperature was now well above freezing, Captain Alderson suggested trying the application of cold air to the carburettors of the two inner engines. This First Officer Richardson did, but after a momentary burst of power, the engines faded again. Hot air was reapplied.

On his return from manipulating the air intake controls located aft of the radio operator's station, the first officer instructed Steward Spence to go down to the rear cabin to collect all the seat life-preservers in case landing became necessary.

12:50. Captain Alderson ordered the radio officer to send out a 'PAN' signal – the second-level distress signal. In a last attempt to restore power to the engines, Alderson asked his first officer to employ the doping system to inject fuel direct into the cylinders – but to no avail. They were now down to 3,000ft, and it was clear to Captain Alderson that they would have no alternative but to 'ditch' in the sea.

12:57. The captain requested the radio officer to send out an SOS; this was followed two minutes later by another message: 'All engines failing through ice. Altitude 1,500ft. Forced landing in a few minutes.' Port Washington control received yet another, at 13:07, stating that the aircraft was still flying on the two remaining engines. These transmissions were acknowledged and were simultaneously received in Bermuda.

At this point, the stewards were instructed to tell the passengers that a forced landing on the sea was imminent, and that they should remain seated and hold on tightly. (In those early days of commercial air travel there were no standardised emergency procedures in place, and no seatbelts were fitted.) One passenger in the aft cabin, Mr Noakes, decided to remain standing, apparently to get a better view.

13:11. On the flight deck Alderson fought to keep the aircraft level as they prepared to ditch. Although the seas were moderate, they were rougher than he had anticipated, and there was a confused swell making landing conditions far from ideal. The approach was made at 110mph, with the outer engines giving sufficient power to make a controlled landing; flaps were ordered to be half out, but they had not quite extended to this point on contact with the ocean. As the aircraft alighted, the swell was estimated to be between 3 and 10ft. Although strongly constructed, these machines were designed to alight on the waters of sheltered harbours, not in open ocean conditions such as these.[12] The aircraft bounced twice, and the final impact was taken just aft of the 'step' beneath the promenade cabin. Alderson was in little doubt that damage had been done as they came down. The flight crew were thrown forward in their seats, and Captain Alderson sustained a head injury; unfortunately, the standing Mr Noakes had been propelled violently forward, making contact with an interior bulkhead which caused a very serious gash to his head. The purser, Mr Williams, had been standing at the rear of the promenade deck; he also had been thrown to the floor, but managed to help the Noakes' forward.

13:12. A short message was sent out by the radio officer saying that they had come down in the sea: 'Landed OK. Switches off. Stand by.' Water was now entering the hull at a considerable rate, and it was clear to Alderson that the boat was going down. Radio Officer Chapman managed to get off a final signal stating simply: 'Sinking'. Alderson opened the top escape hatch to the rear of the flight deck, then descended the ladder into the pantry and ordered everyone to abandon the aircraft. It had been just two hours and thirty-six minutes since the *Cavalier* had taxied out from Port Washington.

Meanwhile, back at Long Island, as soon as it became clear that the *Cavalier* was going to have to make a forced landing, a major rescue operation was mounted. Port Washington was in radio contact with the Imperial Airways station manager in Bermuda. Captain Powell, himself a former flying boat commander, was known for his consummate navigational skills, and he would soon be key to coordinating the rescue effort.

Two flying boats were scrambled – the Pan American Sikorsky S-42, *NC16735 Betsy* from Bermuda under Captain Lorber, and a US Coastguard flying boat from Long Island – as well as a B.17 Flying Fortress bomber based at Langley Airfield, Virginia. All were forced to return to base due to darkness and deteriorating weather conditions. The Royal Canadian Navy destroyer HMCS *Saguenay* set sail from Bermuda, and the United States Coastguard dispatched two cruising cutters – the *Mendota* and the *Champlain* – and two patrol boats, the *Argo* and the *Icarus*, while the US Navy gunboat USS *Erie* (*PG-50*) also responded and headed for the scene.

Merchant shipping in the area was notified, but all were many hours steaming from the vicinity of the downed aircraft. These included the steamship *Alamar*, the *City of Rayville*, the *General Lee*, the tanker *Virginia Sinclair*, and another tanker, the *Esso Baytown*. The *Esso Baytown* was en route in ballast from Boston, Massachusetts to Baytown, Texas; she was owned and operated by the Standard Oil Company of New Jersey and was under the command of Captain Frank H. Spurr. As soon as the *Esso Baytown's* distress auto-alarm self-activated, the radio operator, Andrew Hamilton – who had been off duty at the time – went into action. He at once advised the skipper, who altered course towards the first reported position of the casualty and ordered full speed at thirteen knots.

The exact details of what happened at this point on board the stricken *Cavalier* – which was now rapidly taking on water – are for obvious reasons somewhat sketchy. Certainly, all passengers and crew were safely evacuated with the help of the crew as the flying boat settled in the sea. One of the passengers, Edna Watson, later stated:

> By the time the steward had the door open, the water was already pouring in and the floor of the cabin was knee-deep in water. I literally had to step into the ocean. The plane sank in about fifteen minutes, not fast, you know it just settled slowly. We had climbed on top and the men pulled the injured men up.

They were soon forced to scramble clear as the *Cavalier's* fractured hull broke in two and sank beneath the waves. It is thought that Mr Miller may have been stunned by contact with part of the boat's structure as he jumped; together with Mrs Miller, Mrs Ingham and Miss Smith, he had been given a seat life preserver by Steward Williams, but he was not wearing it, and although Steward Spence attempted to save him, he was seen by Miss Smith to disappear beneath the waves: he was the first to perish.

Captain Alderson had fetched the four crew-type rubber life preservers from the navigator's compartment and handed them to the other passengers. Although the *Cavalier* was equipped with twenty-two seat-type preservers and six crew-type preservers, only eight – four of each – could be gathered before the boat sank. This left Captain Alderson, Mr Talbot and Steward Spence without any form of life preserver.

Captain Alderson instructed them all to 'keep together'; fortunately, by joining the preservers together and forming a circle, these provided sufficient buoyancy to support everyone. (Life rafts were not carried in these early days of civil aviation, nor indeed pyrotechnics, emergency position indicating radio beacons (EPIRBs), personal strobe lights, or any other means of attracting attention, although the Empire boats were some of the first aircraft to carry a basic flight data recorder – or 'Black Box' as it is now called.)

At first, the sea state was moderate, and – thanks to the commander's decision to try to gain the Gulf Stream if ditching became unavoidable – the water was a survivable 66° to 68°F. Had they landed outside the Gulf Stream, the temperature would have been much lower, and their chances of survival would have been greatly reduced.[13]

It is thought that First Officer Richardson and Steward Spence did all they could to look after the badly injured Gordon Noakes; however, about an hour after darkness fell, he succumbed and died in Steward Williams' charge, and his body was released from the group and sank.

About two hours later, the young Spence apparently became restless and excited, and repeatedly swam away from the group. He then started to thresh the water furiously, and although he was brought back and held between Richardson and Mrs Watson, he quickly became delirious and (according to later accounts) he 'lost his reason'; he died shortly after 21:00 in First Officer Richardson's arms.[14]

Meanwhile, Captain Alderson had lost consciousness; the indefatigable Edna Watson kept him alive by holding his head above the waves.

The remaining survivors clung together in the dark as best they could. Mrs Watson fought to keep up their spirits by encouraging them to sing and using her skills as a physiotherapist to periodically massage some warmth back into their stiffening muscles. In a radio interview twelve hours after the survivors arrived in New York, Richardson attested:

> I would like to say very strongly that during the whole of this time one lady passenger, the – all the ladies were frightfully good – Mrs Watson of Bermuda was absolutely holding us together. She was absolutely God-sent. She was so cheerful and marvellous that I didn't think that a woman – or a man – could behave like that.

The survivors had jettisoned most of their clothing to reduce drag, and there was a moment of light relief when Richardson spotted his trousers floating past in the swell and managed to rescue his pipe.

The hours crawled slowly by, with the ever-present threat of shark attack, which was heightened by the presence of the bodies of the three deceased in the vicinity. They did their utmost to push this fear to the back of their minds. Staying afloat became increasingly challenging as the winds strengthened and the seas became rougher.

At some point during the evening – no one knows exactly when – the survivors thought they heard an aircraft on one or possibly two occasions, and later – possibly around 21:00 – spotted the lights of passing ships, together with searchlights, but some miles away. (It was thought that one of these may have been the gunboat, USS *Erie*.) Despite their frantic efforts to attract attention, the ships steamed steadily on, and disappeared over the horizon. This must have been a huge psychological blow; then a very cold rainstorm came upon them, and their spirits began to flag.

At around 23:00, after nearly ten long hours – the little group spotted a large ship heading in their direction, its searchlights sweeping the seas. By this time, according to Richardson, 'the wind was rising a bit and the spray was in our faces quite a lot'. The vessel seemed to turn towards them, and so in a concerted effort they shouted at the tops of their voices 'One, Two, Three – AHOY!' Richardson and Chapman decided to strike out from the group and swam towards the ship, waving and shouting.

Suddenly, the tanker's deck crew thought they heard – through the cacophony of wind and spray – the distant sound of human cries. Captain Spurr immediately ordered the engines to be stopped; the arcs of the searchlights sliced round through the dark and, to the crew's astonishment, the beams picked out two tiny figures. Captain Spurr immediately ordered the lowering of one of the lifeboats – in itself not an easy manoeuvre in the mounting seas – and the rescue crew rowed as quickly as possible towards the bobbing heads. Neil Richardson said later: 'They saw me and heaved me in which was a very wonderful moment for me, especially when I heard a man say, "There's another one there, chief", and I thought that's the finest thing I ever heard.' It was truly a miracle.

What had happened was this: Captain Taffy Powell, operations manager at the Imperial Airways station in Bermuda, was in the routine of logging the positions of flying boats en route. As soon as he had

A TANKER COMES TO THE RESCUE OF SURVIVORS OF THE CAVALIER

Artist's impression of the dramatic rescue of the RMA *Cavalier's* survivors by the crew of the tanker *Esso Baytown*. (*LIFE Magazine, 6 February 1939; drawing by Howard Brodie*)

received the SOS from the Bermuda wireless station, Powell was able to triangulate, from the 12:00 position given by the *Cavalier's* flight crew and a radio bearing obtained by Cable & Wireless,[15] the aircraft's position on ditching as 37° 17′ north, 69° 45′ west.

Captain Powell remained in constant touch with Port Washington. Meanwhile, he had been calculating the likely speed and direction of drift of any survivors in the current of the Gulf Stream as the hours passed, and was simultaneously plotting the course of the *Esso Baytown* towards them.

At around 23:00 he relayed a message to Captain Spurr, the master of the tanker, to say that he thought they had just passed the estimated position of any potential survivors and that they should turn around. Powell's calculations could not have been more accurate.

The rescue itself was far from straightforward. Chapman and Richardson were pulled aboard the lifeboat first, and they then directed the boat to the remaining eight survivors. Captain Alderson was still unconscious when they were pulled from the sea. The swell had been steadily increasing ahead of the gale that was to follow, and this presented something of a problem getting the occupants of the lifeboat safely aboard the tanker. However, according to the *Esso Baytown's* report, 'this was accomplished in a ship-shape manner by slinging a safety belt under the arms of each survivor to assist in the climb up the Jacob's ladder hung over the tanker's side.' In a radio interview given on arrival in New York, First Officer Richardson described the process slightly differently: 'We had a bumpy trip up the side of the ship – you know – on the end of the rope, rather like – like fish.'

Once aboard the *Esso Baytown,* the survivors were placed under the care of Chief Steward Fricker and his team. In fact, Fricker happened to be a former RAF pilot, and was thus well placed to understand the situation of his charges. Indeed, Captain Spurr later commented: 'I have never had a finer steward's department. They did a wonderful job'; and according to Richardson 'We had nothing but kindness and attention and everything we wanted from them.'

The USS *Erie*, which had now arrived on the scene, radioed across to the tanker: 'Have doctor. Suggest any sick survivors be put aboard *Erie*

The rescuing lifeboat crew from "ESSO BAYTOWN". Reading left to right: Chief Officer Olaf Anderson, Thomas J. Brady, John Goodwin, Stanley H. Taylor, John Thomaschek, Howell L. Smith and Joseph R. Minor, Bos'n.

(*Standard Oil Company, The Ship's Bulletin, January-February 1939*)

as we expect to arrive New York late Sunday afternoon. Congratulations on rescue,' to which the response came back: 'Survivors not able to be transferred, but would like doctor to come aboard.' This was duly carried out, and the medic was able to minister to Mrs Noakes, Mrs Miller and Captain Alderson. Records state that the rescue was completed at 02:02 on 22 January.

The fact that the rescue was accomplished at all was a feat of extraordinary skill on the part of the crew of the *Esso Baytown*, and in particular of her master, Captain Spurr.

The role that Captain Taffy Powell played in pinpointing the position of the survivors was likewise critical to its success and cannot be overstated. As Roly Alderson wrote many years later: 'Our rescue was a miracle … No ship or aircraft – in those days – could navigate to that sort of accuracy.'[16]

The brief entry in Captain Alderson's pilot's log for the last flight of the RMA *Cavalier* reflects his typically Churchillian reluctance to indulge in

Mr. H. J. Esselborn, Manager Operating Division, extending congratulations to Captain Frank H. Spurr aboard the 'ESSO BAYTOWN'.

(*Standard Oil Company, The Ship's Bulletin, January-February 1939*)

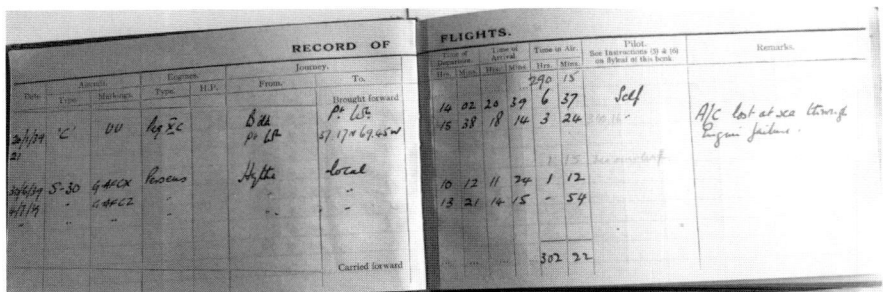

R.A.'s original flight logbook entry recording the loss of RMA *Cavalier*, 21 January 1939. (*Author's collection*)

prolixity. It reads: 'From: Pt Washington To: 37:17 N, 69:45 W – Time of Departure: 15:38** – Time of Arrival 18:14 – Time in Air: 3:24 – Pilot: Self – Remarks: A/C lost at sea through Engine failure' (**Times in GMT)

Captain Taffy Powell arrived from Bermuda on the Sunday Pan American Sikorsky S-42 service, in the company of the wives of First Officer Neil Richardson and Radio Officer Patrick Chapman; they were ferried out to meet the *Esso Baytown* as she entered New York the following day to a frenzy of media coverage.

SS *Esso Baytown* arrives in New York to the glare of the world's media. (*Standard Oil Company, The Ship's Bulletin, January-February 1939*)

Vol. 6, No. 6   LIFE   February 6, 1939

THREE OF THE CAVALIER'S SURVIVORS—MISS NELLIE SMITH, MRS. GEORGE INGHAM AND MRS. EDNA WATSON—WAVE TO NEW YORK FROM THE RESCUE SHIP "ESSO BAYTOWN"

Above: Survivors from the RMA *Cavalier* wave from the deck of the *Esso Baytown* on arrival in New York. (*LIFE Magazine, 6 February 1939; International*)

Right: The RMA *Cavalier* survivors arriving in New York. Note First Officer Neil Richardson smoking his pipe, which he managed to retrieve from his trousers as they floated past in the hours before the rescue. (*Standard Oil Company, The Ship's Bulletin, January-February 1939*)

Survivors of plane crash: Front row seated, left to right, Mrs. George Ingham, Mrs. Edna Watson, M. R. Alderson, pilot of the "CAVALIER", Patrick Chapman, radio operator. Rear standing, left to right, Neil Richardson, first officer of plane, David Williams, steward, C. A. Talbot, passenger.

Miss N. T. Smith, Mrs. Ingham and Mrs. Watson aboard "ESSO BAYTOWN" waving to relatives on Coast Guard cutter. The two other survivors, Mrs. J. Gordon Noakes and Mrs. Donald Miller were under medical care.

Capt. M. R. Alderson, Cambridge graduate, ace Imperial Airways pilot since 1932, kept survivors together in water, later weakened, was unconscious when found. Above: he talks to New York reporters.

Reporters interview R.A. on arrival in New York. (*LIFE Magazine, 6 February 1939; International*)

The crew were transferred under escort to the Hotel Shelton to recuperate.

This was the first ever loss of a scheduled passenger-carrying aircraft in the ocean, and the drama was worldwide front-page news. 'Air Liner Sunk in Atlantic – Three Lives Lost' ran the headlines of *The Times* in London on 23 January.

The sinking of the *Cavalier* – the fifth Empire boat to be lost – spelt the end of Imperial Airways' involvement in the Bermuda to New York route.

R.A. leaving the pier in New York after the downing of the *Cavalier*, accompanied by the niece of Mr Paul Bewshea, Imperial's New York representative. (*Author's collection; Acme*)

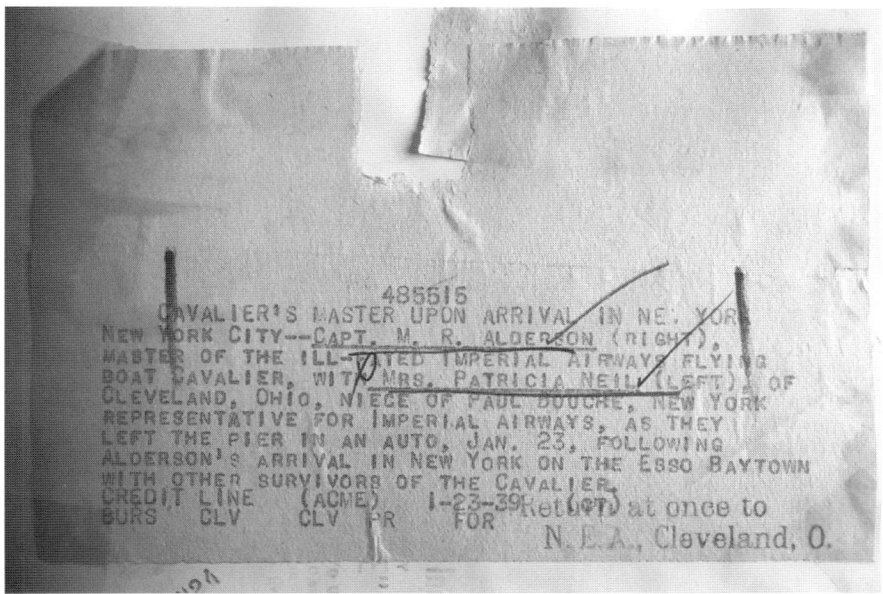

485515

CAVALIER'S MASTER UPON ARRIVAL IN NEW YORK
NEW YORK CITY--CAPT. M. R. ALDERSON (RIGHT),
MASTER OF THE ILL-FATED IMPERIAL AIRWAYS FLYING
BOAT CAVALIER, WITH MRS. PATRICIA NEIL (LEFT), OF
CLEVELAND, OHIO, NIECE OF PAUL DOUCHE, NEW YORK
REPRESENTATIVE FOR IMPERIAL AIRWAYS, AS THEY
LEFT THE PIER IN AN AUTO, JAN. 23, FOLLOWING
ALDERSON'S ARRIVAL IN NEW YORK ON THE ESSO BAYTOWN
WITH OTHER SURVIVORS OF THE CAVALIER.
CREDIT LINE (ACME) 1-23-39.
BURS CLV CLV PR FOR

Return at once to
N.E.A., Cleveland, O.

Obverse of photo above. (*Author's collection*)

'CAVALIER'
('AVE ATQUE VALE')

CAVALIER, YOUR NAME WILL FOREVER LIVE:
WE OF THESE ISLANDS CANNOT SOON FORGET
THOUGH OTHERS MAY, YOU WERE THE FIRST: TO
US
A PIONEER IN THIS THE AGE OF AIR:
WHERE LANDS ARE LINKED AND FRIENDSHIPS
CLOSER TIED.
LONG DID WE TOIL PREPARING YOUR ABODE.
OUR LOVELIEST ISLAND WILLINGLY WE GAVE
TO BE YOUR HOME. ARRIVED, CREATED NEW
YOU MADE YOUR MAIDEN FLIGHT, YOUR
EAGERNESS
IN STARTING FRIGHTENED WATCHERS IN THEIR
BOATS
AS SKIMMING O'ER THEIR MASTS YOU CLIMBED
THE AIR,
AND SAILED, BREATHTAKING IN YOUR GRACE AND
EASE
O'ER ALL OUR LENGTH, THAT PERFECT SUMMERS
DAY.
YOUR BEAUTY HAS NOT DIMMED; WE STILL RECALL
YOUR SPLENDOUR, STRENGTH AND POWER, BUT
GREATER STILL THE
RAGING FORCE OF NATURE HARD BESET
AND THRUST YOU DOWN. NO FAULT OF YOURS.
YOU ARE
FORGIVEN. ONLY IN OUR MEMORY
GLIDES IN THE BLUE THAT GRACEFUL, SILVERY
SHAPE,
THAT SILENT VISION. LOVELY AS A DREAM

(Eulogy to the *Cavalier*, written at school in 1939 by
13-year-old Miss Osborn, of Bermuda)

At a regular monthly meeting of the

Chamber of Commerce of the State of New York

held February second, nineteen hundred and thirty-nine, the following minute, presented by William J. Graham on behalf of the Executive Committee, was unanimously adopted by a rising vote:

Whereas, The Chamber of Commerce of the State of New York since its founding in 1768 has been actively identified with the development of the American Merchant Marine and has given recognition to outstanding deeds of heroism incidental to the duties of navigators and seamen; and

Whereas, The American tanker

"Esso Baytown"

owned by the Standard Oil Company of New Jersey and bound from the Port of Boston to Baytown, Texas, on January 21st last, in the face of peril and difficulties,

did rescue ten survivors of the airliner "Cavalier"

of the Imperial Airways, Ltd., which met disaster over the Atlantic Ocean while en route from New York to Bermuda; therefore be it

Resolved, That the Chamber, in meeting assembled, hereby records its

appreciation of the masterly skill and seamanship

of the captain of the "Esso Baytown" who is a lieutenant commander in the Merchant Marine Naval Reserve, and its recognition of the important parts played by other officers, the radio operator and the seamen, particularly those who so ably manned the lifeboat, in effecting the rescue; and be it

Resolved, That the Chamber hereby also expresses its

admiration of the men who manned the "Cavalier,"

who, calm in disaster, inspired those in their charge, through long hours of fear and helplessness, with the courage to fight to live; and be it

Resolved, That both the American Merchant Marine and the airway transportation service, respectively, may justly feel proud of the courage and resourcefulness of those who, living up to the finest traditions of the sea, made possible the rescue, and the Chamber hereby inscribes their names on its roll of honor:

Captain Frank H. Spurr, of the "Esso Baytown" who directed the rescue; First Officer Olaf Anderson, who commanded the lifeboat, and his crew: Joseph R. Minor, boatswain; Howell L. Smith, John Tomaschek, John Goodwin and Thomas J. Brady, able bodied seamen, and Stanley H. Taylor, ordinary seaman; and Andrew R. Hamilton, radio operator.

Captain M. R. Alderson, of the "Cavalier;" First Officer Neil Richardson, Patrick Chapman, radio operator; David Williams, steward, and Robert Spence, steward, who lost his life after heroically assisting passengers; and be it

Resolved, That this expression of recognition by the Chamber be engrossed and presented to Captain Frank H. Spurr and also that copies of it be sent to the others above named or to their families; and be it further

Resolved, That the Chamber herewith expresses its deep sympathy to the families of those who lost their lives in the Cavalier disaster.

Richard W. Lawrence
President

B. C. Davis Jr.
Secretary

New York Chamber of Commerce Resolution dated 2 February 1939, regarding the rescue of the survivors of the RMA *Cavalier* by the crew of the *Esso Baytown* on 21 January 1939. (*Author's collection*)

Chapter 7

War (1939–1945)

The *Cavalier's* survivors arrived back in New York aboard the SS *Esso Baytown* on 23 January 1939.

Having been interviewed, the American survivors were conveyed home by taxi under police escort; the Bermudian residents and the *Cavalier*'s crew returned to Hamilton by sea aboard the *Monarch of Bermuda* a few days later, to a tumultuous welcome.

It quickly became apparent from all the press interviews which followed the *Cavalier* incident that although there had been many acts of bravery and selflessness while the survivors awaited rescue, the true heroine was Edna Watson.[1]

Indeed, passengers later referred to her as 'the bravest woman alive'. She had ministered to all their needs throughout their long hours of exposure in the open ocean, when they had little hope of ultimate survival, 'demonstrating gallantry and indefatigable determination'. Survivor Nellie Smith – also from Bermuda – later told *The Royal Gazette*: 'Mrs Edna Watson was the life of the party. She absolutely kept us going, talking and joking.' Watson was reported as swimming among the group, 'massaging muscles that had gone stiff with cold'. She had kept their spirits up by encouraging them to sing, and had undoubtedly saved the life of

Mrs. Edna Watson, Bermudian, was bravest, most lauded of all. Said she: "We had fun. We sang, we laughed, we joked, we gossiped."

Edna Watson, heroine of the *Cavalier* disaster. (*LIFE Magazine 6 February 1939; Acme*)

Captain Alderson by supporting his head above the waves when he lost consciousness; indeed, he was still unconscious when the little group were finally found by the crew of the *Esso Baytown*. A few months later, on 4 August 1939, in his last official act, the outgoing Governor, Sir Reginald Hildyard presented Watson with the Royal Humane Society's Silver Medal. The citation reads: 'At great personal risk she saved the life of the captain by supporting him when the aircraft was forced down.'

Captain Alderson's condition had initially given cause for concern, but it was not long before he was well enough to head back to England to continue his recovery and undergo a full debriefing on the ditching with the Imperial Airways management. During the month of February, Alderson was required to give evidence to the official enquiry; meanwhile, much speculation swirled around the circumstances of the *Cavalier* accident, amid talk of lawsuits against both the commander of the aircraft and Imperial Airways Limited.

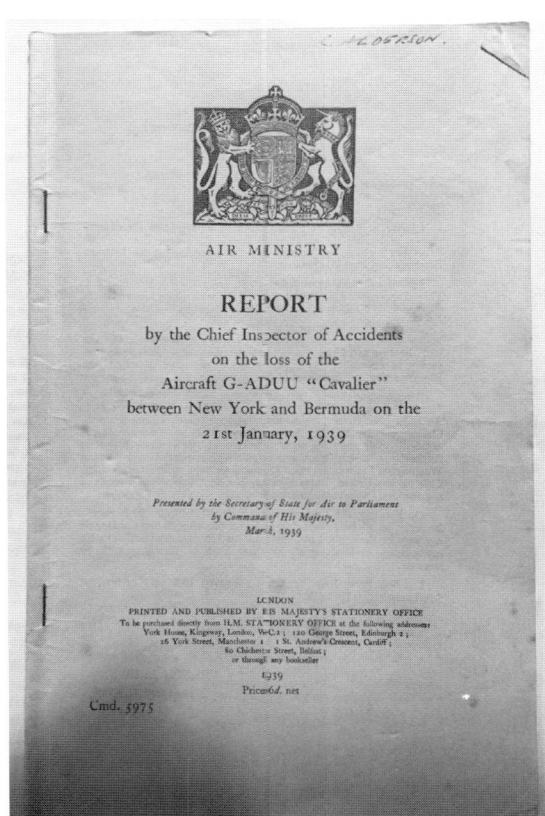

R.A.'s original copy of the Air Ministry's Report into the loss of the RMA *Cavalier*. (*Author's collection*)

At a sitting in the House of Commons on 15 February 1939, Hansard records the response given by Sir Kingsley Wood to a question tabled by Mr Simmonds:

> The Chief Inspector of Accidents is at present conducting his investigation of the accident to the flying boat *Cavalier*, and he is not expected to return to this country until the end of the month. As soon as his report is available, a statement will be issued giving a summary of the general conclusions.

On 28 February 1939, the official report of the incident, prepared by the Chief Inspector of Accidents,[2] Wing Commander Vernon Brown, was presented to the Secretary of State for Air at the British Air Ministry.

Report No. C.A. 92 of The Accidents Investigation Branch is prefaced by the following letter, quoted verbatim:

> AIR MINISTRY,
> February 28th, 1939.
> The Secretary of State for Air,
>
> SIR,
> I have the honour to submit herewith my report on the circumstances attending the accident to Imperial Airways Empire boat Cavalier which, on January 21st last, was lost at sea between Bermuda and Port Washington.
>
> I sailed to New York on January 28th and arrived on February 3rd. There I was met by the British Air Attaché with whom I immediately proceeded to Washington.
>
> As explained in paragraph 1 of the Report he had, on your instructions, conducted a preliminary enquiry in New York. I have had the benefit of the report of this enquiry, and take this opportunity of expressing my appreciation of the way in which the Board carried out their part of the investigation.
>
> After reading through the evidence that had already been obtained I called upon Mr Noble, the Chairman of the Civil Aeronautics Authority, Mr Hester, the Administrator, and Colonel Sumptersmith, Chairman of the Air Safety Board; I also discussed the accident with the two representatives of the Civil Aeronautics Authority who had been appointed

as observers. Before leaving Washington I also called upon Lieutenant-Commander Reichelderfer, Chief of the United States Weather Bureau, from whom I received a great deal of valuable information.

On February 8th I proceeded by air from Baltimore to Bermuda in order to make certain enquiries at the airport there. During my stay in Bermuda I obtained the further evidence necessary for my purpose and left again for New York on February 12th by steamer.

I sailed from New York on February 18th and arrived at Southampton on the 24th.

I am, Sir,
Your obedient Servant,
VERNON BROWN,
Chief Inspector of Accidents.

The full report runs to twenty-one pages together with Appendices and is therefore not reproduced here. However, an abridged summary of conclusions, criticisms and recommendations is as follows:

Principal Conclusions

- All crew were properly qualified and physically fit.
- *Cavalier* and its equipment were in a fully airworthy condition prior to departure.
- The flight was properly despatched at 10:38 hours in accordance with all regulations.
- The local weather conditions/data/forecasts available fully justified the captain in undertaking the flight.
- When the engines faded, nothing that the flight crew could do ultimately had any effect, and due to the lack of power it became necessary to alight on the water.
- The fading of the engines was the result of carburettor trouble due to icing.
- The sea conditions were too severe to make a good landing possible; the damage caused by the impact resulted in the hull flooding and subsequently sinking.

- There were in all twenty-two seat-type life preservers and six crew-type life preservers. None of the passengers were wearing the former when the boat landed, and it was only possible to equip four of the passengers with these.
- Mrs Watson was given a crew-type preserver. Mr Miller was not wearing his lifebelt when he entered the water and was the first to die.
- The four crew-type preservers were fetched from the navigator's compartment by the captain. The captain, Mr Talbot and Steward Spence were never in possession of life preservers.
- Although only eight life preservers were used (i.e., four of each) these provided sufficient buoyancy to support everyone when hands were joined and legs entwined.
- Mr Noakes sustained a serious injury on impact when standing, contrary to the steward's instructions. He subsequently died.
- Steward Spence was apparently a very highly strung young man and wore himself out assisting others. He became delirious and lost his reason and died in First Officer Richardson's arms.
- No blame for the accident can be attributed to either the captain or the first officer who behaved with great coolness throughout.
- The radio message sent out at 12:23 hours, '… may have to earth', referred to earthing the aerial due to the severe static (not 'may have to land').
- If the captain had not continued on his course to Bermuda, the chances of rescue would have been reduced. Moreover, as the water temperatures fell by approximately 10 degrees for every 100 miles nearer New York the chances of survival would have been progressively less.
- All British regulations under which this flying-boat was operated were complied with.

Principal Criticisms and Recommendations

The investigating Board feel that if, as they think, this was indeed the cause of the accident, the Exactor system of throttle and mixture controls must have aggravated it…

[The Board has made the following recommendation:] The Exactor control system should be studied in the light of the remarks made in paragraph above.

(a) An immediate modification should be made to the Short 'C' class flying boat whereby the crew may have more adequate control of the oil temperature ... (or) alternatively the oil temperature should be governed by a thermostatic viscosity controller to achieve the same purpose;

(b) For emergency conditions an ample additional supply of heat under the control of the crew should be provided in order to raise the temperature of the incoming air before it reaches the carburettor jets. As a necessary adjunct to this, a carburettor air temperature indicator visible to the pilots is essential so that the supply of extra heat may be turned on before icing commences.

The board found 'that no instruction is given by Imperial Airways to passengers as to action to be taken in an emergency...' The recommendations are as follows:

(a) Desirability of instructing passengers as to method of fastening life-belts and as to location of emergency doors and hatches.

(b) Question of use of belts. This is important on trans-Atlantic air services, as all US Air Lines insist on passengers being strapped in at the take-off and landing, and there is much criticism unless it is at least pointed out that belts are available.

(c) Provision of additional life-saving equipment such as life rafts, lifeboats, pyrotechnic signals, rockets, and waterproof emergency radio set.

The Chief Inspector of Accidents also recommended that serious consideration should be given to the question of carrying a separate navigator.

As can be seen from the above report, many of the safety procedures and equipment that we now take for granted on modern commercial aircraft were introduced as a direct result of the downing of the *Cavalier* on 21 January 1939 – the first ever loss of a scheduled passenger aeroplane in the ocean.

In the wake of the official Air Ministry Report, any suggestion of culpability on the part of Captain Alderson immediately dissolved and talk of lawsuits abruptly ceased. Indeed, the actions of the commander and his crew were fully vindicated and there was now nothing but praise, both in the press and indeed from the very top of Imperial Airways. A personal letter to Alderson from the Chairman of Imperial Airways, Sir John Reith, dated 24 March reads as follows:

> Dear Captain Alderson,
> The report of the Committee of Enquiry into the *Cavalier* accident, over which Sir John Salmond presided, has now been received and I am happy to tell you that the references therein to the conduct of yourself and your crew in the awful ordeal to which you were recently subject are such as any airman would be proud of. They reflect in fact the greatest credit on you all.
> The Board of this Company join me in congratulating you not only on your escape but on upholding the highest traditions of British seamanship, or establishing those of airmanship – whichever way you prefer the matter to be put. The actual observations are as follows:
> 'We are satisfied that throughout Captain Alderson used all proper skill and exercised good judgment under abnormal conditions.
> 'We feel bound to pay tribute to the calmness, courage and fortitude of the crew … Captain Alderson gave his lifebelt to a passenger and undoubtedly suffered from exposure and the mental strain involved.'

Reith concludes his letter with the fullest praise for all members of the crew, with the committee recommending that they 'be granted a considerable period of leave on full basic and service pay'.

TELEPHONE: VICTORIA 2323.
TELEGRAMS: IMPAIRLIM, LONDON

AIRWAY TERMINUS,
VICTORIA STATION,
LONDON, S.W.1.

24th March, 1939

Dear Captain Alderson,

The report of the Committee of Enquiry into
the Cavalier accident, over which Sir John Salmond
presided, has now been received and I am very happy
to tell you that the references therein to the
conduct of yourself and your crew in the awful
ordeal to which you were recently subject are such
as any airman would be proud of. They reflect in
fact the greatest credit on you all.

The Board of this Company join me in
congratulating you not only on your escape but on
upholding the highest traditions of British seamanship,
or establishing those of airmanship - whichever way
you prefer the matter to be put.

The actual observations are as follows:

"We are satisfied that throughout Captain
Alderson used all proper skill and exercised
good judgment under abnormal conditions."

"We feel bound to pay tribute to the
calmness, courage and fortitude of the members
of the crew .... Captain Alderson gave his
lifebelt to a passenger and undoubtedly
suffered severely from exposure and the mental
strain involved."

"Radio Officer Chapman carried out his
duties with great skill and courage. He was
able to send messages .... which contributed
materially to the ultimate rescue of six out
of the eight passengers and four out of the
five members of the crew."

Letter to R.A. from Sir John Reith, Chairman of Imperial Airways, 24 March 1939
(page 1). (*Author's collection*)

"The conduct and bearing of First Officer Richardson, Radio Officer Chapman and Steward Williams appear to have been exemplary and courageous in all respects."

I am writing similar letters to First Officer Richardson, Radio Officer Chapman, and Steward Williams.

The Committee recommended that all members of the crew should be granted a considerabl period of leave on full basic and service pay, and this will be arranged. You should regard yourself therefore as being on leave on full pay for an indefinite period.

Captain M. R. Alderson,
135 Gloucester Court,
Kew,
Surrey.

Letter as opposite (page 2). (*Author's collection*)

REPORT: *TIME MAGAZINE* Monday 3 April 1939

The day before the four-engined, Bermuda-bound *Cavalier* went down to a crash landing on the Atlantic last January, her Cambridge-educated skipper, thin-faced Captain Marmaduke R. Alderson, wrote a troubled and prophetic report to his employer, Imperial Airways Limited, of London:

'During the past few weeks, I have been very concerned over the unsatisfactory functioning of *Cavalier*'s engines.... I make this separate report in the hope that the Engineering Department may give serious attention to the problem. The essential fact is that ... it is impossible to maintain the power output from any engine, and there is no doubt in my mind that the principal cause of this is ice-formation on the butterfly throttle.... The carburettor heating systems ... have been checked repeatedly for correct functioning but it seems that they fail inherently.'

Last week the British Air Ministry made public its official findings on the crash in which three of *Cavalier*'s company were lost, the other ten rescued after a precarious ten hours in a stormy sea. As everybody had surmised, *Cavalier* was forced down when her engines failed because of carburettor ice, to prevent which her engine builders had failed to provide adequate heating equipment although US designers have long had the problem whipped.

Imperial appeared to have come to grief through smug blundering by its directing personnel. The Air Ministry recorded that Skipper Alderson had reported trouble through carburettor icing as early as last October, had told of one flight in which he had to pump the throttles for three and a half hours to break away ice.

His warnings got no results, although a remedy was at hand in any US engine. Pilots of two Empire boats flying European routes had reported the same trouble. 'Captain Alderson,' said the Air Ministry's report, 'was disturbed that the gravity of the situation was not more fully realised.… These incidents … resulted in some research being immediately put in hand by Imperial Airways.'

That Skipper Alderson was not to blame for what happened after his warnings was an obvious finding, and the Air Ministry made it. Strangely enough the report found the ship airworthy, made no specific criticism of Imperial's management. But when Imperial sends out a new flying boat on the run, revamped to fit the Air Ministry's recommendations, it will follow generally the practices observed by Pan American Airways on the same line.

In addition to being protected by effective carburettor heaters, passengers will be instructed in fastening life belts, since most of *Cavalier*'s passengers left without them or carried them in their hands. Passengers will also be strapped in seats on take-offs and landings, life rafts with rockets, emergency radio and provisions will be carried.

Prize ray of sunshine in the Air Ministry's findings: felicitation of Captain Alderson for heading doggedly for Bermuda, once he was in trouble, instead of turning back to Port Washington. The reason: the water in the Gulf Stream, where he came down, was warm; it was much colder back toward New York.

It was May 1939 before the dust had settled and Roly's life began to gradually return to some sort of normality. His employers now granted him privacy and some well-deserved leave before returning him to normal duties.

Captain Alderson took to the air once more on Friday, 30 June at Hythe, aboard one of the two long-range S.30 boats *G-AFCX*, named *Clyde*, for a seventy-five-minute local flight, just to ease himself back into the left-hand seat. It did not take long – after all, he had by now flown over a million miles as pilot-in-command during his aviation career to date. The following Tuesday he was at the controls of *Clyde's* twin sister *Clare G-AFCZ*[3].

During these days of summer 1939, competition between Pan American and Imperial for domination of the flying boat routes was as fierce as ever. Just the previous week, Pan American had inaugurated both an airmail service flight from the US to the United Kingdom, and a passenger service between the US and France. They followed this a week later by starting a passenger service from Port Washington (New York) to Southampton. In all cases these flights were undertaken using the huge new Boeing 314 Clipper flying boats.

Meanwhile, Roly was evidently back on form and ready for work. In the early hours of Monday, 17 July, the S.30 boat *Clare* lifted off into a crepuscular sky, bound for Italy. An hour or so into the flight, there was a minor glitch with the W/T equipment which caused them to return to base, but this was soon resolved, and *CZ* took off again at 08:36. After a four-hour leg down to Marseilles, they finished the day's flying at Bracciano. Next day, after brief stops at Brindisi and Athens, they alighted at Alexandria. *CZ* pressed on to Tiberias, Habbaniyah and Basrah. The route was then retraced, landing back at Hythe three days later on 22 July.

A similar trip followed, and in August Roly flew the longer run aboard *G-AETY, Clio*, on past Basrah to Bahrein, Dubai, Jiwani, and finally Karachi – and from there back to Southampton. The round trip took seven days. Then the world changed.

On Sunday, 3 September 1939, the United Kingdom declared war on Germany.

On that very same Sunday, the flying boat *Clyde* took off from Poole, bound for St Nazaire in Brittany, then onward to Marseilles; Captain Roly Alderson was in command. *Clyde* routed as before, down through France, Italy, Greece, Egypt, Israel, Iraq, and finally to Imperial's hub at Karachi, capital of the Sindh – still part of the British Raj.

The flying for Roly through the following months was relentless – sometimes to Alexandria and back, sometimes continuing on southwards, following the Nile through the Sudan and Uganda, and thence to Lake Victoria in Kenya; or eastwards to Karachi, or maybe on again, across India to Calcutta, then Rangoon, Bangkok, Penang and finally Singapore.

It must have been with some wry satisfaction, therefore, that Alderson received a personal letter in early November from Sir John Reith, the Chairman of Imperial Airways. It was dated 3 November 1939 – exactly three weeks before BOAC was officially established.

It was sent from the Grand Spa Hotel, Clifton, Bristol – the new HQ – and read as follows:

> Dear Captain Alderson,
>
> Mr Runciman[4] and I wish to put on record to you a note of our personal appreciation and of the Company's indebtedness for the great efforts you made in carrying on the Empire services during the very difficult period before the war started.
>
> We all realised how critical the position had become owing to a shortage of boats and still more of pilots. It would obviously be some time before the situation could be eased, and meantime the Company had commitments to discharge or anyhow to do its best to discharge.
>
> To you it meant prodigious flying hours with an overworked fleet, latterly with weather and operating conditions at their worst.
>
> There was a good deal of public criticism over the inevitable delays, and very little public appreciation of what was being achieved against great odds.
>
> We hope you will look back on that strenuous time with satisfaction; you are certainly entitled to. It marks the end of the first stage of All-up Empire Mail services. And we wanted you to know that we are proud of what you have done and are grateful to you.
>
> This message is intended also for the junior navigating officers, radio officers and crew who served with you.
>
> Yours sincerely
> (signed) J.C.W. Reith

Notwithstanding such words of praise, Alderson was intent on recovering his equilibrium after the events of 21 January – and that included replacing some of the personal items lost or damaged during that episode.

Being a bachelor with no dependents, and with an engineer's eye for craftsmanship, Roly Alderson could always be relied upon to be wearing hand-lasted McAfee shoes on his feet and a quality timepiece on his wrist. When the *Cavalier* had come down earlier that year, Roly lost his shoes, but was still wearing on his wrist a Jaeger-LeCoultre *Reverso* watch (as worn, incidentally, by Edward VIII in his short reign in 1936) and, although it survived the ordeal and came ashore with him in New York, it was no longer in serviceable condition. When he returned to England, the watch was claimed – as a trophy, perhaps – by a close female friend. Obviously a replacement was required, and on 17 December, while on a stop-over in Alexandria en route between Hythe and Kisumu in the long-range S.30 *Clyde G-AFCX*, he called on Wolf Horowitz, in Avenue Cherif Pacha. Horowitz was a Romanian who had settled in Alexandria; he became one of the leading jewellers in Egypt and acted as an agent retailer for Patek Philippe and Jaeger-LeCoultre. Records note that 'he served the elite, as well as the Royal Courts of King Fouad 1 and King Farouk 1'. Roly selected a classically understated Patek Philippe *Calatrava* wristwatch in a rose gold case – which he continued to wear for the next fifty years.[5]

On 9 May 1940, Roly headed off aboard the S.30 boat *Cathay G-AFKZ* from Hythe to Poole, bound ultimately for Basrah and Tiberias. They crossed France, landing briefly at Biscarosse on the French Atlantic coast, and ended the day's flying at Marseilles. The very next day – as Alderson and his crew headed on down to Bizerte in Tunisia, and thence to Malta, where they touched down in Marsaxlokk Harbour and stayed for forty-eight hours – Germany invaded France, Belgium, the Netherlands and Luxembourg, so by the time they had swapped machines in Alexandria and were en route back to England aboard *Castor G-ADUW*, things were really hotting-up.

Their next trip started from Poole on 31 May, aboard the S.23, *G-AEUH, Corio*.[6] This was the long run to Singapore and back by way of Alexandria. On 5 June, when *Corio* and her crew were in Karachi, the Germans had launched their major offensive, entering Paris on 14 May – and within nine days France had been defeated. The outlook was bleak: the massive evacuation of Allied troops from the beaches of Dunkirk had taken place at the turn of the month, and on 10 June Italy had declared war on Britain. The rapidly evolving situation in Europe necessitated an immediate re-evaluation of the flying boat routes, so this long trip aboard *Corio*, which had routed through to Egypt via Biscarosse, Marseilles, Lake Bracciano, Brindisi, Athens and Crete was their last through French and Italian airspace.

Together with the other C-Class crews now effectively trapped in Northeast Africa by the war, Alderson remained on the routes to the south and east of Egypt for the next three months. The flights south through Africa now sometimes took them on from Lake Victoria to Mombasa, Dar es Salaam, Lindi and Mozambique, finishing at Durban.

For a time, Roly kept a car in Durban for use on these trips, which he shared with a fellow boat pilot, a 'larger than life' Irishman by the name of Paddy Sheppard. Unlike the retiring Alderson, Sheppard was something of a wild card, and it was not long before the Irishman successfully managed to stall the vehicle in the middle of a railway crossing, where it was promptly obliterated by an oncoming steam train. Sheppard was fortunate in being able to jump clear and survived to tell the tale.

When this tour ended, Alderson was forced to return to the UK from Durban in a more leisurely fashion – by sea, aboard the SS *Sterling Castle*, finally docking at Liverpool on 7 October 1940.

By early November, Roly was back on duty, this time on the Hythe to Lagos run. These were very long hours: between 07:04 hours on 7 November and 07:08 hours on 8 November, Roly Alderson flew from Poole to Bathurst – twenty-one hours and twenty-seven minutes in

the air in a period of twenty-four hours. Over the next few days, he rotated back and forth several times between Bathurst, Freetown and Lagos.

It was on one of these trips running down the coast of West Africa that Roly and his crew managed to give the Nazis a bit of a fright.

They were flying their Empire S.30 at a modest altitude, a few miles off the

'Down-time' – R.A. aboard SS *Sterling Castle*, returning from Durban, September–October 1940. (*Author's collection*)

coast between Bathurst and Freetown, when they spotted an Allied shipping convoy steaming southwards ahead of them. This was not an uncommon sight on this route, as Allied shipping continued to ply between the United Kingdom, West Africa, and on down to the Cape. As they came up towards the convoy, they spied the unmistakable silhouette of a U-boat, its conning tower just above the surface, stalking the convoy and closing in. Roly did not hesitate … he decided to attack.

Alderson was well aware that the one threat the *Kriegsmarine* U-boat commanders dreaded, above all, was the sight of a fully armed counter-submarine RAF Sunderland flying boat; he was also well aware that the S.30 looked, from a distance at least, exactly like a Sunderland.

He put the unarmed aircraft into a steep dive, and they tore down through the sky – straight at the German submarine.

This was more than the U-boat commander had bargained for: the crash-dive that ensued evidently caused chaos and consternation in the U-boat, for it disappeared, never to be seen again. The convoy continued on its way, blissfully unaware of how close it had come to potential catastrophe.[7]

On 28 June 1940, General de Gaulle had been recognised by the British government as the leader of the Free French – which included the French states of Chad and Cameroon in West Africa. In November, de Gaulle travelled from London – where he had been given sanctuary by Britain – to French Equatorial Africa, in order to attend meetings with the French Governor and High Commissioner.

On the conclusion of these meetings, de Gaulle needed to return to England, and the responsibility for his safe passage back was handed to Captain Alderson. Accordingly, the general boarded the flying boat *Clyde* in Lagos on the Nigerian coast on 19 November and, amid tight security, *CX* took to the air at 05:29, landing at Freetown at 14:08, a flight of some eight hours and forty minutes. This should have been a brief overnight stop – but there was trouble afoot.

Roly, his crew and the general went out for a meal in the evening. De Gaulle and Roly's first officer ordered the same dish, while Roly and the remaining crew made a different choice – and became violently ill. Although it could not be proved, it has been suggested in some quarters that this may have been an unsuccessful attempt upon the life of de Gaulle. Those affected were sufficiently incapacitated to cause their

Short S.30 *G-AFCX Clyde*, in which R.A. flew General de Gaulle from Lagos to Poole, UK, 19–22 November 1940. (*Short Bros*)

planned departure to be delayed, and they stood down for an extra day to recover.

On 21 November, *CX* headed off from Freetown in the morning, for the three-hours-plus hop to Bathurst (now known as Banjul) in British Gambia, arriving just after 11:00. They stayed overnight – this time without drama – and continued the following evening on the long fourteen-hour leg to Gibraltar. The final ten-hour flight to the UK was the one posing the greatest risk, so at 22:21 the same evening Alderson and crew, with their precious cargo safely aboard, departed the safe haven of 'The Rock' under cover of darkness and roared off into the night.

The route of *CX* took them in a wide arc out into the Bay of Biscay, well clear of occupied France and the ever-present risk of Luftwaffe interception. The *Clyde* landed safely at Poole at 08:25 the following morning, where General de Gaulle disembarked and returned to London. Judging by the letter he sent to Captain Alderson the following week, he felt safe and well looked after by the crew; he also alluded to the suspected poisoning incident at Freetown.

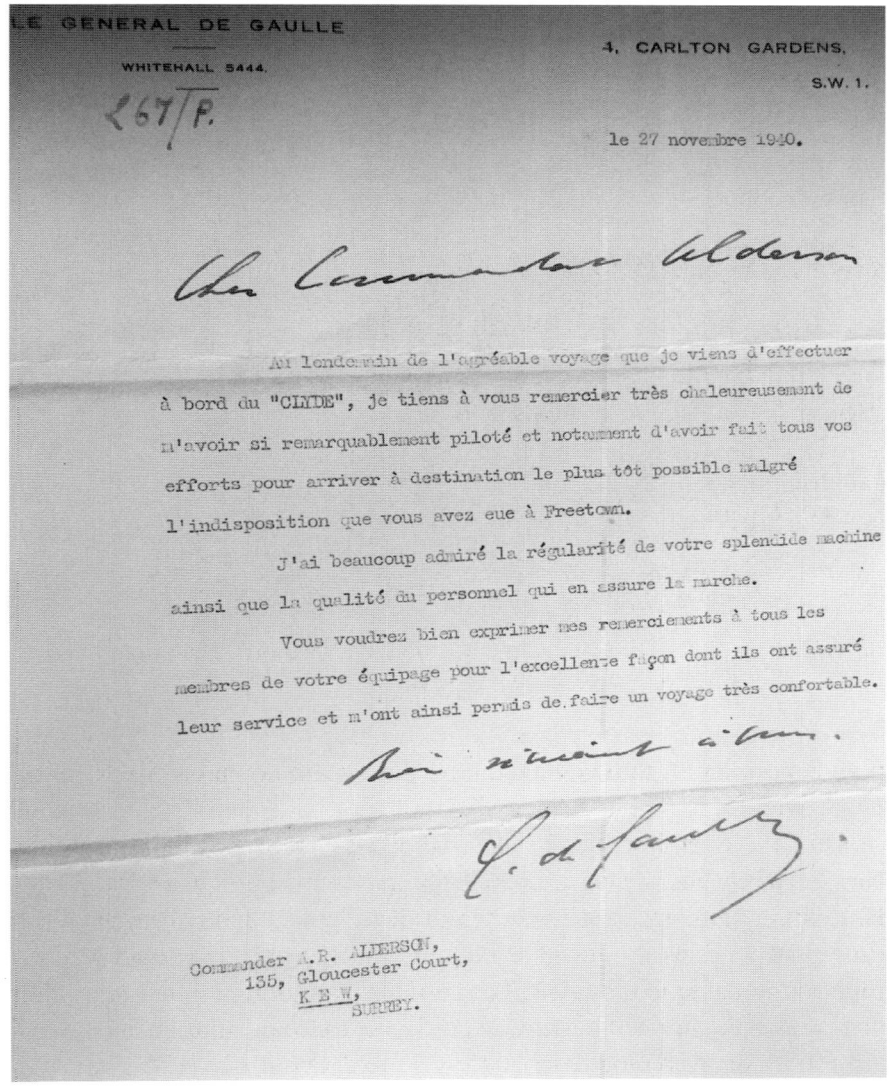

Letter from General de Gaulle to R.A., thanking him for returning him safely back to the UK from Lagos aboard *Clyde*, 19–22 November 1940. (*Author's collection*)

Having deposited the Leader of the Free French at Poole, Roly made the short hop from Poole, leaving *CX* snugged down at Hythe while he went off for some well-earned 'R & R'. He would no doubt have been sorry to hear that the *Clyde*, which had looked after them all so gallantly, was destroyed in a gale just three months later while moored in the Tagus, just off Cascais near Lisbon.

Roly's final long-haul round-trip excursion of 1940 – this time back on board the S.30 boat *Clare* (*CZ*) – was down once more to Lagos, but this time routing via Lisbon, La Luz, and Gando in the Canary Islands, before running across to Bathurst and down to Freetown. This was followed by a trip to Lisbon in the S.30 *Cathay* (*KZ*) on 29 December, arriving back in Hythe on New Year's Eve. This flight was Roly's last in command of an Empire flying boat. But there were bigger things on the horizon.

January 1941 – On 5 January, the tragic news came through that Amy Johnson – the heroine British aviatrix who had done so much to champion the female domination of the skies in the early 1930s – had lost her life when the Airspeed Oxford she was delivering for the RAF came down in the Thames in mysterious circumstances; her body was never found. Roly had of course known her when she worked at Stag Lane, the de Havilland base at Edgware, so would have been very sad to learn of her demise.

The war in Europe was now well into its second year. Roly had been flying the Empire boats on the long-distance routes with little respite since returning to flying duties after the *Cavalier* incident in January 1939. Returning home to spend some time with family and friends would have been very welcome, particularly in these uncertain times. Unfortunately, these pleasures were to be short-lived.

In these first days of the new year, one of Roly's most pressing duties was to visit his young brother Gerald, and his old flying buddy from Cambridge days, Bobby Anderson and his family. Roly had been best man at Bobby's wedding and was godfather to Bobby and Elsa's 3-year-old son Anthony.

Gerald and Bobby were good friends; they were both RNVR lieutenants, attached to the Fleet Air Arm. During this period of the war, it was considered too risky to train young pilots in British airspace, so the Empire Air Training Scheme was devised to provide the safer flying environments of Canada, the United States and other overseas bases. Thus, in a few days' time they were due to head off by sea to RNAS *Piarco* (HMS *Goshawk*) in Trinidad, in the West Indies, to undergo concentrated flying training on Fairey Albacores (similar aircraft to the better-known Swordfish bombers) – so these days together were precious to them all. Little did they all know what was to come.

On 15 January the *SS Almeda Star* set sail from Liverpool, bound for Trinidad. She had been built in 1926 and was a London-registered vessel of some 15,000 tons belonging to the Blue Star Line. On board were the ship's crew of 166, together with 194 passengers, including 142 ratings and officers of the Fleet Air Arm. Among them were Gerald, Bobby, Elsa and little Anthony.

On the morning of 17 January, the *Almeda Star* was pounding west in heavy seas some 35 miles north of Rockall, a rocky outpost on the western edge of the Outer Hebrides. At 07:45 she was attacked by the German U-boat *U-96*[8] under the command of Captain Heinrich Lehmann-Willenbrock. The first torpedo struck the *Almeda Star* amidships. She was badly damaged but was not sinking. *U-96* fired another about twenty minutes later, which hit her stern, and this was followed by yet another an hour or so later; although she did not founder, she was totally disabled, and the crew managed to get four of the lifeboats away. *U-96* now surfaced, and fired around thirty incendiary shells, half of which made their mark. A final torpedo was launched at 09:55; this proved to be the *coup de grace,* and within minutes the *Almeda Star* had gone to the bottom.

The SS *Almeda Star.* (*Blue Star Line*)

A single SOS message had been sent from the *Almeda Star* at 07:49, and seven British destroyers were immediately dispatched. When they arrived on scene several hours later nothing was found – no wreckage, no debris, no survivors. All 360 souls lost their lives that morning.

This event must have dealt a terrible blow to Roly. At 33, he had already suffered the loss of both his parents, a baby sister and two of his brothers. Now, in one fell swoop, he must bear the grief of the deaths of his last surviving brother Gerald, his best friend and former flying buddy Bobby, Bobby's wife Elsa, and his little godson Anthony. The letter of condolence Roly received from Buckingham Palace would have been scant comfort in his deep sorrow.

After this tragedy, the only way open for Roly was to throw himself back into his work. Since returning from Bermuda after the *Cavalier* incident, he had logged another 1,200 hours on the S.23 and S.30 boats, and was hence one of the airline's most experienced flying boat captains. He was now selected for a new and highly important role – as one of a

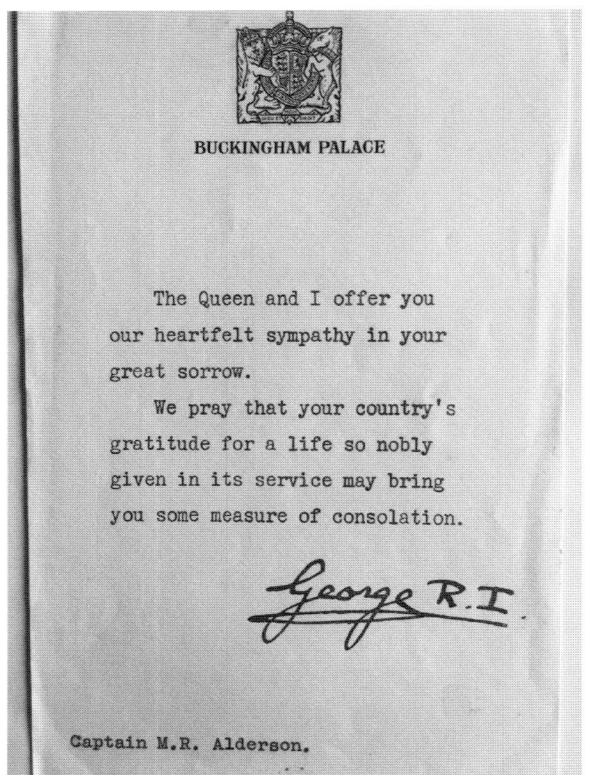

BUCKINGHAM PALACE

The Queen and I offer you our heartfelt sympathy in your great sorrow.

We pray that your country's gratitude for a life so nobly given in its service may bring you some measure of consolation.

George R.I.

Captain M.R. Alderson.

Letter of condolence from Buckingham Palace to R.A. on the loss of his brother Lieutenant G.A. Alderson RNVR aboard the SS *Almeda Star* on 17 January 1941. (*Author's collection*)

tiny group of elite captains responsible for the new Boeing Clipper 314A flying boats.

In August 1940, the Under Secretary of State for Air, Harold Balfour, had agreed to purchase three of these massive machines – which had originally been allocated to Pan American Airways – from the United States government, at a cost of £259,000 each. Winston Churchill was said to have been incandescent that Balfour had sealed the deal without consulting the Cabinet. However, it ultimately proved to be a wise move, as these machines were vital in maintaining the Anglo-American alliance throughout the remaining years of the Second World War (later in the war, Churchill flew on both *Berwick* and *Bristol,* and declared himself highly impressed).

The three 314As acquired by the British Purchasing Commission were to be operated by the British Overseas Airways Corporation and were primarily intended for the UK to West Africa route, as existing flying boats could not travel this route without stopping in Lisbon. The sale made a small net profit for Pan Am – priced at cost plus 5 per cent – and provided a vital communications link for Britain.

These were truly enormous aircraft: 106ft long, with a wingspan of 152ft – three-quarters the span of a modern Boeing 747 jumbo jet – and weighing in at 22.44 tons (empty). They were powered by four Wright twin-cyclone 14-cylinder radial engines of 1,600 horsepower each, had a range of 4,700 miles, and could cruise at 180 miles an hour at an altitude of over 19,000ft. The cavernous interior boasted six passenger areas, including a dining room and a VIP suite, and the spacious flight deck was designed for a crew of five: captain, first officer, navigation officer, radio officer and flight engineer. Indeed, so monumental were the dimensions of these behemoths that the flight engineer was actually able to walk *through* the wings in order to carry out in-flight maintenance on the engines should this be required.

These boats were not simply big: they were also highly technically advanced and consequently very demanding of their flight crews. F. Robert van der Linden, curator of Air Transportation and Special Purpose Aircraft at the Smithsonian National Air and Space Museum has been quoted thus: 'These planes were beautiful, but they were hard to fly.' They not only required skill and experience from their pilots – Boeing's test pilot, Edmund 'Eddie' Allen (the first to take a 314 off the water, in June 1938) commented that keeping the boat straight in

Boeing 314 Clipper lifting off. (*The Boeing Company*)

Cockpit and pilots' controls aboard Boeing 314A Clipper *NC18607*. These two photographs were taken the day before the aircraft was handed over by Boeing to captains Gray (Pan American) and Alderson (BOAC) on 3 April 1941 in Seattle. (*The Boeing Company*)

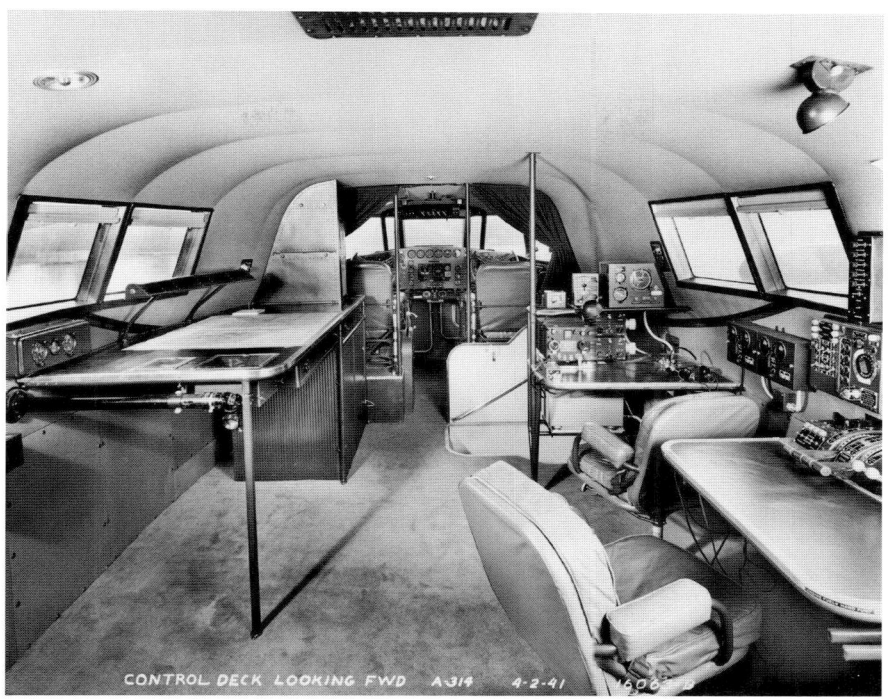

The spacious control deck aboard Boeing 314A Clipper *NC18607*. (*The Boeing Company*)

the air was 'akin to herding a reluctant buffalo' – they could also be tricky to handle on the water, particularly on a downwind taxi, due to the large 'sea-wing' hydrostabilisers, and dipping a wing-tip into the water was a very real potential hazard. (Boeing was aware of this danger and designed watertight wingtips to guard against this eventuality.) One of the 314s most experienced pilots was quoted as saying: 'No one in the operations department had any idea of the hazards of flying boat operations. The main problem now was the lack of the very high level of experience required of seaplane pilots.' On account of this, only the cream of the flight crews, with thousands of accumulated hours on flying boats to their credit, were selected for duty on the Boeing 314s.

In February, captains Kelly-Rogers and Roly Alderson headed out to Seattle in the US Pacific Northwest, where the Boeing Aircraft Company was based. The next few weeks were spent on familiarisation. These large, complex machines were, in many respects, very different from the C-Class boats the aviators were used to. Although not perhaps as aesthetically pleasing as the graceful Empire boats, they were by all accounts fit for purpose. The mammoth aircraft were assembled at Boeing's Plant 1 on the Duwamish River in Seattle and towed to Elliott Bay for taxi and flight tests.

The first flight of the new model for delivery to BOAC – the Clipper 314A – took place on 20 March. On 3 April the first of these new flying boats for Britain – *NC18607* – was piloted from Seattle down to San Francisco by Captain Harold Gray, the senior pilot at Pan American Airways, with Captain Alderson in the right-hand seat. Two days later, Gray and Alderson flew her to San Pedro, Los Angeles, thence across the States to Miami in Florida, and finally alighting in New York on 8 April.

This was the first boat handed over to BOAC, being registered *G-AGBZ* and given the name *Bristol*. This boat was soon under the

R.A. (fifth from left) with captains Harold Gray (Pan American) and J.C. Kelly-Rogers (BOAC) and members of the BOAC flight crew in New York, 8 April 1941 – with the first Boeing Clipper 314A *NC18607* (soon registered *G-AGBZ* and named *Bristol*) in the background. (*Author's collection*)

Photograph of Boeing 314A *NC18607* in New York, 8 April 1941, signed by Captain Harold Gray. This boat soon became BOAC's *G-AGBZ Bristol*. (*Author's collection*)

command of Captain Kelly-Rogers and on 22 May, with Alderson acting as supernumerary captain in the right-hand seat, she arrived in Bermuda on her inaugural flight to the UK. To celebrate this first visit, a dinner was held at the Belmont Manor Hotel.

Among the guests were Captain Don Bennett (pilot of the transatlantic record-breaking *Maia* composite seaplane, and later of Pathfinder Force fame) and Roly's old friends Taffy and Marion Powell. This would have been a déjà-vu for Roly – it was his first visit to Bermuda since the loss of the *Cavalier* in January 1939. In spite of his reticence, he was welcomed with open arms by the Bermudians, who treated him as their very own returning hero.

Two weeks earlier, on 8 May, Roly had taken the left-hand seat for the first time aboard one of the new boats – this time it was *NC18608*. He took her for two local flights out of New York – two hours forty minutes, and one hour forty-seven minutes, and again on 11 May for an hour-and-a-half. This machine would become *G-AGCA, Berwick*. This was the second boat.

R.A. with J.A. at the Belmont Manor Hotel, Bermuda. (*Author's collection*)

Bang on schedule, a month later, the third 314A was ready to be handed over. On 9 June, with Harold Gray again at the controls, *NC18610* departed Seattle for San Francisco, with Roly acting as co-pilot. As before they routed down via San Pedro and Miami, arriving in New York on the 15 June, after a total of twenty-eight hours and forty-eight minutes flying time.

BOAC Boeing 314A *G-AGCA Berwick* (formerly *NC18608*) in her wartime livery, on a take-off run. (*The Boeing Company*)

These were pivotal moments in the war between the United Kingdom and Germany. Two weeks earlier, on 24 May, early on in the Battle of the Denmark Strait, HMS *Hood* was lost, foundering with 1,415 of her complement of 1,418 hands. This was a massive blow to the country's morale, as the *Hood* had been considered invincible. However, the score was soon evened up when three days later the great 50,000-ton German battleship *Bismarck* was finally sunk in a coordinated attack on the morning of 27 May. On 1 June there was more bad news for the Allies when the fierce battle for Crete was lost: this was a terrible defeat for the Allies, who lost almost 4,000 soldiers. In addition, over 11,000 Allied troops were captured during the engagement.

Meanwhile, back in America, the Boeing boat *NC18610* had morphed into her British identity as *G-AGCB, Bangor*. She was now officially handed over to BOAC's representative, Captain Alderson, and on 9 July Roly took off from New York on a local flight to sort a few minor issues. His log for that day reads: '*G-AGCB*; N.Y.; local: 1.25; (Pilot) Self; Test – compass swing'.

On 13 July, the great flying boat lifted off from New York harbour with her new commander in charge, on a two-hour fifteen-minute run down to Baltimore, the new east coast BOAC base. There they remained for ten days, to allow the Boeing technicians to make some final checks and adjustments.

On July 23 at 10:50 local time, *CB*, with Captain Alderson and his crew, took to the air once more – finally en route for the UK. They landed at Botwood, Newfoundland, after a flight of eight hours and ten minutes, stopped overnight, and then headed out over the Atlantic. It was a long flight: they had departed just before 23:00 and touched down at Foynes, on the River Shannon on Ireland's west coast, shortly before 11:00 the following morning, after eleven hours and forty minutes in the air.

For Roly, there was no resting on his laurels. Three days later, he and his crew set off again – this time on the long run down to Nigeria, via Lisbon. Of course, there was no crossing of France or Italy now that war was in full spate across Europe, and great care had to be exercised to reduce the chances of interception by the Luftwaffe. The route south from their base at Foynes therefore took them well clear of the Western Approaches of the English Channel, in a wide arc out into the Bay of Biscay, before they turned east again as they closed Lisbon. Likewise, these flights were all now undertaken under cover of darkness, and radio silence was maintained. Although the Portuguese remained neutral, they were content to allow these civilian British flying boats to continue to use Lisbon as a staging post between the UK and North Africa, for it was still a long run down to Bathurst from there – usually about fourteen hours.

During these summer days of 1941, the RAF were furiously fighting off the Luftwaffe over Britain and France. On 9 August – the day after Roly had landed the Boeing back on the River Shannon after the first return flight to Bathurst – the *supremo* British fighter ace Douglas Bader[9] was shot down over France in his Spitfire. He bailed out successfully – but only after leaving behind one of his prosthetic legs which became stuck in the cockpit. (He was captured on landing, and ultimately ended up as a prisoner in Colditz Castle, after making a number of unsuccessful escape attempts.)

The crews of these three big Boeings – *Bristol* (*BZ*), *Berwick* (*CA*) and *Bangor* (*CB*) – would routinely change over at Foynes. As one machine arrived, another would leave, so it was a very rare occasion to see all three moored up together.

Rare wartime photograph of all three BOAC Boeing 314As, *Bristol, Berwick* and *Bangor* moored up together on the Shannon at Foynes. (*Author's collection*)

Baltimore, on the eastern seaboard of the US, was now BOAC's maintenance base, set up specifically for the three 314As. The machines were required under the terms of the purchase agreement to return after every 120 hours of flying for valve descaling and routine servicing. In the summer months, they would fly from Baltimore to Botwood (Newfoundland) and on to Foynes; they would then depart on a round-trip to Lagos via Lisbon and Bathurst, then back to Baltimore from Foynes by way of Botwood. In the winter, the Newfoundland facility could not be used due to ice, so they would route back via Bermuda, the Azores and Lisbon to Foynes; they would then return to Baltimore by way of Lisbon, Bathurst, Lagos, Belém (Brazil), Trinidad and Bermuda.

Through the rest of 1941 the flying routine was again unrelenting, a constant roundabout of swapping machines and routes. On one tour in November, Roly moved across to the right-hand seat and acted as supernumerary captain to John Kelly-Rogers, the most senior of the 314 skippers, on board *BZ*. This boat, the *Bristol*, as *NC18607*, was the first of the fleet to be delivered to BOAC, into the care of Captain Kelly-Rogers – so she was really 'his boat', in the same way that the *Bangor* was really 'Roly's boat'.

This time they took a slightly different route: from Bathurst they flew for twelve hours across the Atlantic to Natal – on the eastern tip of Brazil – then to Belém and on to Bermuda via Trinidad. Roly managed to catch up briefly with his oldest friends in Bermuda, as well as with a couple of the *Cavalier* survivors. This was a brief forty-eight-hour stay, then it was the six-hours-plus run to Baltimore for the routine maintenance schedule. During this period, Baltimore effectively became Roly's 'home-from-home' – as he probably spent more time in the United States than he did in the UK – but at least he had the company of his friend Ross Stainton, who was managing the 314As for BOAC at Baltimore (Roly and Ross had both joined Imperial in 1933).

Three weeks later, on 6 December, Roly picked up *BZ* from the Baltimore Boeing base and headed back to Bermuda. The following day, while Roly was in the air on the twenty-hour overnight transatlantic flight to Lisbon, the Japanese attacked Pearl Harbor; by the time he had landed on the Tagus, the United States had declared war on Japan; and by the time Roly landed back at Foynes three days later, Germany and Italy had declared war on America. In five dramatic days, the whole course of the war had changed.

This overworked pilot was now due some proper leave back home; he had not had a real break since July. He returned to the very empty flat in Kew which he had formerly shared with his brother Gerald. It was a sad time; he missed Gerald – they used to go flying together, skiing with friends in Switzerland, fishing in Scotland, shooting in Sussex; and he missed his best friend Bobby Anderson – they had shared such great adventures in the air.

Still, life must go on. It was wartime, and he was due back at the flying boat base in Foynes by the middle of January. After he had seen in the New Year of 1942 with his sister in Sussex, Roly returned to Kew; he packed a bag – not forgetting his 'oversized' Longines pilot's watch.[10]

He then locked up the flat and headed out of London on the afternoon express train bound for Bristol. He planned to stay with an uncle and aunt for a couple of days before continuing on to Foynes via the Whitchurch 'Shuttle'.[11]

(The following is a romance in the truest sense. It is recounted in the present tense, in an attempt to convey the emotions surrounding it. This is not fiction: every detail, every word – as far as they could recollect – was related years later by the two characters involved.)

R.A.'s 'oversized' Longines aviator's watch, worn while flying the Boeing 314A boats throughout the Second World War. (*Author's collection*)

As the train steadily builds up steam and heads out of Paddington Station, Roly cannot help but notice a trim young lady occupying the seat opposite him in the carriage. For some time, he attempts to read his book, but – unusually for this self-disciplined young man – he finds it impossible to concentrate. He takes a furtive glance in her direction: she is evidently several years his junior, casually but elegantly dressed – no ring on her finger, he notes – and taller than average. He takes another surreptitious look across at his fellow passenger (for in this compartment there are no others), and this time he meets her eye doing the same thing – and it takes his breath away.

After a few moments, having at least partially recovered his equilibrium, he manages to stammer out a few halting words: 'Are you, umm ... are you alighting at Bath ... or are you going on?'

'Yes, I am getting off at Bath – I work at the Admiralty Office there. How about you?' she asks coyly from under her eyelashes.

'No, I am going on ... er ... to Bristol' replies Roly.

After what seems to Roly like just a few minutes (but which was in fact hours), the steam train begins to lose pace as it emerges from Box tunnel and makes its approach down the valley towards Bath station.

'Perhaps I can help you with your case?' asks Roly as the girl gets up from her seat. 'Thank you so much – how kind,' she says shyly. Roly reaches for the case lying on the overhead rack, swinging it down between them. As the train judders to a halt, wreathed in steam, he opens the carriage door and steps down onto the platform with the bag, holding the door open with his spare hand.

'Thank you' she mumbles, unable to think of anything else to say.

'It has been my pleasure,' he responds, holding her gaze – and her bag – for a second longer than strictly necessary.

'Goodbye' says the young lady.

'Goodbye' replies Roly.

The young lady picks up the case, turns towards the gate marked 'Exit', and disappears.

Roly, feeling a little giddy, and with the girl's strangely mellifluous voice still echoing in his head, steps up into the carriage, and settles back into his seat. The steam engine gives a long blast on its whistle, and the train begins to trundle slowly out of the station. He then realises that he never even asked her name…

A couple of days later, and Roly has been quite unable to put the young lady on the train out of his mind. He only has a few days' leave left before resuming duties on his transatlantic flying boat operations, and for the last two days he has been walking the streets of Bath close to the Empire Hotel, near Pulteney Bridge – which had been taken over by the Admiralty in 1940 – in the forlorn hope of 'accidentally' bumping into this mysterious young lady. The Admiralty Office is his only clue – but he cannot simply march into the Empire Hotel and declare that he is looking for a tall, slim young lady with no name. For what must be the sixth or seventh time this day, he approaches the hotel's imposing entrance; he stops disconsolately beside a wooden bench, and is on the point of sitting down when, out of the main entrance steps the young lady he has been seeking. Roly hesitates for a second, then turns towards her. He has taken no more than a couple of steps when she turns in his direction, looks up .. and their eyes meet.

'Hello!' says Roly, 'The girl on the train! I am not letting you go this time. How about dinner tonight?'

Joan Branfoot, shortly after becoming
Mrs Joan Alderson. (*Author's collection*)

The tall, slim young lady – her name is Jo – says 'Yes, that would be lovely!'

And so began a whirlwind wartime romance.

By 15 January 1942, with a spring in his step, Captain Alderson was reporting for duty back at Foynes flying boat base on Ireland's west coast, to rejoin his boat, *CB*.

On precisely the same day, Prime Minister Winston Churchill – having completed his talks with President Roosevelt following the Pearl Harbor attack – was on his way from Virginia to Bermuda aboard *CB*'s sister flying boat, *CA*. Soon after the flight departed for Bermuda, the Prime Minister came up to the *Berwick's* flight deck – as usual smoking a fat cigar. Captain Kelly-Rogers on this occasion chose to waive the rules and let him continue – apparently 'even allowing him to strike a match when his cigar went out'.[12]

When Captain Kelly-Rogers made radio contact with the accompanying American fighter escort, Churchill asked if he could speak to them, but Kelly-Rogers ruled it out as being too much of a security risk. Churchill then took the controls of the huge craft – under the watchful eye of the commander – and, according to Kelly-Rogers, he allowed the PM to execute a couple of gentle turns before taking back control. As they approached Bermuda 'the Prime Minister remained in the seat while I executed the landing' Captain Kelly-Rogers later recalled. 'This is a privilege which is not normally accorded to passengers, but conditions were ideal and I was able to handle all controls myself.'

Churchill was met on arrival by the Governor, Lord Knollys, and taken to Hamilton aboard a Royal Air Force launch. From there he went to Government House and prepared for his address to the Bermuda Parliament. He told the Members of the Colonial Parliament that 'you in Bermuda happen to be called upon to play a part of especial importance and distinction. Everybody has to do his duty to the cause – first to the British Empire, but above that to the world cause.' He went on: 'I wish to express to you my strong conviction that these bases are important pillars of the bridge connecting the two great English-speaking democracies. You have cause to be proud that it has fallen to your lot to make this important contribution to a better world.' He concluded his remarks by expressing his profound gratitude to Bermuda and Bermudians.

Having flown to Bermuda by flying boat, Churchill came to the conclusion that it might be preferable to continue on to England by air. However, on the morning of their planned departure, it seems that he was entertaining some doubts as to the wisdom of his decision:

> I woke up unconscionably early with the conviction that I should certainly not go to sleep again. I must confess that I felt rather frightened. I thought of the ocean spaces, and that we should never be within a thousand miles of land until we approached the British Isles. I thought perhaps I had done a rash thing, that there were too many eggs in one basket. I had always regarded an Atlantic flight with awe. But the die was cast. Still, I must admit that if at breakfast, or even before luncheon, they had come to me to report that the weather had changed and we must go by sea, I should have easily reconciled myself to a voyage in the splendid ship which had come all this way to fetch us.

Churchill went on to record that 'Roosevelt had also expressed concern about the dangers of the voyage. Our presence in Washington had been for many days public to the world, and the charts showed more than twenty U-boats on our homeward courses.' The flight which was about to take place was later dubbed 'The most daring flight of the whole war.'

Sometimes – particularly in still waters – it took considerable skill (and some heart-stopping moments) to get these immense boats to 'unstick' on take-off, and Friday, 16 January was one of those days. The *Berwick* had a full load of fuel on board, in addition to its precious cargo of VIPs, which on this occasion included not only the Prime Minister but also Sir Dudley Pound, Chief of the Naval Staff, Sir Charles Portal, Chief of the Air Staff, Lord Beaverbrook, Minister of Aircraft Production, and

Sir Charles Wilson. However, Captain Kelly-Rogers managed to get the huge machine airborne without issue. Said Churchill later:

> It was, as the captain had predicted, quite a job to get off the water. Indeed, I thought that we should hardly clear the low hills which closed the harbour. There was really no danger; we were in sure hands. The flying-boat lifted ponderously a quarter of a mile from the reef, and we had several hundred feet of height to spare.
>
> […]
>
> There is no doubt about the comfort of these great flying-boats. I had a good broad bed in the bridal suite at the stern with large windows on either side. It was quite a long walk, thirty or forty feet, downhill through the various compartments to the saloon and dining-room, where nothing was lacking in food or drink. The motion was smooth, the vibration not unpleasant, and we passed an agreeable afternoon and had a merry dinner.

The latter was certainly true: the menu is known to have consisted of shrimp cocktail, cold buffet, chicken, ham, beetroot, Bartlett pears with cream, and coffee. From his remarks, it seems that Winston had forgiven Harold Balfour for his unsanctioned purchase of the Boeings in 1940.

The flight plan was intended to take them to Pembroke Dock in South Wales. However, as the *Berwick* approached Europe, Captain Kelly-Rogers discovered a navigational error which had led them too far south of their intended track. By this time, they were just minutes from the port of Brest, which bristled with German defences.

The Nazis had been on the lookout for them, so when an unidentified foreign aircraft was picked up approaching the Brest peninsula from seaward, Luftwaffe fighters were scrambled to investigate; fortunately, they never located their target.

As soon as Captain Kelly-Rogers had realised his error, he had turned the *Berwick* smartly to port, maintaining radio silence for the next hour as they headed north. Danger was never far away, and they had yet another near miss as they approached the naval base at Plymouth. Instead of approaching from the west, they were coming in from the south and

Cartoon by S.D. Moon, referring to Churchill's flight from Bermuda to the UK aboard the flying boat *Berwick G-AGCA* on 16–17 January 1942 (signed by Winston Churchill). (*Author's collection*)

were not expected from that quadrant. As Churchill later laconically recalled: 'This had the result, as I was told some weeks later, that we were reported as a hostile bomber coming in from Brest; six Hurricanes from Fighter Command were ordered to shoot us down – but failed in their mission.'

As *CA* alighted in Plymouth Sound on the morning of 17 January 1942, and the Prime Minister was whisked off back to London by train, Captain Alderson was in Foynes, making preparations to depart for Lisbon aboard *CB*. At 01:02 the following morning, *Bangor* left the Shannon base, thundering off into the darkness. They flew the southbound winter route, as usual making a wide sweep west out into the Bay of Biscay, to reduce the chances of enemy interception. After the seven-hour run down to Lisbon, it was straight on to Bathurst and Lagos, then the long seventeen-hour leg across the lonely wastes of the Atlantic to Brazil before heading north up to Trinidad and Bermuda, finally alighting at Baltimore for a week of scheduled maintenance at the BOAC base.

On 30 January, while Captain Alderson and his crew were in Baltimore waiting for *CB* to return to service, the war in the Far East claimed more flying boat victims: the Empire S.23 boat *Corio G-AEUH* – which Roly had taken all the way from Poole to Singapore via Alexandria in June 1940 – was shot down and destroyed by Japanese fighters in West Timor, killing thirteen of the eighteen on board.

Meanwhile, back at the Admiralty in Bath, Jo Branfoot had been doing a little bit of sleuthing on this charming but mysterious person who apparently 'flew boats'. Roly had told her that his brother had been lost on the *Almeda Star* the previous January. It was not difficult for her to trawl through the 'Missing at Sea' records. Everything checked out.

Roly and his crew had been away a month before they touched down once more on British waters, returning direct to Lisbon from Bermuda – a long leg of over nineteen hours – and thence back up to Foynes and straight across to Poole. It was now 14 February. The war was at its height all over Europe, Africa and the Far East, and the next day Singapore fell to the Japanese.

Miss Jo Branfoot had not been far from Roly's thoughts in the weeks he had been away – and it was, after all, St Valentine's Day. He was due back in Poole on 18 February, so he just had time to fit in a brief visit to Bathwick Hill, where Jo was lodging with her uncle and aunt, barely a mile from her workplace in the centre of Bath. Those precious days flew by, but Roly was in love, and he headed back to Poole revitalised.

Roly's next run was down to Nigeria and back to Foynes. Two days after arriving back, he and his crew made the short hop down to Cork and back to collect a changeover crew. Roly carried out a local test flight the following day, before flying *CB* the 170 miles up to RAF Castle Archdale,[13] which was located on the eastern shore of Lower Lough Erne. This base was equipped with maintenance facilities, and a flying boat dock where these machines could be serviced without removing them from the water.

This tour was followed by ten days' leave. Roly went straight down to Bath – and proposed. The answer was the one he had been dreaming of, and the die was cast. When he returned to Foynes to rejoin his crew on board the *Bangor*, Captain Marmaduke Jonathan Rowland Alderson (34) was engaged to Miss Joan Branfoot (23). Jo was the youngest of five: the other four were the proud bearers of several forenames, but by the time her parents came to their last-born they seemed to have run out, so they just called her Joan – and then (somewhat in the Alderson fashion) promptly shortened it to Jo.

The following duty for Roly was the long maintenance trip with *CB*, entailing the southern route (as it was winter and Newfoundland was therefore still ice-bound), all the way via Brazil to the Boeing facility at Baltimore. He was not back into Ireland until late April and had not seen his new fiancée for over a month. The same day that Roly and his crew were in the air between Lisbon and Foynes, 20 April 1942, was one of the darkest in the history of the RAF. They had sent forty-seven Spitfires out to Malta, but almost every single aircraft was destroyed on the ground by the Luftwaffe.

It was Saturday, 25 April, before Roly finally arrived in Bath from Ireland. He had collected his sleek drophead Lagonda from his uncle's house near Bristol, and duly pulled up at 4, Bathwick Hill, where Jo was lodging. Shortly before 23:00, they were sitting in the Lagonda at the top of Lansdown Hill, quietly savouring each other's company after weeks of separation, when the air raid sirens began to howl. A few minutes later, they saw a flash to the west, followed by the sound of a distant explosion – it must be another attack on Bristol. Then they heard the unmistakable drone of multiple approaching aircraft, shortly followed by a string of Pathfinder flares which lit up the night sky.

Within minutes, the centre of Bath below them was being pummelled by wave upon wave of German bombs.

This was the beginning of what became known as the *Baedeker Blitz*; after the first attack, the eighty Luftwaffe aircraft returned to occupied France to refuel and rearm, making another raid before dawn, and a third on the Monday morning. During the course of this Blitz hundreds of properties were either badly damaged or totally obliterated, and over 400 lives were lost.

Alderson was not due back on duty until the middle of May. The engaged couple had set a date to be married – 20 June 1942. As time was short, they decided they must go up to Yorkshire, so that Roly could meet his prospective in-laws. At first, Jo's father did not think much of her choice of an 'air boat pilot' for a husband. (When Jo had asked Roly what he did for a living, he had said simply 'I fly boats', to which she replied – predictably – 'But boats don't fly!'). Fortunately, however, Roly and his future father-in-law soon found common ground: both men shared a passion for fly-fishing and tennis – indeed, Jo's father Clive was no slouch at the latter, having played in the men's doubles at Wimbledon in 1923 – and they became firm friends.

This sojourn with Jo's parents at Stonegrave House, in the Ryedale district of North Yorkshire, was a happy interlude for them both. They

R.A. en route wartime style to have Banns of Marriage read, Yorkshire Dales, May 1942. (*Author's collection*)

cycled the 20 miles across the moors to have the Banns of Marriage read, in preparation for their wedding a few weeks later.

When they had parted once more and Roly was back in the flat in Kew, he wrote his last letter to Jo as a bachelor, in which he reflects on the sorrows of his past which have been swept away: 'it's like emerging from a long dark tunnel now that I can suddenly let myself think of you once more. In fact, the sunshine is a bit too dazzling.' He finishes the letter by saying: 'Darlingheart, you have everything I've got.'[14] Roly was a very private person, not known for his effusiveness – but there was no doubt that he had found love.

All too soon it was time for Alderson to return to his flying, and by 19 May, he was back in the left-hand seat of one of the Boeings – this time *G-AGBZ, Bristol*. The Newfoundland base was now ice-free again, so they departed Poole for Botwood via Foynes, then on to Bermuda, before retracing their route back to the Shannon. Within forty-eight hours, they had roared off to Lisbon, then to Bathurst and finally Lagos. Roly and his crew were very soon heading back in a northerly direction, alighting in Poole harbour just before 08:00, having been airborne for in excess of thirty-three hours of the last fifty-two – not untypical of the punishing schedules flown by these crews.

The *Bristol* was soon refuelled, and, with a different commander in the still warm left-hand seat, she stormed out of Poole's protected waters, bound for Stranraer on Loch Ryan, on the southwestern edge of Scotland. There, two days later on 17 June, *BZ* was boarded by Winston Churchill, and he headed off once more for vital talks[15] with President Roosevelt in America. The boat routed direct across the Atlantic to Baltimore, returning Churchill to the UK ten days later – this time via Botwood, Newfoundland. This was Churchill's only Atlantic round trip by air during the war.

But Captain Roly had an important appointment to keep. While Churchill was on his way to the United States aboard *BZ*, Alderson was en route to North Yorkshire to marry his sweetheart. The ceremony was held on 20 June at Stonegrave Minster, adjacent to Jo's parents' home, the service being conducted by Roly's uncle, the Reverend Augustus 'Gus' Alderson.

Being wartime, the wedding party was small – for the most part made up of Jo's family and close friends. Of Roly's family, only his one surviving sibling Dorothy and her husband, Arthur F. St. G. William

'Willie' Orpen, were present, no doubt accentuating the absence of his brother Gerald and best friend Bobby, lost at sea the previous year.

Of the wedding, Jo's elder sister Dulcie, a VAD nurse, later recalled:

> I had, of course, to go in uniform. I doubt whether I had any civilian clothes left – they tended to disappear in wartime, with coupons making dressing difficult for civilians. Her bridegroom was in the uniform of a BOAC captain and his best man, his brother-in-law, was in very similar uniform, that of a captain R.N. The bride looked smashing, the sun shone, and no bombs were dropped this time.[16]

In fact, Willie Orpen was still wearing the three stripes of a Commander RN – not being promoted to captain until three weeks later. He was currently in command of the Havant class destroyer HMS *Hesperus*, and the following year was promoted to Western Approaches Command where he became Chief Staff Officer.

R.A. and J.A. on their wedding day, 20 June 1942. (*Author's collection*)

Another family member conspicuous by his absence was Jo's brother, Tony. Captain William Anthony Ridley Branfoot, 3rd The King's Own Hussars, had been among those forced to surrender on the fall of Java two months earlier. Tony spent the next three-and-a-half years as a Japanese prisoner of war and was so badly beaten by his captors for standing up for the rights of his men that he was only able to walk with the aid of crutches; his torture included the confiscation of his crutches, and the smashing out of all his teeth out with the butt end of a rifle. When he finally arrived home in December 1945, he weighed just six stone. For his services in captivity, he was recommended for the DSO, but due to a petty War Office policy this was denied (although he was subsequently awarded the military MBE).

For the newly married couple there was a honeymoon of sorts, in spite of the rigours of wartime. This took the form of a few days at Roly's sister's house in Sussex – with a cook! Too soon, it was all over: Jo was installed in the fourth floor flat at Gloucester Court in South London and by late morning on Sunday 5 July, Captain Roly was once again airborne in *CB* – 'his boat' – heading across from Poole to the base at Foynes. Here, some technical adjustments were made as they awaited orders, followed by a two-hour test flight on the morning of 14 July. This was of course Bastille Day in France: when an enormous crowd gathered illegally in Marseilles, waving French flags and singing the national anthem *La Marseillaise*, two women were shot dead. Unbowed, General de Gaulle led Bastille Day celebrations of his own in London.

The following evening after another test flight, *CB* tore off into the night on the long run out across the lonely wastes of the North Atlantic, bound for Newfoundland. As they settled into the journey, the weather began to steadily deteriorate. At around 02:00 – between 600 and 700 miles into the flight, but still safely before the 'PNR'[17] – Alderson took the decision to abort the trip and return to Foynes. The *Bangor* touched down in the early morning light at 06:08, after over nine hours in the air. The typically cryptic remark in Roly's flight log states 'Ret. Weather.'

Later that day, just before 21:00, the colossal Boeing once more rose from the waters of the Shannon and thundered away into the gloaming. This time, all went according to plan, and *CB* alighted at Botwood after fourteen hours and thirty-five minutes. This was another 'maintenance flight', so by the next evening *CB* was safely snugged down at Boeing's

Baltimore facility, there to remain for a week while the engineers carried out their servicing routine.

The return flight back across the Atlantic was unremarkable – apart from its precious cargo. This time, *CB* carried not a VIP but a consignment of Havana cigars. By now, Roosevelt and Churchill were friends and allies in every sense, and Roosevelt was well acquainted – from the clouds of blue smoke permanently surrounding the British Prime Minister – with Churchill's weakness for the finest cigars that Cuba could muster. As there was now a regular and dependable transatlantic delivery route, Roosevelt had decided that his friend should not go short in these critical times. The cigars were duly delivered on board by special messenger from the White House and, on arrival at Poole, were securely placed, together with the diplomatic mail, in the bullion hold on the train straight to London. (Unbeknown to the public, this secret supply chain continued for the rest of the war.)

And so, the awful circus of war continued. There seemed to be tragedy at every turn. On 25 August 1942, Prince George, Duke of Kent, took off from Invergordon on the east coast of Scotland in a S.25 Sunderland Mk III Flying Boat. The official line was that the Duke was on a morale-boosting visit to RAF personnel stationed in Iceland, although the real truth will never be known, and the event is to this day shrouded in mystery. There was a highly experienced crew on board, all chosen specifically for the trip. The machine took to the air at 1.10 pm. Being a flying boat, its standing orders were to fly over water whenever possible, therefore only overflying land when absolutely necessary. The planned route would follow the coastline up to the northernmost tip of Scotland, and then turn to the northwest over the Pentland Firth towards Iceland. About an hour-and-a-half into the flight, and apparently in good visibility, the aircraft crashed into Eagle's Rock near Dunbeath at a height of around 650ft. The Sunderland exploded on impact, and of the fifteen passengers and crew on board, only the rear gunner was spared.

War continued to vent its fury, and there was no let-up for anyone – least of all for the little group of British aviators continuously criss-crossing the Atlantic in the three monster Boeings, between Britain, Africa and the United States. The work was critical to the war effort, transporting VIPs, mail, top-secret documents – and, of course, Havana cigars. The hours were routinely horrendous: often the flights were of fifteen hours or more in duration, sometimes much longer. Alderson's flying log for 8–9 November 1942 reads: 'From: Bermuda To: Lisbon Time of Departure: 09:45 Time of Arrival: 15:46 Time in Air: 22:01'.

Twenty-two hours in the air, which with pre-flight preparations and post-flight shutdown, would mean a full twenty-four-hour shift.

Roly Alderson saw little of his new bride over these months at the height of the war – he was mostly in the air. He did, however, manage a few days at home at the end of September; by late November, Jo knew she was with child. This was wonderful news for the couple, and especially for Roly, who had suffered so much personal grief. This was a new beginning for him, and he felt buoyed up by the prospects ahead of them.

As 1942 rolled into 1943, it was more of the same for the BOAC Boeing 314 crews. Meanwhile, the American-operated 314s were also busy with some important duties. The Casablanca Conference was due to take place from 14 to 24 January in Morocco, and President Roosevelt needed to be there. So, on 11 January, Roosevelt boarded the 314 *C-143* named the *Dixie Clipper*; it took off from Miami, taking the southerly route via Trinidad and Belém, thence across the Atlantic to Bathurst in British Gambia. There the President transferred to a C-54 land-plane for the final leg to Casablanca. The conference was of great historic importance: it announced to the world that the Allies would accept nothing less than the unconditional surrender of the Axis powers.

In the same month, the Boeing 314 became the first airliner to complete a million miles of transatlantic flight. These flights were never without risk, however. Just a few weeks after Roosevelt's return flight – he celebrated his sixty-first birthday in the air over Haiti – another American 314, the *Yankee Clipper*, the pride of Pan-Am's fleet, which incidentally had been christened by Mrs Roosevelt, was en route from New York via Bermuda and the Azores when it crashed on landing on the River Tagus at Lisbon. The Pan-Am launch on stand-by was quickly on the scene, and was soon joined by two more – one belonging to BOAC and the other to Pan-Am. The huge aircraft was critically damaged and soon sank. Of the thirty-nine on board, only fifteen survived.

On 5 March 1943, Roly and his crew departed Poole once more, bound as usual for Foynes, thence down to Lisbon, and ultimately Lagos. All proceeded as normal until they arrived back in Lisbon in the early hours of 14 March. A storm blew up overnight as the *Berwick* lay to her mooring just off Cascais on the Tagus, and such was the violence of the weather that *CA* sustained damage to one of her engines. Roly kicked his heels at the Hotel Palacio in Estoril for three weeks while they waited for a replacement unit to be flown out and fitted – a complex operation, particularly in wartime conditions. By 4 April *CA* was ready to go, and they thundered off on the return trip to Foynes, finally touching down in Poole harbour at 11:28 on 5 April.

There were now risks, too, from the Luftwaffe. Until late 1942, so-called 'civilian' flights between Portugal and Britain had been spared – but the enemy now stepped up their aggression. The BOAC DC-3 *Ibis* was particularly unlucky: on 15 November, she was jumped by a single Me 110 fighter and sustained considerable damage; she limped on to Lisbon and landed safely. Then on 19 April, she was again attacked, this time by six Me 110s; although badly damaged, she evaded her attackers by flying at 50ft above the ocean until she got to Lisbon, where she was able to seek shelter and underwent repairs.

In the very early hours of 28 May 1943, Alderson and his crew alighted on the Tagus aboard *Bangor*, mooring up as usual at Cascais for a brief stop and to refuel. Often they stayed over, either at the Hotel Atlântico at Cascais, or at the Estoril Hotel Palacio. These were popular meeting places for those passing through – which, as Portugal was officially neutral, included Germans as well as Americans and Brits. These venues were therefore hotbeds of intrigue and were known to be frequented by undercover agents from both sides.

Earlier in May, the famous British actor Leslie Howard had arrived in Lisbon for a promotional lecture tour; he was still staying at the Atlântico in Cascais when Roly flew in on 28 May aboard *Bangor*. Howard finished his tour by the end of the month and prepared to return to England. On 1 June, the same DC-3 that had been involved in the two previous incidents, BOAC's *Ibis*, *G-AGBB*, took off from the recently opened Portela Airfield, just north of Lisbon, at 07:35. Aboard Flight 777A were thirteen passengers and four crew. On the passenger list was Leslie Howard, Howard's friend and accountant Arthur Chenall, and a gentleman by the name of Tyrrell Mildmay Shervington. The latter was a director of the Shell-Mex and BP Oil Company in Lisbon, but covertly he was also agent H.100 of the Special Operations Executive's Iberian operation. At around 11:00, some 200 miles northwest of Spain, the DC-3 was set upon by eight Ju-88s of *Kampfgruppe 40* and was shot down in flames: there were no survivors. Another wartime mystery unsolved. Had the Germans known that Shervington was an SOE spy? Or were they after actor Howard, who was believed by Joseph Goebbels, Germany's Minister of Public Enlightenment and Propaganda – who had been personally ridiculed in Howard's 1941 film *'Pimpernel Smith'* – to be 'the most dangerous British propagandist'? It has also been suggested that Howard's friend Arthur Chenall, who somewhat resembled Winston Churchill, may have been the target, mistaken by agents as the 'thickset man smoking a cigar' boarding Flight 777A to Bristol. On hearing the news, Churchill wrote in typically scathing fashion: 'The death of the fourteen civilians including Leslie Howard was a painful shock to me … the brutality of the Germans was only matched by the stupidity of their agents.'

The following day, 2 June, a Short Sunderland flying boat of the Royal Australian Air Force 461 Squadron, on maritime patrol operating out of Mount Batten in Plymouth Sound, was intercepted in the same area of Biscay by a flight of eight Ju-88s operating from an airfield near Lorient – quite possibly the same eight that had brought down Flight 777A the previous day. The Sunderland had been searching for signs of wreckage from the *Ibis* when it was attacked. A furious battle ensued, in which three of the German fighters were shot down, with three others believed damaged. The Sunderland was badly shot up but managed to struggle back to England, making a forced landing close to the beach at Praa Sands in Cornwall; one of her crew perished.

The RAF Sunderlands were having a tough time of it in these weeks of early summer 1943. Just the previous week, one had been lost off Clare Island on its return to the Lough Erne RAF flying boat base after a routine Atlantic patrol, with the loss of all eleven crew members on board. Then, on 30 June, yet another crashed into Lough Erne with the loss of two lives; fortunately, the other nine crew were saved.

The war continued unabated in Europe, in North Africa, and in the Far East – but the Allied forces were slowly gaining ground. There were now two major successes to celebrate. The first came on 13 May, when the Axis forces surrendered in North Africa. Three days later, while Roly and his crew were waiting in Lagos with *CB,* the news came down the line that a successful raid deep into Nazi Germany had been carried out by 617 Squadron. They succeeded in destroying two massive dams in the Ruhr valley on the night of 16/17 May, using the revolutionary

'Bouncing Bombs' designed by Barnes Wallis.[18] Although the cost of the raid was high – eight aircraft lost and fifty-three airmen killed – the success of Operation Chastise gave another much-needed boost to morale at home, and the legend that was *The Dam Busters*[19] was born.

On Wednesday, 23 June at precisely 10:33 hours, Roly throttled back the four mighty 1,600 horsepower Wright Twin Cyclone engines, and *CB* carved a gentle scar in the calm waters of Poole harbour, thus ending yet another long 'Horseshoe Route' trip across to Baltimore via Lisbon, West Africa, the West Indies and Bermuda, returning by way of Newfoundland and Foynes. They had been away from England since 20 May.

Roly was due a few days' leave, and he lost no time in heading straight up to see his young pregnant wife, who had been staying with her parents at Stonegrave in Yorkshire. It was a long, slow journey through a war-weary England, and Roly finally arrived at Stonegrave House on Thursday. It was, of course, a joyous reunion – but sadly very short-lived. In the early hours of Saturday morning, Jo unexpectedly went into early labour, and it was not long before a tiny girl was born. She was premature and obviously very weak, and Jo's mother Evelyn – a former GP – feared for her survival. While Evelyn and the housekeeper tended to the tiny newborn (for there was no time to summon a doctor), Jo suddenly announced that she was about to give birth to a second. Evelyn's professional pronouncement was that this was 'just the afterbirth' – but she was wrong, and a second little girl was soon delivered. No one had been aware that Jo had been carrying twins – not even Jo's medically trained mother. With no professional intervention available, the tiny sisters were simply too premature, and within a few hours both had given up the struggle. Georgina and Elizabeth were buried in an unmarked grave in a corner of Stonegrave Minster churchyard, just a stone's throw from where they were born. This was a heart-breaking experience for the couple, but at least Roly had been there for Jo, and they were able to comfort each other in their sorrow. Roly went to Helmsley two days later to register the deaths; but duty called, and by 2 July he was back on board *BZ* in Poole, bound once again for West Africa.

On the morning of 28 July 1943 – while Captain Alderson was finally home on leave, keeping Jo company at Stonegrave as they grieved together for the lost twins – a BOAC Sunderland, *G-AGES*, while on a flight from Lisbon back into Foynes – with eighteen passengers and a cargo of 30,000 letters from British prisoners of war in Japan – crashed into the slopes of Mount Brandon in County Kerry. Of the twenty-five men on board, ten died and the remaining fifteen crew and passengers suffered injuries. This terrible incident was not, however, caused by enemy action – it was understood to be the result of a navigational error, compounded by fog.

In spite of the precautions taken, the three British Boeings were now more than ever at risk from enemy attack over the Atlantic, particularly over the Bay of Biscay. They invariably flew these legs under cover of darkness, maintaining complete radio silence and keeping well away from occupied France.

It was on a flight while returning from Lisbon to Foynes that Roly and his crew had a brush with the Luftwaffe. On this occasion they were chased by a lone German fighter, which they fortunately managed to evade, suffering only minor damage after a burst of machine-gun fire. They had a lucky escape: no one was injured, and the Boeing alighted safely on the Shannon four hours later, the only evidence of the attack being a line of bullet holes in the fuselage. The damage was soon repaired and the 314 was once again ready for service.

The Boeings and their crews continued to ply their routes down to West Africa and across to the United States through the remaining months of 1943. The enforced rest periods in Baltimore for the 314 crews while maintenance was attended to at the BOAC facility would have been a welcome break for these overworked airmen – but nevertheless it was frustrating for Roly, with a young wife waiting at home in England. He found it hard to stand idle and made use of his three-week lay-over in November by racking up thirty-four hours on another type – the Beechcraft AT-7 Navigator (a C-45 variant).

Generally, any major work on these big flying boats took place in the US, but sometimes necessity indicated serious attention back in the UK. One such occasion occurred in mid-January 1944 after a run up from Poole in *BZ*: Roly's log for 22 January reads 'Test after E/Change'.

By this time, extra crews were needed on the BOAC 314A routes, and over the next eight months Roly allocated the left-hand seat to several other pilots, while remaining in command on the right. Various names now appear in his logbook: Stacey, Rogers, Burgess, Peacock. The routes remained broadly as before, with occasionally a minor change to the itinerary to include, for instance, Nassau – en route from Trinidad to Bermuda – or Horta in the Azores, as a stop to break up the long leg between Bermuda and Lisbon.

By late spring 1944 the tide was beginning to turn against the German war machine, and preparations were afoot for the Allied invasion of Europe. There were some nasty surprises still in store for the Allies, however. On 28 April, Exercise Tiger – which was a full-scale rehearsal for the Normandy landings off the south Devon coast – ended in complete disaster, with the fleet of American tank-landing ships being attacked by German E-boats. A total of 749 American servicemen lost their lives that day. Also, the Germans had another terrifying weapon up their sleeve: in early June, they unleashed the first of the 'Doodlebugs' – the V-1 flying bombs – on London.

However, the Allies were gaining traction, and 6 June saw D-Day – the beginning of Operation Overlord – with the landing of 155,000 troops on the beaches of Normandy. For the pilots of the BOAC Boeings, it was a full summer, so the faster northern route over the Atlantic was the option of choice: Foynes to Botwood, on to Baltimore, then back to Botwood and direct back to Foynes.

Roly Alderson's days on the wartime Boeing 314As were now drawing to a close. Since that first flight from Seattle to San Francisco with Captain Harold Gray on 3 April 1941, in *NC18607,* Captain Alderson had, over a period of nearly three-and-a-half years, been in command for some 3,200 hours in the air, covering over half-a-million miles, the equivalent of twenty times around the world. His tally was now up to 9,500 hours.

Captain Alderson's last flight in one of these giants – after a five-day scheduled service stop in Baltimore – was back to Foynes via Botwood on 3–4 September 1944. An old friend and colleague, Captain Dennis Peacock was taking over, and occupied the left-hand seat: Roly was nevertheless in command. It was fitting that this final run was aboard 'Roly's boat', *G-AGCB Bangor.*

Roly arrived home to Jo at the flat opposite Kew Gardens, where they at last had the opportunity of spending three valuable weeks together. They had now been married for over two years – two long years of war chaos, during which they had seen little of each other, and in the middle of which they had faced the tragedy of losing their first-born twins.

In October, Captain Alderson reported at Bristol Whitchurch Airport – the wartime BOAC base – where he carried out two short familiarisation

Poole 1942.

Denis Peacock, Bernard Frost, Roly Alderson & Tommy Farnsworth

R.A. with three Boeing 314A pilot colleagues, Poole 1942. (*Author's collection*)

flights in the left-hand seat of an Airspeed Oxford. This was by way of preparation for more long-distance work, this time flying C-47s out to Africa and beyond.

On Wednesday, 1 November, he began a 'Blind Approach' training course at RAF Watchfield, near Wootton Bassett in Wiltshire. The aircraft of choice for the 'BAT' was the Oxford. This machine was a low-wing monoplane, powered by a pair of Armstrong Siddeley Cheetah X air-cooled radial engines of 340hp each. It was specifically developed for use in a variety of training roles, including navigation, night flying and instrument flying, and was equipped with a blind-flying panel, incorporating an airspeed indicator, altimeter, artificial horizon, directional gyroscope, rate of climb indicator and turn indicator.

On the first day Roly occupied the left-hand seat, while the instructor, Flying Officer Hyslop, sat in the right. A number of different instructors accompanied him over the next five days, and by Monday the 'BAT' course had been completed.

At 09:30 hours on Tuesday morning, Alderson took off from Whitchurch Airport on a familiarisation flight aboard a Douglas C-47 Skytrain commanded by Captain Sherwood. The C-47 *Dakota* was a development of the civilian DC-3; these ones were equipped with two Pratt & Whitney 1,200hp engines. The following day he was in command, practising landings and take-offs, and on the following Tuesday he went up to Croydon to collect a C-47B, *G-AGKE*, for delivery back to Bristol. Within an hour of landing, he was in the cockpit of a different C-47 trying his hand at – according to his log – 'Heavy Landings'.

Roly clocked up a few more hours out of Whitchurch over the next two weeks. On 13 November, Alderson was fine-tuning his skills on the Dakota *G-AGHO* when the Allies scored another major victory over Hitler: the RAF finally managed to sink the pride of the German fleet, the battleship *Tirpitz* known by Churchill as 'The Beast' – again using bombs designed by Barnes Wallis. On seeing the reconnaissance photographs after the sinking, a staff officer was heard to remark: '*Sic transit gloria mundi*' (So passes away earthly glory).

On 3 December, in the captain's seat of the C-47A *G-AGIU,* Roly rolled down the runway and took off on the short half-hour hop to Hurn Airport, just outside Bournemouth. The following morning required what Roly called a 'sparrow-fart' start. Captain Alderson and his crew would be in Rabat in Morocco by the end of the day, after a brief refuelling stop for the Dakota at Lisbon. The team were back at Whitchurch two weeks later, having called in at ten different aerodromes in seven countries; they had logged sixty-five flying hours, swapping aircraft at their final destination – Lagos (Nigeria) – for the trip home.

Roly spent a well-earned Christmas break back with Jo, who was once more expecting. The due date was the beginning of June, and they desperately hoped that this time everything would proceed smoothly. They had recently moved to a new home on the edge of Ringwood, just 8 miles from Hurn Airport, which would be much more convenient when the time came.

Returning to Bristol after the break, it was now more of the same – all on Dakotas, all on the same route – for the next three months. The last flight on this type for Alderson was in March, to Madrid and on to Lisbon, from where he made another 'sparrow' departure the next day, stopping again at Madrid, then Hurn, and finally arriving back at Bristol Whitchurch in time for afternoon tea.

Alderson was now appointed Flight Captain of the Line, responsible for the fleet of Avro Yorks and Lancastrians on the Australian, African and Indian routes. This necessitated certification on a variety of different aircraft types. After Easter, he undertook three familiarisation flights with Captain Jones on the York,[20] and the next day was in the driving seat doing landings for his 'B' licence endorsement, with night landings ticked off the day after. This was followed by four days on a Handley Page Halifax – and the next day, 8 May, Winston Churchill announced the surrender of Germany: this was 'VE Day' – Victory in Europe.

A week after VE Day Roly moved straight on to the Avro Lancastrians. Like the York, these were fitted with four Merlin XXIVs, powerful 12-cylinder liquid-cooled supercharged units of 27 litres each. After an hour-and-a-half of landings for his ticket endorsement and a 'Test Flight', *G-AGLV* thundered off down the runway at Hurn – next stop Lydda (twelve hours), then on to Karachi (nine hours). Roly was acutely aware that the due date for the birth of the baby was nearly upon them – it was important that he be close by; he landed back at Hurn on 20 May.

On 2 June, Roly carried out just over three hours of test flying in the Lancastrian *LX*, and was back home in Narrow Lane, Ringwood, by teatime. That night – right on cue – Jo went into labour; all went well, and by the following morning – Sunday, 3 June 1945 – the Alderson family had grown to three. The baby girl was named Josephine Clare, but, of course, following family tradition, they immediately swapped her names around – and then called her 'Clari'. The child was fortunately blissfully unaware that she had – just possibly – been named after the S.30 C-Class long-range flying boat with the registration *G-AFCZ*. This was a wonderful day for Jo and Roly – they had suffered the heart-rending tragedy of losing the twins two years previously, and of course Roly had borne the loss of nearly his entire family by the time he and Jo had met. This was truly the beginning of a new chapter for 37-year-old Alderson.

Other than swapping over to different Lancastrians – *LF, LT, LW, LX, MD* – Captain Alderson plied this route for the next six months

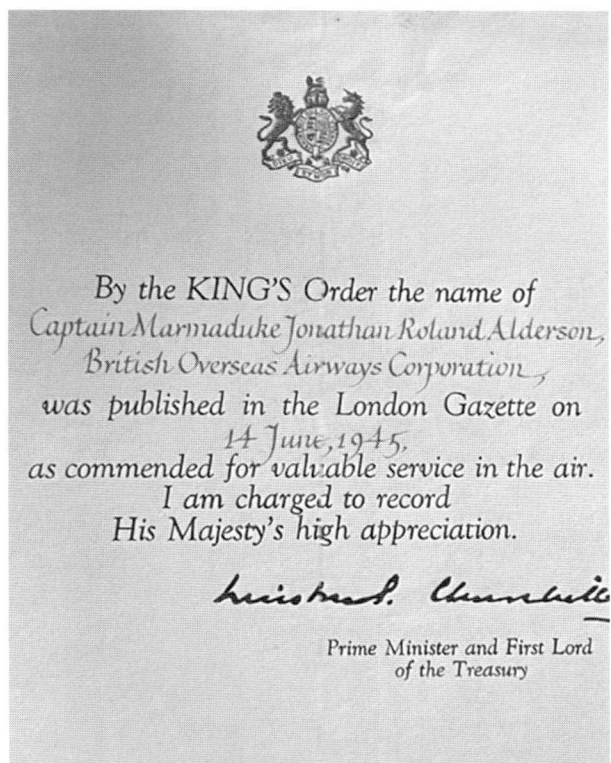

By the KING'S Order the name of
Captain Marmaduke Jonathan Roland Alderson,
British Overseas Airways Corporation,
was published in the London Gazette on
14 June, 1945,
as commended for valuable service in the air.
I am charged to record
His Majesty's high appreciation.

Prime Minister and First Lord
of the Treasury

The King's Commendation 'for valuable service in the air', 14 June 1945 (signed Winston Churchill). (*Author's collection*)

with steady regularity; on 15 July, he clocked up his 10,000th hour of flight – just a month after he had received a commendation from the King, signed by Winston Churchill, 'for valuable service in the air'.

During this period, several apocalyptic world-changing events were to take place: on Monday, 6 August – when Alderson was doing some local flying out of Hurn in the Lancastrian *MD* – the first atomic bomb was dropped on Hiroshima. Three days later, on 9 August – while Roly was resting on a no-fly day in Karachi – a second obliterated Nagasaki. On 2 September – another no-fly day for Roly, once again in Karachi – Japan surrendered, marking the official end of the Second World War.

Chapter 8

BOAC D.F. (1945–1949)

In November 1945, Captain Alderson switched to the Johannesburg run, piloting Yorks on proving flights; this was no problem, as he had gained the appropriate endorsement in April.

These tours lasted between eleven and fourteen days, originating at Hurn, with the first stop being at either Castel Benito – an RAF base at Tripoli in Libya – or Malta. They would then fly on to Almaza Air Base,

The crew of Avro York *G-AGNL* at Hurn, prior to departure for Johannesburg, 8 February 1946. (*Author's collection*)

just outside Cairo, and on to Khartoum, before continuing to Nairobi, finishing up at Johannesburg in South Africa.

It was for one of these flights that Roly invited George Errington[1] to join him as supernumerary co-pilot down to Johannesburg, and back as far as Cairo. George then took the opportunity to swap onto a BOAC Lancastrian for the run back to Hurn. Roly and George had been friends since the 1930s and shared much in common. Like Roly, George had a background in aeronautical engineering, and he felt strongly that the only proper way to learn to fly was by becoming an aeronautical engineer first. George had joined the aircraft company Airspeed[2] in 1934, becoming their Chief Test Pilot in 1939, and in fact had been responsible for much of the incident-packed testing of the Horsa glider, as well as flying the prototype Airspeed Oxford. (When de Havilland took over Airspeed in 1951, George moved to Hatfield, where he was later involved in the flight testing and delivery of Comets.)

On this particular trip, having dropped George off at Cairo, the York detoured over to Lydda (Israel) before continuing to Malta and on to RAF Northolt, London, before returning to Hurn. In March, Roly hurtled down to Malta in the Lancastrian *G-AGMG*, arriving back in Hurn before midday the next day. As with the detour to Lydda, this trip was not routine. The mission's reason is unknown, although many of these post-war flights were shrouded in secrecy.

Alderson then took the York *NL* down to Rome via Marseilles, and the next day on to Foggia on the Adriatic coast, an hour's flight time to the southeast, before the direct flight back into Hurn. Now that he was finally living close to his workplace, Roly was at least able to return quickly to his wife and child after a tour.

Finally, after twelve long years of prodigious flying hours, Captain Alderson's protracted runs out to the far-flung dominions of the British Empire were drawing to a close. In May, he completed a final long flight out of Hurn in the Lancastrian *MM* to Calcutta, routing by way of Lydda, Karachi and Delhi, and returning via Karachi, Baghdad and Lydda. Although he would spend the next twelve months still in the cockpit, it was mostly in English airspace; major changes were now occurring in Roly's aviation career.

In 1943, the UK government had formed the Brabazon Committee, to make important decisions on the future direction of post-war commercial aviation. One of the members of the committee was Sir Geoffrey de

Havilland, head of the de Havilland Aircraft Company, who used his personal influence, together with his company's expertise, to champion the development of the first jet-propelled passenger aircraft. The committee ultimately accepted his proposal (the 'Type IV') and in 1945 awarded a development and production contract to de Havilland. This was designated 'Type 106'. A design team was formed within de Havilland in 1946 under the leadership of chief designer Ronald Bishop, who had also been responsible for the wartime Mosquito fighter-bomber. The Ministry of Supply ordered two Type 106s in 1946 and BOAC followed suit.

Meanwhile, however, BOAC were urgently in need of commercial passenger aircraft to serve their post-war needs. BOAC was backed financially by the UK government, but the coffers were empty. The pressure was on to find aeroplanes which had the capability to serve the long-distance routes, the transatlantic ones being the priority – and ideally these needed to be British aircraft, so as to avoid spending dollars on American machines. As for the 'Jet Age', this was as yet not a reality – there was considerable development still to be undertaken.

In order to fulfil this brief, BOAC decided to form what they termed the 'BOAC Development Flight' – known within the organisation as the 'DF'. This was to comprise a small team drawn from within their own ranks, ideally to include someone with a deep grounding in aeronautical engineering, combined with extensive seat-of-the-pants piloting experience. Serendipitously, there was just such an individual based at Hurn: Roly Alderson was approached, and was duly appointed on 12 August 1946, his thirty-ninth birthday (or at least – if family rumour were to be believed – the beginning of his thirty-ninth birthweek). There is a characteristically terse acknowledgement of the appointment in Alderson's logbook: 'Appt. to D.F. 12/8/46'.

The next twelve months was a busy time for Roly in his new role, shuttling between Bournemouth and Hatfield, as well as Croydon, Radlett and Farnborough. It was imperative that Roly was efficient with his time. Fortunately, he had at his disposal a BOAC Airspeed Oxford *G-AIRZ*, which he always piloted himself and which became his own personal means of transport. (*G-AIRZ* was later sold to Hunting Aero-surveys and crashed into a hillside in Luxembourg on 18 July 1952 while on a survey mission, killing both the pilot and the photographer.)

On four occasions – possibly because the Oxford was elsewhere – Roly borrowed an RAF Proctor III, *HM347*, for brief day trips to Woodley, Croydon and Aldermaston; on another, while on a day visit to RAF Radlett (the Handley Page base), he had his first-ever flight in a glider. This was in one of the 3,800 Airspeed Horsa gliders built for the RAF and used to ferry troops for the D-Day landings and at Arnhem. The pilot was Flying Officer Pike, and they were towed behind a Halifax. What? Alderson not in control? And no engine? This would have certainly been one for Roly's scrapbook.

On New Year's Eve 1946, Roly drove the short distance to Hurn Airport and took the left-hand seat in an Avro Tudor for a quick local flight of forty-five minutes. The Tudor was of considerable significance, being the first-ever pressurised British passenger aircraft. This particular machine, registered *G-AGRE* and named *Star Ariel*,[3] had arrived in September and was the first to be delivered to BOAC; it was in the process of undergoing evaluation.

In early January Alderson departed for Kenya. He travelled down to Nairobi – on this rare occasion as a passenger. As he normally did when

R.A. with colleagues at the Muthaiga Club, Nairobi, Kenya, November 1945/February 1946. (*Author's collection*)

stopping over here, he stayed at the Muthaiga Club, the establishment notoriously frequented by the 'Happy Valley Set' of the 1930s.

The trip was a fact-finding and testing trip, part of his Development Flight brief. Nairobi was on the established BOAC route down to South Africa, and the fact that the airfield was in the tropics and stood at an elevation of nearly 5,500ft above sea level had a material effect on the performance of aero engines. Roly made the return trip in mid-January aboard another Tudor, *G-AGRD*, on this occasion as co-pilot to Captain Garside. This Tudor had just been delivered to the BOAC Development Flight for performance trials. Garside and Alderson departed Nairobi just after 06:00 on 16 January, touching down at Almaza, Cairo some ten hours later.

They took off again shortly after midnight for the five-hour run to Malta, and after breakfast continued on to Hurn – back home for afternoon tea. After the heat of Africa, captains Garside and Alderson arrived home to one of the worst winters of snow and sub-zero temperatures in living memory. The deep freeze continued until late March and put a stop to the majority of operational flying.

Official welcome at Almaza, Egypt, during flight trials in Avro Tudor 1 *G-AGRD*, 16 January 1947. (*Author's collection*)

Resupplying the Avro Tudor 1 *G-AGRD*, 'Egypt-style', Almaza, 16 January 1947. (*Author's collection*)

Avro Tudor 1 *G-AGRD*, Almaza, Captain Garside centre right, 16 January 1947. (*Author's collection*)

Meanwhile, back on the home front at Ringwood, Roly's wife Jo was now expecting their second child, and Christopher Jonathan Rowland Alderson arrived – slightly behind schedule – on 28 March. Predictably, the long names were ditched, and they called him 'Kit'. The following day Cambridge won the boat race. On both counts, Roly was delighted.

In August 1947, an opportunity arose to add another aircraft type to Alderson's list – the Lockheed Constellation. Roly had rejected the Avro Tudor, which had failed to live up to expectations – it had stability issues, and he deemed it unsuitable for commercial passenger operations. BOAC cancelled their order for sixteen of the aircraft.

The American Constellation was now the obvious commercial passenger aircraft of choice for the transatlantic route, as there was no other British machine currently available to this specification. The Constellation was capable of carrying a payload of 20 tons, with a range of 3,500 miles at a cruising speed of over 320mph. Although the purchase was politically highly controversial, BOAC was permitted to proceed with an initial order for five of these planes. As the

BOAC's Lockheed Constellation *G-AHEM*. (*Lockheed/BOAC via Airhistory.net*)

DF Manager, Alderson found himself acting as supernumerary – after two familiarisation flights – from Montreal to New York's LaGuardia Airport aboard *G-AHEM*, and then New York to London Airport via Gander (Newfoundland) in *G-AHEJ*.

Roly arrived home from this delivery flight on 17 August. Six days later, a major tragedy occurred involving the prototype Avro Tudor 2, *G-AGSU*. Avro's chief designer, Roy Chadwick, was killed when it crashed on take-off. His death was a very great loss to British aviation. Chadwick had been responsible for the design of many notable aircraft, not least of which was the Lancaster bomber, as well as the York – which was heavily involved in the Berlin airlift – and many others.

Through the rest of the year and on into 1948, Alderson became ever busier in his new role at the Development Unit. This entailed many trips between Hurn, Croydon, the Aeroplane and Armament Experimental Establishment ('A&AEE') at Boscombe Down, and RAF Bitteswell in Leicestershire – the latter having just been established as a flight development centre especially for jet and turbo-prop engines. The majority of his visits, however, were to de Havilland's HQ at Hatfield and the Royal Aircraft Establishment at Farnborough. Most of his commuting was done by air – often in the Airspeed Oxford, *G-AIRZ*, but increasingly in a Miles Gemini 1.A, *G-AKHW,* which had been purchased in October by BOAC for the use of management. The Gemini was a handy little four-seater monoplane, ideal for Roly's frequent travelling.

Meanwhile, Roly never missed an opportunity to keep his hand in on the larger machines as part of his aircraft performance evaluation role, regularly occupying the left-hand seat in Avro Yorks and Lancastrians, Handley Page Hastings' and Hermes IVs,[4] and Vickers Vikings. On 9 April Roly drove the short distance to Hurn to test the interesting-looking, bulb-nosed *G-AIFF,* a Bristol 170 Freighter which had been flown over from its base at Filton.

He was aloft for fifty-five minutes: his log has nothing recorded in the 'Remarks' column, but *FF* crashed in May the following year 16 miles off Portland Bill, killing all seven of the Bristol Aeroplane Company flight crew and engineers onboard. The exact cause of the accident was never established, although it was believed to have been some form of structural failure. This theory was supported by the fact that the commander of a surfaced submarine had witnessed the aircraft crashing into the sea, and saw a large piece of the aircraft, thought to be part of the wing, coming down separately.

The Bristol 170 Freighter *G-AIFF,* flight-tested by R.A. on 9 April 1948. (*BAE Systems*)

As 1948 drew to a close, Captain Roly had not ventured out of UK airspace since the Constellation delivery trip in August the previous year. It was evidently time for a little overseas run. On 3 November he climbed aboard the Lancastrian *G-AGMM* on a proving flight from Hurn to Colombo in Ceylon, acting as supernumerary captain. It was a thirty-hour flight taking two days. He remained in Ceylon for nine days, dealing with some family business relating to the Alderson estate holdings in the south of the country. Never one to miss the chance of some sport, Roly had been mindful to load his shotguns into *MM's* hold, as the snipe shooting there was always particularly good sport. He left on the return flight from Colombo on 12 November, again acting as supernumerary on a different Constellation – *ME* – and touched down back at Hurn three days later.

Chapter 9

Comet (1949–1955)

On one of his regular trips to Bristol, Roly met up again with a long-term friend Don Aldington, who had been a wartime Ministry of Aircraft Production Inspector at Filton. Don was one of three brothers who had owned the Fraser Nash car company prior to the start of hostilities. Immediately after the war ended, the Bristol Aeroplane Company took a controlling stake in Fraser Nash (AFN), having decided to branch out into quality vehicle manufacture. The Aldingtons remained agents for Bristol cars, and in 1949 Roly took delivery of a new Bristol 400 coupe.

Meanwhile, the development of the de Havilland 106 – now named 'Comet' – had been gathering pace, and the maiden flight of the first prototype – designated 'G-5-1' – took place out of Hatfield Aerodrome on 27 July 1949 and lasted thirty-one minutes. At the controls was de Havilland's chief test pilot, John 'Cat's Eyes' Cunningham,[1] with Captain 'Tubby' Waters in the right-hand seat. It happened to be Cunningham's thirty-second birthday, and by an extraordinary coincidence, it was also the birthday of Sir Geoffrey de Havilland himself. History does not relate what form the celebrations took at Hatfield that evening!

The British designed and built DH 106 was heralded as the world leader in the new era of jet air travel. The prototype G-5-1, now sporting its official registration letters *G-ALVG,* was the star attraction at the second Farnborough International Air Show just a few weeks later in early September, which Alderson attended as a guest of de Havillands.

As the Comet was to be the first pressurised passenger jet aircraft, much of the technology was new, necessitating exhaustive testing which was being carried out at Hatfield employing stress test rigs and water tanks. BOAC had ordered ten Comets, and Roly Alderson was therefore in close and regular contact with de Havilland to monitor progress. He continued to be very busy with the Development Flight and was regularly commuting

R.A. with Sir Geoffrey de Havilland at Farnborough International Air Show. (*Author's collection*)

by air – sometimes to the Handley Page base at Radlett, sometimes to RAF Martlesham, the base of the 'Bomb Ballistics and Blind Landing Unit' – shortly to be renamed the 'Armament and Instrument Experimental Unit' – and regularly to Filton Airfield on the western outskirts of Bristol, which was the principal servicing base for the BOAC fleet. Alderson's logbook gives an insight into a typical busy day, flying the Miles Gemini: '*Hurn to Pebsham (near Hastings) – 0:55 mins; Pebsham to Hurn – 1 hr:02 mins; Hurn to Filton: 40 mins; Filton to Hurn: 44 mins*'.

As it was unlikely that the new DH 106 jet would be ready to enter service until 1952, BOAC was continuing to use American and Canadian aircraft, and had recently added the Canadair DC-4M Argonaut[2] and the Boeing 377 Stratocruiser to its fleet.

On Thursday, 23 February 1950, Roly ran over from Hurn to Filton in the Gemini to test-fly *G-ALSA*, one of the new 377s which had recently gone into service. Captains May, Stacey and Alderson were all on the flight deck and took it in turns to put the 377 through its paces. Roly had a busy visit and stayed at Filton until the following Tuesday.

R.A. with Canadair DC-4M Argonaut, *CF-TEL*. (*Author's collection*)

Two days after getting back from Filton, Roly was once again over at DH's base at Hatfield. It was 2 March, and at 11:45 in the morning he took off on his first flight aboard a Comet. This was the prototype 106, recently registered *G-ALVG*. He and John Cunningham were aloft for an hour and a quarter, with Roly taking the controls for fifteen minutes; they were back down for lunch at exactly 13:00.

On 13 March, Roly squeezed in an hour at Hurn on a new Handley Page Hermes IV, carrying out three take-offs and landings.

This was a new type for BOAC, similar to the Hastings, and the airline had ordered twenty-five – although due to issues they ultimately only took delivery of nineteen. On Friday 17 March he flew over to Hatfield in an Oxford – *G-AIAT* on this occasion – touching down at 10:25. After a briefing with Cunningham, they were soon aloft once more in the prototype Comet *VG* for an hour and forty-five minutes; Roly took the controls for thirty-five minutes. This was groundbreaking stuff, and there was much to discuss. By the time they had finished it was too late to return to Hurn, so Alderson stayed the Friday night at Hatfield and flew home the next morning.

R.A.'s Bristol 400 beside Hermes IV *G-ALDB* at Hurn Airport, 13 March 1950. (*Author's collection*)

There was always much evaluation to be done within the Development Flight, both in regard to BOAC fleet aircraft and route-proving. The following week saw captains Field and Alderson heading off down to Nairobi via Castel Benito and Khartoum for performance evaluation on the Hermes IV – in this case *G-ALDB* – which was shortly to go into service. On this trip, Field was in the left-hand seat, with Alderson acting as supernumerary. While at Nairobi the two captains carried out a series of test flights over two days, in order to assess how the high altitude of this tropical airfield affected the performance of the four Bristol 763 radial engines. The following week, four hours into the return leg from Khartoum, *DB* developed engine problems, forcing them to return to Khartoum. Alderson's typically concise flight log entry records the incident: 'Ret. Eng. U/S'

Due to the necessary repairs and subsequent test flights, it was a week before they finally landed back at Hurn. (*DB* was destroyed in a crash-landing two years later in France, en route from Blackbushe Aerodrome to Egypt – fortunately without loss of life.)

In the early hours of 14 July – exactly twenty years to the day after he had taken his brother Guy on his first flight in the ancient Cirrus

Moth – Roly's wife Jo went into labour with their third child. Roly drove her to the cottage hospital at Fordingbridge, and by mid-morning, Clari (just turned 5) and Kit (now 3-and-a-bit) had a baby brother. The French shared the celebrations: after all, it *was* Bastille Day! Jo and Roly had run out of names, so they christened him Mark – and, true to family form, nicknamed him 'Polo'. One of the godparents chosen for Mark – aka Polo – was Lesley Errington, the wife of Roly's test pilot friend George Errington.

The summer months of 1950 saw Alderson visiting de Havilland's at Hatfield on a regular basis, developing an ever stronger and more effective working relationship between DH and the BOAC Development Flight. Apart from maintaining his own flying currency and Instrument Rating on the firm's Airspeed Oxfords, Roly spent a week as supernumerary on one of the Stratocruisers, *G-AKGH*, on a run from London to New York (Idlewild) via Shannon and Gander (Newfoundland) and back.

His return to England marked the beginning of a new chapter in Roly's aviation career. BOAC's 'Comet Development Unit', under Roly Alderson's leadership, was formed in September 1950. This seemed to be a sensible move by BOAC, and a logical progression for Captain Alderson. He had been working closely with de Havilland since his appointment to the newly formed Flight Development Unit four years

R.A. with his young family, early 1951. (*Author's collection*)

BOAC's Boeing 377 Stratocruiser *G-AKGH Caledonic*. (*San Diego Air & Space Museum*)

previously. During the Comet's gestation period, he had learned more than anyone outside de Havilland about the technical aspects of the project; to add to this, his flights with John Cunningham had furnished Roly, as a highly experienced pilot, with first-hand knowledge of the handling characteristics of this brand-new concept aircraft.

Roly lost no time in getting to grips with the new challenge. On 19 September he was once again up at de Havilland's Hatfield base. This time he logged three hours and twenty minutes in the air aboard *VG*, during which he was in command for an hour and twenty minutes and completed three landings and take-offs.

Roly's home life was no less busy. As the Comet would be operating from London's new major airport, he decided to move the family from Ringwood to Sunninghill, near Ascot racecourse, less than half-an-hour's drive from what was to become known as Heathrow Airport, in advance of the fleet's establishment.

The winter months flew by. On 9 January 1951 the first production aircraft, *G-ALYP*, underwent its first flight, and was then lent to the

Comet Unit for development flying. The production Comets – including *Yoke Peter* – differed slightly from the two prototypes, being equipped with four-wheeled bogies which replaced the large single-wheeled main landing gear.

Roly went up in *G-ALZK* – the second prototype – twice on 7 March with captains Cunningham and Boyce, and on the same day in *YP* with Captain Boyce.

On 2 April, *ZK*, which had been designated G-5-2 by de Havilland and officially registered in the previous July, was duly handed over to the Comet Unit at the new London Airport. Twelve days later, Captain Alderson settled into the left-hand seat, took the Comet down the runway and eased her into the air for a two-hour forty-minute flight, which included three landings at Stansted. *ZK* was now destined for 500 hours of crew training and route-proving work with Roly's Comet Unit.

On 24 May, Roly was at London Airport again to orchestrate BOAC's first development flight, according to the press release, 'preparatory to the introduction on this service of the de Havilland Comet, which is to

Comets *G-ALZK*, *G-ALVG* and *G-ALYP* in formation flight above cloud, 7 March 1951. (*Author's collection*)

Comet *G-ALZK* over the new London Airport (now Heathrow), March 1951. (*Author's collection*)

Early Comet trials, India/Pakistan – John Cunningham (holding hat), R.A. on right (with tie). (*Author's collection*)

Comet's beautifully contoured engine air intakes. (*Henry Hensser, MBE, Photographic Officer, BOAC*)

operate between Britain and South Africa' – the so-called 'Springbok Route'. *ZK*'s flight on this day was a return trip to Ciampino (Rome), with Captain Rodley at the controls.

As commercial jet travel was now on the cusp of becoming a reality, so the interest in the highly promising Comet project in the world's press increased. This was a very busy time for Roly. Crew familiarisation and training gathered pace, with the two senior pilots, captains Majendie and Rodley leading the way.

Taxiing after first landing at Ciampino (Rome), Comet *G-ALZK*, 24 May 1951. (*Author's collection*)

R.A. (centre) arriving at Ciampino aboard *G-ALZK*, 24 May 1951. (*Author's collection*)

G-ALZK refuelling after first landing at Ciampino, 24 May 1951. (*Author's collection*)

Welcoming committee for *G-ALZK*, Ciampino, 24 May 1951. (*Author's collection*)

'*È stato sicuramente un volo veloce!*'. (*Author's collection*)

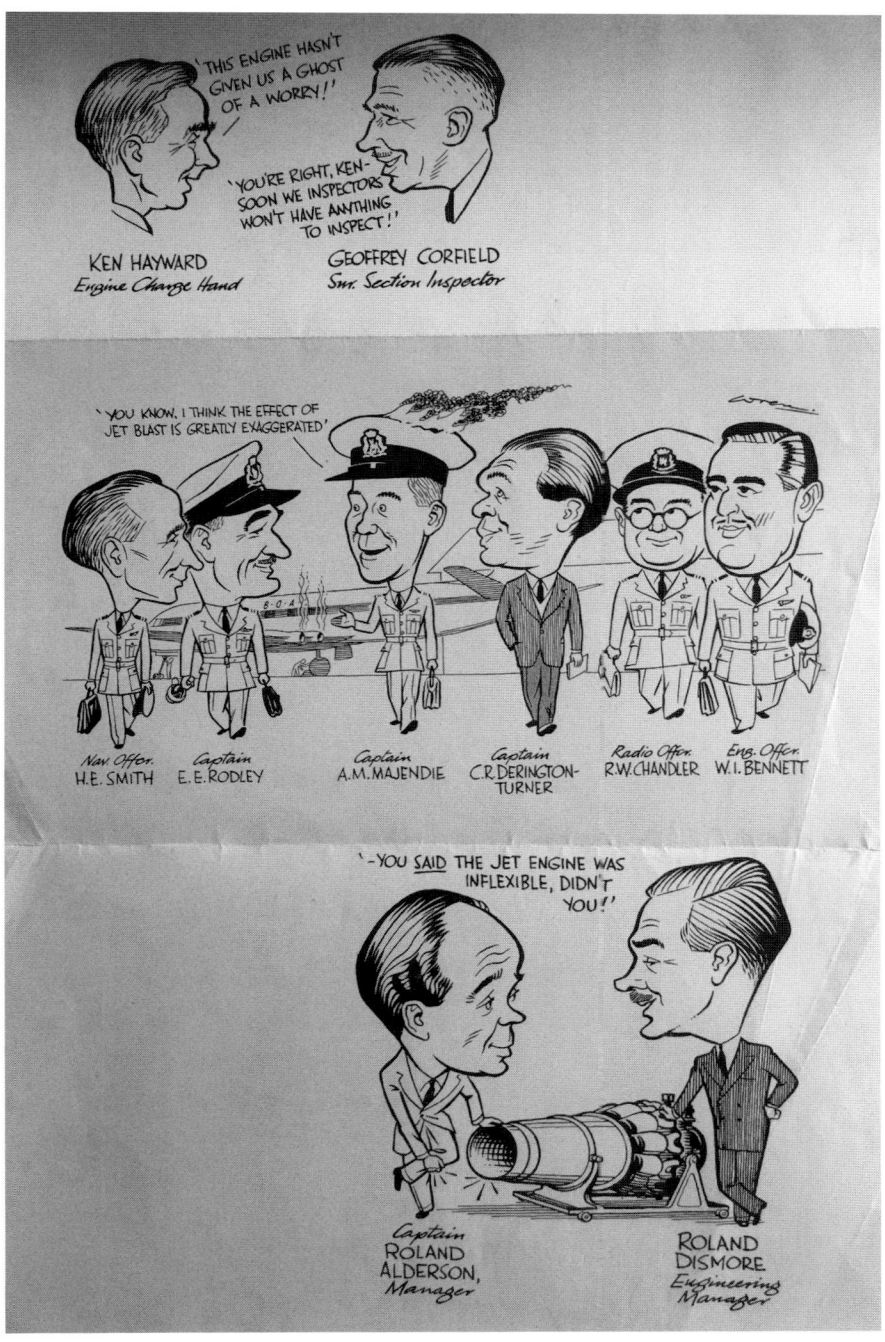

The principal members of the new BOAC Comet team. (*Author's collection*)

On 17 July, *ZK* took to the air from London Airport, bound for South Africa. In command on this groundbreaking flight was Captain Alastair 'Michael' Adair Majendie, who had been appointed to the Development Flight shortly before the Comet Unit's inception. Roly Alderson was in the right-hand seat, acting as supernumerary captain. *ZK* hurtled off down the runway, propelled by its four Ghost 50 Mk1 turbojet engines, lifting gracefully into the air at exactly 17:30 hours, and touching down at Cairo Airport at 22:48, just five hours and eighteen minutes later.

Fifty-seven minutes on, after a quick refuel and check-over, *ZK* blasted off again, this time bound for Entebbe in Uganda. After just over five hours in the air, Entebbe was another brief stop-over for fuel, and they were in the air once more in less than ninety minutes, this time with Roly piloting. Entebbe lies at a height above sea level of nearly 4,000ft, so this stop was of some importance, in order to monitor the performance of the Comet in the thinner air at this higher altitude.

From Entebbe, the final destination was Palmietfontein, Johannesburg, in South Africa – a four-and-a-half-hour flight in the

Comet *G-ALZK* at Farouk Airport, Cairo, 17 July 1951. R.A. centre, with briefcase. (*Author's collection*)

Comet *G-ALZK* at Entebbe Airport, Uganda, 29 July 1951. (*Author's collection*)

Comet. Johannesburg is higher still, at some 5,500ft, so again a useful test for the airliner. The overall flight time from London was seventeen hours and thirty-three minutes.

On 20 July they headed north to Pietersburg, in the Limpopo province of South Africa – another high-altitude landing strip, over 4,000ft above sea level. As the Comet and her crew were to be based there for a few days, Roly took the opportunity to go on safari in the Kruger National Park.

On 27 July, *ZK* returned to Johannesburg, then took off once more heading north to Lusaka, then Livingstone – both in Zambia – and finally ending the day's flying back at Entebbe, after a day's total of just over eight hours in the air. The crew stayed overnight at Entebbe, departing early at precisely 07:00 for a three-hour leg to RAF Wadi Seidna in Sudan. *ZK* thundered off to the north two hours later, touching down at Cairo at 14:47.

Departure the following morning was at 07:59, for the three-hours and forty-eight-minute run to Rome's Ciampino Airport; less than two hours later, Majendie and Alderson were airborne once more on the final leg back to London Airport, which was accomplished in just under two

R.A. at Kruger National Park, while on a proving flight in Comet *G-ALZK*, 21–26 July 1951. (*Author's collection*)

hours and fifty minutes – similar to the flight times of today, some seventy years later. The Comet was cutting journeys by air by at least 50 per cent, often much more.

On 10 October, *ZK* flew the flag as the first Comet flight to Singapore; the next proving flight, on 19 October, covered over 16,000 miles. By now, the Comet had completed 470 hours in the air. The Comet crew were fully occupied over the remaining months of 1951 with further familiarisation, training, and route-proving, in the build-up to the Comet entering service as the world's first passenger-carrying jetliner. The first Certificate of Airworthiness issued to a turbojet-powered civil aircraft was granted to *G-ALYS,* the fifth production aircraft, on 22 January 1952. This was a highly significant milestone.

The Comet Development Unit was in the process of morphing into the Comet Fleet, and Alderson was now officially appointed as BOAC's Comet Fleet Manager – incidentally the only fleet manager with a current commercial flying licence. He was in overall charge of a sizeable team of both flight and ground personnel, and he found himself aboard on many of the route-proving flights down through Africa and across to the Far East during this period.

The first jet airliner schedule flight carrying fare-paying passengers took place between London and Johannesburg on 2 May, and it was *Yoke Peter* that took this honour. Captain Majendie was in command from London to Beirut; on the leg between Rome and Beirut, the plane established a new world record by reaching 525mph. Captain Marsden then took over

BOAC Comet Fleet team, London Airport 1952 (under construction in the background is the Queen's Building, later Terminal One), R.A. centre, flanked by Crew Training Captain E.E. Rodley and Fleet Engineering Manager Roland Dismore. (*Author's collection, Flight, 6 March 1952*)

from Beirut to Khartoum, and Captain Alabaster completed the journey via Entebbe and Livingstone to Johannesburg. The total flying time for the 6,663-mile trip was twenty-three hours and twenty-six minutes, and *YP* arrived into Johannesburg fourteen minutes ahead of schedule. BOAC's Chairman, Sir Miles Thomas, was on board *YP* for the final leg from Livingstone to Johannesburg.

Shortly before this, Sir Miles had written an article for *The Aeroplane's* 2 May issue:

> All this development work has been under the able eye of Captain M.J.R. Alderson, and the idea of forming a small unit with an entirely new type of aircraft and gradually building it up into a fleet section seems to work well.
>
> It has been a most interesting experience grooming the Comet for service. Its presentation to the public has required very delicate handling, because, although it is a very remarkable aircraft, it was important not to get any feeling of mysticism or magic into its make-up.

R.A. with Sir Miles Thomas, BOAC Chairman, after the first scheduled Comet flight to Johannesburg, 2 May 1952. (*Author's collection*)

It is, in fact, a very fast aeroplane, well-behaved aerodynamically and very comfortable in so far as its passenger amenities are concerned. It has posed few new problems, intensified some old ones, but it seems to reflect the characteristics of its sponsors and designers in having delightful manners and a most effective performance.

In mid-May, it was *G-ALZK* that lifted smoothly off the main runway at London Airport, under the command of Captain Majendie with Comet Manager Roly Alderson at his right elbow. On this occasion – instead of carrying scientific equipment – the Comet was fully equipped with seats and catering facilities for thirty-six passengers. This time the payload consisted of sixteen crewmen, four engineers and four BOAC observers. The final destination was Singapore, with stops at Cairo, Karachi and Bangkok – incidentally all the major stopping-off points on the old Imperial Airways 'Overseas Division 3' route that Roly had plied

MALAYA'S NATIONAL NEWSPAPER: ESTABLISHED 1845

SINGAPORE, MONDAY, MAY 19, 1952.

THE COMET'S HERE—IN 19 HOU AND NO HURRYING

FROM LONDON IN A 'DAY'

PENANG AIRSEARC MAAF PL

Pilot meets the Governor

NETEEN HOURS and 13 minutes flying time after it left London Airport, the first ly equipped de Havilland Comet jet airliner ded at Changi airfield, Singapore, yesterday ernoon at 4.35.

The pilot, Captain M. Majendie, shook ds with the Governor, Mr. J. F. Nicoll, and l: "We were not hurrying at all. This is n ning flight".

The Comet, fastest airliner in the world, which put Britain ahead for many years, would have ved at the scheduled time, 3.30, if a crowd of ted Burmese had not "mobbed" the plane at reen and held it up 90 minutes.

Captain Majendie said: "Our average speed from Rangoon to Singapore was 350 miles an hour."

oman sets t to sail Atlantic

PLYMOUTH. Sun DAVIDSON, 26-year-old lish authoress and ex-heavy, Creamh, Plymouth jolles in her yacht Felicity Ann ea first-ever attempt by man to cross the At-

The Comet which he flew in yesterday is fully equipped with seats and catering facilities for 36 passengers.

The first Comet Singapore crew saw, which landed at Kallang Airport last year, was filled with scientific equipment.

For the first time, air hostesses were carried with the party of 24—16 crew-men, four engineers and observers and BOAC repre-sentatives—who landed yes-terday.

U.K. WAS LOSING £2m A DAY

ABERDEEN. Sun. THE Foreign Secretary, Mr Anthony Eden, said today, that Britain was heading for a financial catastrophe at the rate of £2,000,000 per day when the Conservatives as-sumed office in October.

That was the amount by which the value of British im-

8,000-mile air trip to see her cat

REDS DEFY U.N. AUTHORITY

LESS than a day's flying time from Britain, the Comet touches down at Changi airfield. Below Comet's pilot, (left) and Mr. Alderson, head of the BOAC jet liner team, with the Governor of Singapore, Mr J. F. Nicoll. at the air-field.

PEN R A.F. planes from Butterwor R. launches from Batu Uhan to air/sea search for a Malayan plane which was seen crashing 1¼ miles north of Lone Pine morning.

The plane, a Harvard, was Aircraftsman Allan Leong, a me al batch of local trainees who squadron of the MAAF when it

The Straits Times reporting on the arrival of Comet *G-ALZK* on its first flight to Singapore, where the crew were met by the Governor, Mr J.F. Nicholl. (*Author's collection, The Straits Times*)

so often in the Atalantas back in the 1930s. According to Alderson's flight log, *ZK* touched down at Changi Airfield at exactly 08:54 GMT (16:54 local time) on Sunday, 18 May 1952, where they were greeted by the Governor of Singapore.

Once the Comet fleet had become fully operational during 1952/1953. the world welcomed this new era of jet travel – indeed, the Comet 1 was widely thought to have been one of the most important steps forward in aviation technology and design. The final production aircraft, *G-ALYZ*, first flew in September 1952, and in its first year of commercial operation, the Comet fleet carried over 30,000 passengers, among them the young Prince Philip, who was flown back from the Helsinki Olympics aboard *G-ALYS*.

BOAC's Comet programme, a symbol of Britain's recovery from the war, 'drew tremendous press attention and it engulfed Roly and his team'.[3] The press continued to be beguiled by the record-breaking performance and sleek beauty of the Comet and. as manager of the fleet,

Roly Alderson was never far from their sights – but, true to form, he was ever the reluctant interviewee. As one journalist wrote:

> If you met Roly Alderson – Captain M.J.R. Alderson, to be precise – out of uniform and far, far away from London Airport – you would hardly associate him with aeroplanes. In all probability you would think him a university professor. There is something scholarly in both his appearance and manner. And you would certainly fall under the spell of his charm. But if you tried to get him to talk about himself you would draw blank. He will talk enthusiastically about what others have done; about his own achievements he says not a word.[4]

Meet the man who manages the Comet fleet

FLYING eight miles high between Entebbe and Livingstone on the morning of Sunday, February 8, a Comet on the London-Johannesburg service completed B.O.A.C.'s first 10,000 hours of Comet flying. In command was Captain J. Andrew, a Sussex man.

Less than three years previously another Sussex man had been appointed manager of the unit that was to introduce Comets into the B.O.A.C. services. To-day that man is manager of the Comet fleet, which already operates not only to South Africa but to the Middle East, Pakistan, India, Ceylon and Singapore, and will soon operate to Japan.

If you met Roly Alderson—Captain M. J. R. Alderson, to be precise—out of uniform and far, far away from London Airport—in his native Sussex, for instance—you would hardly associate him with aeroplanes. In all probability you would think him a university professor. There is something scholarly in both his appearance and manner. And you would certainly fall under the spell of his charm.

But if you tried to get him to talk about himself you would draw blank. He will talk enthusiastically about what others have done; about his own achievements he says not a word.

YET in many ways he has had an exceptional career. Born in Sussex and brought up in Yorkshire, he learned to fly with the Cambridge University Squadron in the late twenties. His first job, when he came down from Cambridge in 1929 at the age of 22 with a degree in engineering, was in the design office of the Fairey Aviation Company. He found, however, that design office work did not bring him in close enough touch with actual aircraft, so he studied for the necessary licences and in 1933 was taken on by Imperial Airways as a First Officer.

He rapidly gained a wide and varied experience of flying. The early thirties were a period of expansion. Routes were gradually lengthened, bigger aircraft were introduced. By 1938 Alderson was in command of the flying boat Cavalier, which operated Imperial Airways' only ocean route—a service between New York and Bermuda twice a week. This was the first route on which pure navigation was needed and for some years Alderson had been studying navigation. He had, in fact, added a first-class to his second-class navigator's licence, his ground engineer's licence and his P.M.G. W/T licence.

When the war broke out he was still with flying boats, and in 1940 he was sent to America for the delivery and conversion of the Boeing flying boats which played such an important part in Britain's trans-Atlantic communications. In the next four years he flew 4,000 hours.

Captain M. J. R. Alderson

BACK to Britain in 1944, he was appointed Flight Captain of the Line which operated Yorks and Lancastrians on the Australian, African and Indian routes, and two years later he was selected to manage the B.O.A.C. Development Flight.

Ask him why he was chosen for this post and all he will say is: "I suppose I was the most senior Captain available at the time." He will not deny, however, that he was deeply interested in the opportunities it gave him. For his abiding interest, through all the years he was gaining flying experience, was still aviation engineering. Now his main job was to establish the performance of new types of aircraft and equipment and to prepare operational data for the benefit of those who were flying the aeroplanes in passenger service.

Inevitably he came more and more into contact with the "backroom boys" of aviation and this led naturally to his becoming concerned with the first jet airliner.

In 1950 he was appointed to command a small unit which was preparing for the introduction of the Comet. Group Captain John Cunningham, world-famous de Havilland test pilot, gave Captain Alderson his first instruction in flying the Comet—the first B.O.A.C. pilot to fly in the Comet and the first B.O.A.C. man to handle it. After a little over 18 months' organisation and development work the Comet was in passenger service.

Royal Aeronautical Society

KEEN interest was aroused by the first of the Royal Aeronautical Society's 1953 gatherings, which was held at the Grand National Hotel on February 11. About 70 members and guests were present to hear a symposium on jet propulsion.

Introducing the subject, Mr. John Nash, president of the Southern Africa Division, drew a clear distinction between the operation of the true jet and the gas turbine. With the aid of excellent diagrams, he briefly described the various types of compound compressor and by-pass engines in use or projected, and expressed the view that we are approaching the limiting travel time in jet transport.

Mr. A. O. M. Vialls, who did his aeronautical training at Princeton University, gave a brief outline of some of the principles of supersonic aerodynamics and demonstrated the reasons for the adoption of sweep-back in some jet aircraft.

The improvement in maintenance schedules of aircraft powered by gas turbines was explained in detail by Mr. S.E.G. Quinn, of de Havillands, and Mr. I. R. Lyon, of Shell, described the qualities required for high altitude operation, and pointed out that, because paraffin supplies are limited, as many substitutes as possible have to be found.

The series of talks was rounded off by Major P. Retief, A.F.C. and Bar—South Africa's most experienced jet pilot—who gave an amusing commentary on his experiences in approaching the sound barrier, especially when in an untested aircraft. He left no doubt in the minds of his audience of his disdain for "up-and-down jobs."

Article in *Wings*, March 1953. (*Author's collection, Wings*)

Sadly for the Comet, however, clouds were gathering on the horizon. The first incident occurred on 26 October 1952, when the BOAC Comet *G-ALYZ* failed to leave the ground on take-off from Rome and ran off the end of the runway: two passengers sustained minor injuries, but the aircraft was a write-off. Five months later, a brand-new aircraft christened the *Empress of Hawaii*, which had just been delivered to Canadian Pacific Airlines, was involved in a similar incident at Karachi Airport. On this occasion, the outcome was grim: all eleven passengers and crew were killed.

It was subsequently found that in all probability these two incidents had been caused by the wing profile experiencing a loss of lift at a high angle of attack, and its engine inlets suffering a lack of pressure recovery in these conditions. Consequently, de Havilland re-profiled the wings' leading edges with a pronounced droop, and 'wing fences' were added to assist with air pressure recovery.

This was only the beginning of a series of catastrophic failures. The Comet's second fatal accident occurred on 2 May 1953, when another of BOAC's fleet, *G-ALYV*, came down in a severe thunderstorm just after taking off from Calcutta's Dum Dum Airport, killing all forty-three on board. Eye-witness reports suggested some form of catastrophic structural failure. Subsequent investigations concluded that extreme negative G-forces were encountered during take-off, causing structural failure in the horizontal stabiliser and severe down-loading to the wings; metal fatigue in this incident was ruled out.

Clearly, there was considerable concern, not only within de Havilland, but also at BOAC, whose hopes had been so high for this ground-breaking aircraft. After such an auspicious start and a highly successful first year

The *Daily Express* reports on the first fatal Comet crash (*CF-CUN Empress of Hawaii*) at Karachi on its delivery flight to Canadian Pacific Airlines, 3 March 1953. (*Author's collection, Daily Express*)

in service, things were beginning to look a bit uncertain. However, at this point confidence in the Comet was still sufficient for Sir Geoffrey and Lady de Havilland to put on a special flight for the new Queen Elizabeth, together with the Queen Mother and Princess Margaret in June – the month of the Coronation. The Coronation Honours List published on the first of that month included a citation for an OBE to Captain Marmaduke Jonathan Rowland Alderson for 'Services to Aviation'.

1954 got off to a terrible start: On 10 January, BOAC's Comet *G-ALYP* – the first production aircraft – broke up in mid-air just twenty minutes after taking off from Ciampino, crashing into the sea off Elba with the loss of all thirty-five on board. This was a massive blow, and BOAC voluntarily grounded the Comet fleet pending the outcome of investigations. As the Abell committee could point to no apparent structural defect – and as de Havilland had meanwhile instigated a host of measures to guard against any potential design flaws – flights were restarted on 23 March. Subsequent events, however, proved this decision to be premature. The wreckage of *Yoke Peter* was only located in February, and the recovery operation by the Royal Navy took a further six months – which meant that the forensic examination was at this point in its very early stages.

The final hammer blow fell two weeks later. On 8 April, G-*ALYY*, a BOAC Comet on charter to South African Airways, having lifted off from Rome en route to Cairo, fell out of the sky near Naples, killing all twenty-one passengers and crew. This led to the immediate grounding of all Comets and the revocation of its Certificate of Airworthiness. For now – and until a definitive cause for the losses could be established – the Comet was literally 'dead in the water'.

This was, of course, a terrible time for all concerned – for de Havilland, for Roly and his Comet Fleet team at BOAC, and indeed for the British people, who had taken such pride in seeing this world-beating project come to fruition. Ironically, these events played directly to the advantage of the American aircraft industry, which was now quick to learn from – and take advantage of – the unfortunate events that had befallen their British competitors.

The Prime Minister of the day, Winston Churchill, was determined that the root cause of the failures be established. A long and complex investigation into the Comet accidents was headed up by the RAE (Royal Aircraft Establishment) at Farnborough. In essence, the RAE ultimately concluded that the accidents to *YV*, *YP* and *YY* could be attributed to design and construction flaws leading to structural failure of the pressurised cabins; the square shape of the windows was also an exacerbating factor. Commercial operations with the Comet did not resume until 1958, by which time BOAC had with reluctance ordered several American Boeing 707s, which were more cost-effective, larger, and with a longer range.

One of the most important outcomes of this tragic period in the history of British aviation was the vast amount of knowledge and expertise accrued as a direct result of the exhaustive air accident investigations, and specifically the great leaps forward in the development of investigation processes and protocols. It is precisely because of this that air travel is now so safe, as well as being by far the fastest means of transport available to man.

Chapter 10

Towards Concorde (1955–1966)

As the Comets had been mothballed and were yet to return to commercial service, Roly Alderson's position as Comet Fleet Manager became redundant, and in 1955 he was given a new role, that of BOAC's Technical Manager of Flight Operations. As an additional responsibility, he was also appointed as a panel member of the Air Registration Board, which oversaw the standards for aircraft airworthiness within the United Kingdom.

Roly now found himself responsible for all technical aspects of the Flight Ops Department, encompassing a considerable fleet of aircraft, including ten of the new Douglas DC7-Cs which were introduced in 1956 to plug the 'jet gap'; he was also in charge of the Central Training Unit, as well as advising on the operational aspects of new aircraft types, preparing them for regular service, and for liaison and contact with the MTCA (Ministry of Transport and Civil Aviation) on behalf of the Flight Ops Department.

An order for fifteen new Boeing 707 jets was placed the same year, although it was another four years before BOAC began to take delivery. There were a variety of other piston-engine aircraft still operational, including the Lockheed Constellations, Bristol Britannias, Boeing Stratocruisers, and the trusty Canadair DC4-M Argonauts – one of which, of course, G-*ALHK Atalanta,* was the aircraft which had transported Princess Elizabeth out to Kenya on her honeymoon, and returned her barely a week later as Queen.

Meanwhile, back at de Havilland, they had been busy redesigning and strengthening the Comet, and on 12 December 1955 John Cunningham had achieved the first round-the-world flight in a jet airliner with the new Comet 3, *G-ANLO*. This was a huge achievement after all the setbacks that had occurred earlier, although it was still more than two years before the first two Comet 4 derivatives *G-APDB* and *APDC* entered the arena, heralding the introduction of the world's first scheduled transatlantic jet service in October 1958. *DB* was duly selected to do duty for a royal tour of Canada early in 1959.

Alderson's new posting as Technical Manager presented challenges for his personal life-balance. Having been based at Hurn with the Comet Unit, Roly's work had been confined mainly to the UK – after so many years of enforced absence – and he had been able to spend valuable time with his young family at Ringwood prior to the move to Ascot. Now, in order to become fully conversant with the technicalities of the aeroplanes under his wing, he found himself out of the country for extended periods, making regular trips to the United States to attend certification courses and briefings on the models in service at the manufacturing headquarters of the aircraft and aero-engine companies supplying BOAC – Boeing, Lockheed, Douglas, and Curtis-Wright among others.

This was also a time of change at home for Roly. Kit had – reluctantly – been sent off to boarding school in Oxford, soon to be joined by his younger brother Polo. Kit took after his father – quieter and more reserved than his younger sibling. Polo was a different kettle of fish – full of *joie de vivre* and seemingly forever courting trouble. One day at school, after the mid-morning break, the 8-year-old Alderson Minor kicked a football – his acumen in this activity not apparently being one of his strong points – which inadvertently went straight through the pavilion window. He quickly sought out his older brother for advice: 'Go straight to the headmaster's office and own up,' advised Alderson Major, 'otherwise it will be announced in the Dining Room, and you will be in even deeper trouble.' Alderson Minor did as his brother suggested, and the headmaster – the fearsome and cadaverous *GB* – summarily administered 'Six of the Best' with his cane. This was an instrument of chastisement – today one might say torture – which was always kept close at hand. Alderson Minor soon got his revenge, however: he discovered where the substantial supply of canes was stored, and 're-stored' them out of harm's way.

While Kit and Polo were 'enjoying' boarding school, Roly and Jo headed over once more to Bermuda, guests of Bermuda's 'Civil Aviation Week', which was opened by the Governor on 17 June 1957 to commemorate the twentieth anniversary of the first passenger flights between Bermuda and the United States, operated jointly by Imperial and Pan Am. Among those present was the Director of Civil Aviation, as well as Roly's friend, Taffy Powell, and Captain Armstrong who had been in command of the *Cavalier* on her first flights in 1937. As always, Roly and Jo were welcomed back to Bermuda with open arms.

By this time, Roly had been with Imperial and BOAC for twenty-five years; this achievement was acknowledged by the Chairman of the Corporation, Gerard D'Erlanger. Roly was also one of the longest serving members of the Guild of Air Pilots and Air Navigators of the British Empire,[1] having joined in May 1936. He had served the Guild for many years on the Navigation and Airline committees and had already been admitted into the Freedom of the Guild. He was now appointed a Liveryman and was consequently granted the Freedom of the City of London.

AIRLINE PIONEERS. — Arriving over the week-end were a number of figures connected with the opening of commercial flights between Bermuda and the U.S. 20 years ago. In the group above are (l. to r.), Mr. John Fountain, local B.O.A.C. manager, Mrs. Ware, Captain W. Armstrong, Mrs. Armstrong and Wing Commander E. M. Ware, Civil Aviation Director; (second row), Mrs. Alderson and David Powell; (back row), Captain M. Alderson and Air Commodore G. Powell. Air Commodore Powell (he was then captain) plotted the R.M.A. Cavalier's position when she was forced down at sea and lost in 1939; Captain Alderson was piloting the aircraft. Captain Armstrong commanded Cavalier on her first flights from Bermuda in 1937.

Guests at Bermuda's 'Civil Aviation Week', 1957. (*Author's collection, The Royal Gazette, Bermuda, 17 June 1957*)

R.A.'s certificate in recognition of twenty-five years of service with Imperial Airways and BOAC. (*Author's collection*)

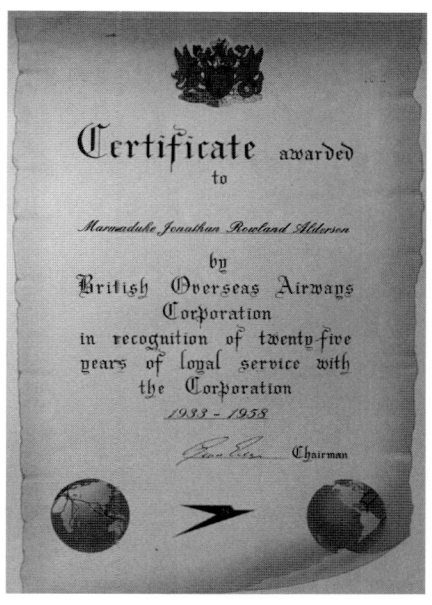

It was in this year that Roly witnessed the return to service of the Comet in the form of the Series 4; it was barely two years before the Boeing 707s started to arrive, heralding the beginning of the real 'Jet Age' and the demise of many of the piston-engine aircraft. The Constellations were retired in 1958, the Stratocruisers in 1959, and the Argonauts the year after. By this time, BOAC had put in an order for seventeen of the beautiful and ground-breaking Vickers VC10 jets.

This was a period of many changes within the management structure of BOAC, however, and Roly needed no reminding of the fact that he was 'pilot-turned-manager'; in fact, he increasingly felt that he was not ideally suited to the 'manager' part. Flying was what he had always loved, and it was a calling at which he had excelled; he was also exceptionally knowledgeable in the field of aviation technology, which suited his exacting and cerebral approach to problem-solving. Although he had developed into a highly respected team leader at the Comet Unit, his reserved nature was not a natural fit with the increasingly management-driven style of BOAC's modern business model. By the early 1960s Roly was beginning to question what the future held for him in this organisation.

Despite the heavy responsibilities of his role at BOAC, Roly made the most of his leisure time. He taught his young family to ski on winter holidays in Austria and Switzerland, and in the summer weeks he often took advantage of the generous BOAC travel concessions by taking them to Bermuda to stay with the Wardman family from the *Cavalier* days. On each occasion, Roly was welcomed by the Bermudians like a long-lost friend, and for him in a way it felt like coming home.

One memorable holiday saw them heading for Barbados. The trip out was in itself an epic adventure for the children. The outward leg took

'The Reluctant Manager'. (*Author's collection*)

them by B.377 Stratocruiser first to Gander, then onwards to Toronto. The 377 had a second deck beneath the main cabin, which on this aircraft was reserved as a VIP lounge, complete with its own bar and comfortable seating. It was with great excitement that the family were escorted below to spend time with the captain, while his first officer remained at the controls. Being able to welcome on board the Technical Manager of the airline together with his family, the commander evidently felt that it was his duty to see that his guests were properly looked after.

After a night in Toronto the family boarded a Douglas DC7-C bound for Barbados; this was not a scheduled flight and, apart from the full flight crew, its only passengers were the five Aldersons. For the children, this was nirvana – the freedom to roam the cabin, building dens between the rows of seats, making announcements on the public address system: 'Zis iz Kruschev speaking; vee heff control ov zis aircruft.' (This was, of course, the Cold War era).

When the DC7-C touched down at Seawell (now Grantley Adams) Airport in Barbados, the family were met by their hosts, Sir John and Lady Stow. Sir John was the current Governor of Barbados: he and Roly had been at Cambridge together and were old friends. The family were ushered into a large black limousine and whisked off under police motorcycle escort to their rather grand holiday accommodation at Government House. The visit was certainly one to remember: fresh mangoes for breakfast, served on the verandah; games of snooker in the billiards pavilion; archery in the evenings on the floodlit lawns; the Royal Box at the Barbados Turf Club horse races. These were among the last gasps of the British Empire – indeed, to the children, it felt like something out of Rudyard Kipling or Rider Haggard.

When time allowed, Roly enjoyed a game of golf as a member of nearby Swinley Forest Golf Club, either with Jo (only on weekdays – at that time, ladies were not permitted to play at weekends), or with the Aero Golfing Society. There was a hard tennis court at home, and regular weekend tennis parties were a feature of those days. Polo remembers the wartime fighter ace Douglas Bader coming to play. When asked by the host's young son if he really had tin legs beneath his long whites, Bader replied: 'Well, why don't you hit them with this tennis racquet of mine, and see?' Polo did – and was met with a sonorous 'Clang!'

There was also an outdoor swimming pool, which was in use from April until September. When it was early (or late) in the season, Roly would don a home-made wetsuit for a brisk swim – even breaking the ice if necessary – before heading over to his office at Heathrow.

Usually, he would commute in his V8 BMW 502 saloon – he had always admired German precision engineering, his war experiences notwithstanding – but on occasion he would take the sublime Mercedes 300SL 'Gullwing'. He continued to be an automotive engineering aficionado, and since his Bentley days had owned a variety of exotic vehicles – and he had not finished yet.

Meanwhile, back at Heathrow, the Boeing 707s were dominating the fleet when the first Vickers VC10 took off on its maiden flight at the end of June in 1962. It entered service two years later, and by 1965 the BOAC fleet consisted solely of jets – 707s and VC10s; all the piston-engine aircraft had been retired from service.

This was nevertheless an exciting time to be at the forefront of developments in aviation. Supersonic flight was on the near horizon. In November 1962, France and the UK signed a treaty to engage in a joint development project, and this was soon followed by the French

R.A. breaking the ice…. (*Author's collection*)

'The Aviator's Choice': R.A.'s Mercedes 300SL '*Gullwing*'. (*Author's collection*)

President Charles de Gaulle, in a speech in 1963, setting in stone the name *Concorde*. The joint Franco-British venture into 'faster than the speed of sound' aviation was born, and on 3 June, BOAC backed this by signing an option for six of the new aircraft.

In September of that year, Roly Alderson crossed to the States to attend the NASA Supersonic Transport Symposium at Langley, Virginia (Langley was a USAF base that Roly was intimately connected with since the *Cavalier* affair in 1939). Roly needed to be fully aware of all global developments in this area of aviation expertise. While at Langley, he spent some time discussing these exciting aeronautical advances with John Glenn, who had been the first American spaceman to orbit the earth on the *Friendship 7* mission.

As supersonic transport was now the next major goal in commercial air travel, it was Roly's responsibility to see that the organisation was fully engaged with developments every step of the way. While ensuring that the BOAC jetliner fleet was operationally fit for purpose, Roly was of necessity peripherally involved in this new and challenging area of aircraft technology, and being an aviation engineer through-and-through, this kept him on his metal – in spite of his increasing misgivings regarding his new role as BOAC's General Manager of Flight Services. Sir Giles Guthrie had taken over as Chairman of the Corporation on 1 January 1964, and brought with him a harder, profit-driven management style.

In April 1964 BOAC issued a Declaration of Intent to purchase eight Concordes, and nine months later production started on the first prototype. Now that BOAC was fully committed, Roly was engaged in liaising with the British Aircraft Corporation designers at Filton – the British half of the Concorde partnership – in detailed work on the layout of the cockpit to BOAC's specification.

For his winter break in 1965, Roly decided on another skiing holiday, this time to the Swiss resort of St Moritz. By this time, Clari and Kit had flown the nest, so it was just Jo and Polo who drove with him to catch the British United Airways 'Roll-on/Roll-off' Bristol 170 Superfreighter[2] (similar to the bulb-nosed aircraft, *G-AIFF*, which Roly had test-flown in April 1948) from Lydd to Le Touquet. As these aircraft carried vehicles, they only catered for a maximum of twenty passengers. Among the contingent on this day was the well-known left-wing journalist and satirist Malcolm Muggeridge, who had worked with Roly's brother-in-law, Bill Deedes.[3] Polo recalled considerable hilarity between Alderson and Muggeridge during the flight, although their political viewpoints were poles apart. Roly always made a point of refusing to be drawn into discussions on matters political.

This holiday proved to be a difficult one for Roly as a father: Polo was 15, and in typical rebellious form he immediately defected from the family trio. On the first evening he discovered girls and dry Martinis. That was just day one.

Polo was by this time a reckless if reasonably accomplished skier, having cut his teeth on the slopes of Lenzerheide at the age of 4. It seems that he was a born risk-taker – not a good combination for a hormone-fuelled teenager with a potential hangover on a skiing holiday. On the second day in St Moritz, the tips of his father's cherished Kneissl skis were ripped off on the downhill racecourse after a series of poorly judged moguls finally hurled Polo high into the air, resulting in a potentially life-changing wipe-out: he miraculously walked away – the remains of the Kneissls under his arm – with nothing but snow up his nose and bruises to his pride. After two weeks Roly and Jo had had enough – they returned to England by car, leaving Junior to make his way home on the Alpine Express in the company of his new-found (mostly female) thrill-seekers.

1965 rolled into 1966. Construction of the six Concorde prototypes was under way, and as BOAC was to be waving the flag for Britain, Roly continued to busy himself with the plans of the cockpit layout for the British flight crews – although it would be another three years before this graceful new bird took to the air.

Over the last decade, with the coming of the jet age, civil aviation's safety record had greatly improved, although freak accidents could never be ruled out. Like other airlines, BOAC was not immune to such events, and on 4 March 1966, Flight 911 from Tokyo, a Boeing 707-436, registered *G-APFE*, disintegrated in mid-air and crashed near Mount Fuji shortly after take-off; all 124 people on board died. The probable cause was thought to be 'abnormally severe turbulence which imposed a gust load considerably in excess of the design limit' – in other words an unusual event which could not be foreseen.

These were Roly's swansong months with BOAC. The love affair was all but over – and, in Roly's eyes at least, worse was to come. On 31 March, Harold Wilson, leader of the Labour Party, won the general election in Britain and was duly appointed Prime Minister. For Roly, it was definitely time to go.

Captain Alderson retired from BOAC after thirty-three years of devoted service. Known throughout as the consummate professional, during his flying career he had piloted 180 aircraft of nearly 50 different models, from the lowly Lynx to the classy Comet; he had flown a total of 37 flying boats and had logged some 11,000 hours in the air. Almost 6,000 of those hours had been spent commanding 'boats'.

At the Corporation's presentation gathering were ninety members of staff; among them were twenty captains, the Managing Director Keith Granville, and the Chairman Sir Giles Guthrie. A tankard from his Flight Services team was inscribed thus:

Presented to

Captain M.J.R.Alderson, OBE,

By his Senior Staff

In sincere appreciation of "Our Boss!"

R.A. and J.A. at R.A.'s retirement presentation, with Sir Giles Guthrie, Chairman of BOAC. (*Author's collection*)

Chapter 11

Twilight (1966–1992)

Like many high achievers, retirement did not initially suit Roly; he had spent his entire life at work – very concentrated work – and to find himself at home without a purpose was anathema to him. It was also difficult for Jo, who could see that this did not sit well with her Roly – he needed to be mentally challenged.

He joined a shooting syndicate in Norfolk; he acquired a trout rod on a chalk stream in Wiltshire, creating an exquisitely crafted one-handed mayfly box to his own exacting specification; he designed and constructed one of the very first effective solar panel systems for heating the swimming pool – but none of it was enough to engage him sufficiently on a cerebral level.

Roly needed to be involved in engineering in some form. He continued to enjoy servicing and maintaining his performance cars – now a new Porsche 911S and a BMW CS Coupe (while Jo was happy to rattle about in a Morris Traveller 'plank-wagon'). He felt keenly the lack of any further involvement with the Concorde project, but nevertheless looked on with some pride as the first prototype – 001 – was rolled out of its hangar in Toulouse on 11 December 1967 in front of more than 1,100 guests.

When he collected his new 911S from his friend Don Aldington at Porsche GB, Don mentioned that his company AFN still held the dormant UK distribution rights for Steib, a German engineering company. Steib was well-known in racing circles for producing a highly advanced and desirable motorcycle sidecar used by BMW; they were also involved in the design and production of innovative agricultural machinery – notably manure-spreading equipment. Don and Roly hatched a plan to take this franchise forward. They duly registered Powerspread Ltd, and got busy during 1967 to launch this new venture.

October 1967 – Foot and Mouth Disease hit the UK. The timing could not have been worse. Alderson and Aldington could not display their products at shows – everything was cancelled – and visiting farms to demonstrate their wares was banned. Very quickly, Don and Roly took the difficult decision to cut their losses and ceased trading. After less than twelve months, Powerspread Ltd was consigned to history.

With hindsight, this may have been a blessing. Aldington already had a busy diary with sales of the hugely successful Porsche 911 – at the time a technically advanced rear-engine sports coupe which was sweeping the board. Roly would have been the first to admit that he was not a born salesman. He was not by nature an entrepreneur – he was, after all, really just a pilot and an engineer.

Meanwhile, he still had responsibilities to attend to in Ceylon. He and his sister continued to be the absentee owners of two estates, and he needed to visit on a regular basis, to ensure that their agents and managers were properly discharging their duties. Roly decided to visit in 1968, taking with him Jo and his elder son Kit, as he thought that the latter might enjoy some game shooting in a more exotic setting. While the boys went off blasting at snipe and 'LBJs',[1] Jo was left on her own in Colombo; how she spent her time, history does not relate. It transpired that this was the final Alderson visit to the country, and it marked the end of a hundred-year-old dynasty.

This confirmed engineer and high-performance car enthusiast was not sufficiently challenged by the Porsche. In a reprise of thirty-seven years earlier – when Roly bought himself an early Christmas present in the form of a de Havilland Gipsy Moth biplane – he made the short trip to Maranello in Egham, returning home with a 12-cylinder Ferrari. Rumour had it that the 330 GTC was very comfortable in its new centrally heated garage.

Due to his unconventional upbringing, Roly had never been one for exhibiting overt affection; nevertheless, he was first to admit that his precious family was his greatest pride, so when Polo was invited by his cousin Bruce Tulloh[2] – a former Olympic long-distance runner and European gold medallist – to be part of the support team for a record attempt on foot from Los Angeles to New York, he was more than happy to help by arranging a concessionary air ticket for Polo to the United States.

While Tulloh was limbering up to start his epic trans-American adventure, Roly's old friend Brian Trubshaw ('Grubscrew' to Roly and other close colleagues) was firing up Concorde 002 at Filton. To the delight of the nation – and, of course, Roly – the supersonic marvel took to the air on its maiden flight, landing a few minutes later at RAF Fairford. 'It was wizard – a cool, calm and collected operation' commented Trubshaw with a grin.

Clari and Kit often felt that Roly gave Polo special treatment as the youngest child – but this was not always the case. When Polo confided one day to his father that he was about to embark on a parachuting course, he was met with the normal pilot's retort: 'What would induce anyone to hurl themselves out of a perfectly serviceable aircraft?' Polo responded that he would prefer to learn to fly, but that it was much more expensive. If Daddy would like to pay for this, he would readily forgo the 'hurling out of the aeroplane' experience. The curt response from Daddy: 'Well, you had better go parachuting, then!' (This particular venture did not end well – but that is another story.)

Meanwhile, Clari had become a successful fashion house entrepreneur, numbering the Lennons and McCartneys among her Weybridge clientele; and Kit was carving himself out a new life in South Africa, with a little help from Paddy Sheppard of the Durban 'Train Wreck' saga.

Roly made one final visit to Bermuda with Jo in early 1976, staying with his old friends the Wardmans at Mount Pleasant in Paget. He took the opportunity to visit Edna Watson, the heroine passenger on the ill-fated *Cavalier* flight of January 1939, and was once again feted by the Bermudian press.

Scroll on to 1980: Polo can finally afford to learn to fly. Emulating his father, he shares a small aircraft with a friend, and within two months of gaining his PPL he is off across the English Channel to Normandy to celebrate Bastille Day – his birthday – with fellow French aviators. Forever the adventure seeker, he casts off the following year in a little wooden yacht, bound for the West Indies. On board is his girlfriend Magles and – sensibly, since they are both pretty green sailors – a third crew member, Paul, who has already completed a transatlantic crossing and so comes with some invaluable experience. Long story short: 'Bay of Biscay/75-knot storm/Knock-down/Polo & Paul swept overboard, saved by safety harnesses/Arrive English Harbour for Christmas – No worries.'

In due course, Roly and Jo fly out to join them in the Caribbean. Paul has by this time moved on, but it is nevertheless a tight squeeze for the

39 years on . . .
Pilot of crippled Cavalier recalls ocean death dive

3 perish after 11 hours in Atlantic

Some people walk around concealing, or forgetting, stirring stories beneath bland exteriors. Such a one is Mr. Roland Alderson, who said when approached for an interview: "I don't know whether it's worth it."

When met in person, he seems like the quiet blue-eyed Englishman he is, visiting old friends in Bermuda with his wife and enjoying rounds of golf which may account, in part, for his fresh complexion.

He is retired in fact.

He wears no label to proclaim him as a hero. And only two people in Bermuda have first-hand memories of his heroic feat of 39 years ago when, as captain of the flying boat Cavalier, he brought down the disabled craft at sea smoothly enough for 13 passengers and crew to escape before it sank.

CLINGING

All but three of them — two American passengers and a British steward — lived to tell the tale, being picked up by tanker after nearly 11 hours clinging to a raft which had improvised from life belts.

On Sunday Mr. Alderson went to King Edward Hospital to see two of the survivors, Mrs. Edna Watson, who is recovering from surgery.

The other one still living here is Mrs. A. Weatherley, who at the time of the ill-fated trip was Mrs. George Ingham. A third woman survivor, Miss Nellie Smith, has since died.

"Two of the crew are dead now," said the captain. "Nail Richardson, the second pilot, was married here, and poor Robert Chapman, the radio officer. The stew and who perished after tiring exertions to help the others was Robert ...

development he had a hand. "I think jumbos are the only other new craft we have had since I retired; I will probably go back to England on one," he said. "Most of the fleet are 707's. I imagine that one of the biggest contrasts between the Cavalier and the jumbos is the cost. You could probably get 10 Cavaliers for the price of one jumbo jet engine."

"I have always been a supporter of Concorde, before I retired I was concerned to a limited degree with the design arrangements for the cockpit.

EFFORT

"I have had nothing to do with it since. I have always been enthusiastic about Concorde as a great effort of both French and British manufacturers. One has to do these things in the interest of advancement, and time ..."

jets, but this is essential for its performance. I am glad the United States landing rights hurdle is over for the moment, but there are still a few other hurdles.

All countries over which Concorde flies want to be sure the supersonic bang does not annoy people. If it is not allowed to fly at supersonic speed over large areas, this will reduce the advantages of its speed.

"At high altitude the bang is very small, and is not likely to annoy people at the height they normally do it."

FLYING BOATS

Going back to flying boat days, the veteran pilot said: "I came to Bermuda originally in 1936, a few months after the service started in the war, I would have come back to flying the Cavalier after ...

pheric conditions."

Speaking of rough weather, he reminded the ex-pilot of that chilly afternoon and evening spent by the Cavalier survivors in the Atlantic on January 21, 1939.

Because the aircraft was a boat, he said, "we had difficulty getting out; the problem was to be floated. The aircraft went down because of the swell."

"A January sea is often building up in front storm or dying down; one, so you don't find the calm weather in the Atlantic.

"We ae lucky to be able to get down without breaking up. We did a certain amount of shouting, trying to attract the attention of the ship which eventually found us and of another that did, though we saw its lights ...

CARRIAGE CAL

When Imperial Airways and Pan American Airways shared the flying boat service between New York, Bermuda, said Mr. Alderson, "the American pilot I would have a carriage in the morning and take to the Belmont where we catch a launch to Darrell's Island.

"I sailed past it the other day but it looked dead; the hangar is left to indicate that there had flying boats here at one time."

Mr. Alderson and his son are guests of Mr. and George Wardman at Pleasant, Paget.

The two men met when Mr. Wardman was American representative here at the time Mr. Alderson arrived in Bermuda to pilot the flying boats ...

CHILLY

"After the war there were enough airstrips for land craft, but we lost some of the advantages of flying boats. You could say that was the end of the Cavalier affair and probably about here ...

HENRY REA TO QUIT?

CAIRO — U.S. Secretary of State Henry A. Kissinger tendered his resignation as President Ford chairman of the National Security Council; the resignation House by the ...

Ex-pilot Mr. Roland Alderson, who brought a Cavalier flying boat safely down at sea en route to Bermuda in 1939.

The Royal Gazette, Bermuda, 10 February 1976. (*Author's collection, The Royal Gazette*)

four of them, living and sleeping on board a boat of under 30ft – but Jo and Roly are up for it. In spite of the cramped conditions, they happily cruise the Virgin Islands together – swimming, imbibing the local rum, catching kingfish and langoustines for the barbecue, watching for the

207

R.A. and Sir Ross Stainton, celebrating fifty years since they both joined Imperial Airways in 1933. (*Author's collection*)

'Green Flash',[3] toasting the future – for Polo and his sweetheart had become engaged at the height of the Biscay storm.

In 1983, the management of the old firm – now re-christened British Airways and known globally as 'The World's Favourite Airline' – held a joint party for Ross Stainton[4] and Roly Alderson, to commemorate fifty years since they joined Imperial Airways together in 1933.

Roly was by now approaching 80: he was travelling less, still playing golf, albeit less often – and still servicing the cars, although the Ferrari had finally gone – and still gamely climbing 30ft ladders to clean the house gutters. Was it, perhaps, time to wind down, take his foot off the pedal, and hand over control to others? A difficult transition for someone who had been in charge of his own destiny, and that of his beloved family, for so long.

Chapter 12

Final Flight (1993)

Early April 1993, Near Ascot, Berkshire

Jo has noticed that, over the past few weeks, Roly has been looking a little peaky, a bit jaundiced, and he seems to be losing weight. Together, they visit the local GP, an excellent doctor who has been looking after the Alderson family for many years – indeed, as his doctor father had done before him. He is giving little away but would like to order some blood tests.

A few days later, Jo receives a telephone call from the GP. The blood tests results are back, and he tells her he has made an appointment with a consultant in Windsor. He suggests that they attend together: Jo – having been a nurse – is able to read between the lines, and the signals are not encouraging.

On Monday morning of 19 April, Jo drives with Roly the few miles to Windsor. The meeting is brief, but the message is clear: pancreatic cancer, advanced, terminal. 'The candle is burning low,' says the consultant as kindly as possible, 'You will have things to do'.

Roly does not, in fact, have things to do. In his typically organised way, he has done it all: will, powers of attorney, estate planning – everything is in place, everything has been taken care of.

Immediate family members are notified that time is short. Clari and Kit are both within easy driving distance. Polo is in the South of France, working on a superyacht; he catches the next available flight out of Nice. He is collected on Friday evening from Heathrow by Clari and driven the 10 miles back to the family home. Kit and his family are already there, as is Clari's daughter. Magles and the children arrive the following morning.

The weather that last weekend in April is glorious. It is unseasonably warm. The birds are singing, and the sound of laughter fills the air as the grandchildren play happily together in the garden; some even brave the bracing waters of the swimming pool. Roly is in good spirits and makes a brief appearance on the verandah to sit in the sunshine, although he is clearly failing.

By Sunday evening everyone has gone home, leaving just Jo and Polo to tend to Roly, who is now exhausted after the wonderful family get-together. It was worth it.

Roly remains in bed on Monday, obviously going downhill. That afternoon, he has a special visitor: his old friend and colleague Ross Stainton. The two comrades spend ten minutes together in private, quietly chatting. When it is time to leave, they shake hands and say, simply, 'Goodbye'.

Jo and Polo take it in turns to sit at Roly's bedside overnight; he is now obviously experiencing some discomfort and is barely conscious. When the doctor calls by the following morning, he decides it is time to set up a syringe driver to keep Roly comfortable. As the morphine dose is gradually increased, so Roly will become more deeply unconscious, although he should be pain-free.

For the next four days and nights, Polo and Jo tend to Roly's needs – a gentle wet shave (Roly had never used an electric shaver), a wash with a warm flannel, a sip of water.

It is the evening of Saturday, 1 May 1993: Roly does not approve of the new May Day Bank Holiday, which had been instigated by (in Roly's words) 'that dreadful Michael Foot' to coincide with Labour Day. The bedroom window is ajar, and pop music can be heard blasting across from the neighbour's garden, where a post-wedding party is in full swing. Roly does not care for pop music either. A Marie Curie nurse has been booked for 22:00, to give Jo and Polo a night off, but Roly does not want to waste her time.

It is precisely 21:33: 'The *Cavalier* is eager to depart', and so on this fine, calm spring evening, with Jo and Polo by his side, Captain Roly gently lifts off…

Order of Service for the Funeral
Of
MARMADUKE JONATHAN ROWLAND
ALDERSON
OBE, MA

('Roly')

'A Very Private Man'

12th – 18th August 1907 – 1st May 1993

On
FRIDAY, 7th MAY 1993
Address by Sir Ross Stainton, CBE

Portrait Photo of R.A. by Dorothy Wilding, c.1942. (*Author's collection*)

Tributes and Memories

Roly was one of the finest men that I have ever known, and I knew him from the time I joined the Imperial Airways in 1934. With his death goes another link with the early days of aviation in Bermuda. He will be sorely missed by his many friends.

Mr Hilary Watson, former Bermuda-based
Imperial Airways employee, and husband
of one of the survivors of the *Cavalier* disaster

Some pilots become instinctively good airmen. A few become good and intelligent airmen and Roly was one of these few.

Sir Ross Stainton, former CEO and Chairman,
British Airways

Roly had a long and distinguished career in Civil Aviation. He was also one of our longest serving members, having joined the Guild of Air Pilots and Air Navigators of the British Empire in May 1936. He served the Guild for many years as a member of our Navigation and then Airline Committee. We all have so much to be thankful for from his life and work in Aviation.

Group Captain John Tritton,
Clerk to the Guild, GAPAN

We were at Cambridge together … and he and I drove together in the 3 litre in the University Speed Trials – no crash hats, no goggles, no nonsense! I also remember the rather gruesome story he told us of flying on the India route at a fairly high altitude when the plane crashed into a sleeping albatross or some such creature. It passed right through the windscreen and injured Rowland quite badly.

Mr Guy Shoosmith, friend and
life-long Bentley aficionado

Roly was a splendid fellow to fly with, he had a quiet air of command combined with a delightful sense of humour. I cannot recall a single difficult moment throughout the whole period we were together.

Mr Eric Draper, former Boeing 314A
flight engineer

Others who were in close touch with Roly for far longer than I was know from first-hand how great his contribution to civil air development was over so many years…My personal indebtedness goes back to India in 1935/36: I was with Indian National Airways which had run into financial difficulties… Our Chief Pilot failed his medical, and Roly came to us for some months. The 'loan' was a complete success. Not only were the Viceroy and Vicereine in safe hands but Roly placed his knowledge and expertise at our disposal and we were able to improve our organisation in many ways. It is not going too far to say that this saved I.N.A. as a company.

Mr Robert Maxwell, former manager,
Indian National Airways and BOAC Cairo Station

In the far-off days…he was looking us up in West Africa whenever a flying boat brought him there. So started a friendship…which was always valued by us.

Sir John Stow, last Governor of Barbados

Our friendship has been a very long one – from our days at Cambridge – the Air Squadron – then de Havilland's – later Hurn…we have so greatly valued and enjoyed our family friendship.

Mr Wilfred Hampton, pioneer aviator

The Taylors count themselves very lucky to have met and known Roly…I'd always guessed that he played a more important part in the aeronautical world than he ever let on – anyone less of a line-shooter it would be hard to imagine.

Mr Francis Taylor, friend

One phrase springs to the minds of all of us privileged to have known Roly – 'One of Nature's Gentlemen'. We met spasmodically after the great 'boat' days but always with warmth and pleasure.

Ms E.R. 'Minnie' Mann,
former Imperial Airways colleague

He will be remembered by older Bermudians for his part in an amazing rescue on Saturday January 21st 1939. His flying skills and nerve were partly the reason why ten people survived the sinking of the flying-boat *Cavalier.*

The Royal Gazette, Bermuda

He was such a dear friend – we are proud to have known him and to have had the privilege of enjoying his company. For me this goes back fifty-five years!

Mrs Freda Wardman,
Mount Pleasant, Bermuda

Scholarly in manner and appearance and loath to talk about his work, Roly Alderson was an intensely private person.

The Daily Telegraph, May 1993

Endnotes

Chapter 1

1. It seems likely that the cause of Dixwell Ian's death was a cover-up by the Royal Navy. The official line was that he 'was found lying in a shell room of a turret, with a severe head injury. It was believed that he had been hit by an ammunition cage', but 'no witness to the accident could be found'. Many years later, Roly Alderson met one of Dixwell Ian's fellow officers, who recounted a very different version of events. He told Roly that he himself had been standing with Roly's brother in one of the gun turrets aboard HMS *Conqueror* 'when a shell exploded in the breach, and a piece of flying shrapnel hit him in the head, killing him instantly'.
2. This carriage clock remains in the possession of the family.

Chapter 2

1. From an interview recorded by R.A.'s son in 1991.
2. The Avro 504N Lynx was the principal RAF trainer of the 1920s. The machine was of wood and fabric construction, and 598 were built. The 504N was fitted with a 160hp Armstrong Siddeley 7-cylinder air-cooled radial engine.
3. Goddard was later to become Air Marshall Sir Victor Goddard KCB CBE DL, having been a senior RAF commander during the Second World War in charge of administration for the air command of Southeast Asia Command (SEAC). After the war he became the RAF's representative in Washington.
4. Cambridge University Air Squadron: Annual Attachment at Old Sarum', *Flight*, 28 June 1928, Major F.A.ce V. Robertson.

Chapter 3

1. From an interview recorded by R.A.'s son in 1991.
2. Saint-Inglevert was an airfield in the Pas-de-Calais region of northern France. It was established by the Royal Flying Corps in the First World War.
3. The de Havilland Company had their HQ at Stag Lane Airfield, in Edgware, North London.
4. This Comper Swift, *G-ABJR*, was destroyed on 28 January 1934 when its new owner crashed at Brooklands; the pilot was killed. The cause was thought to be pilot error.
5. This particular de Havilland DH.9J *G-AARS* was used in the development flying for the powerful 340hp Armstrong Siddeley Serval IV 9-cylinder radial engine. The aircraft crashed on 9 September 1934 and was destroyed; the pilot bailed out and survived.
6. The 'Happy Valley Set' was a group of fun-loving mainly British aristocrats and adventurers who settled in the 'Happy Valley' region of colonial Kenya and Uganda in the 1920s and 1930s.
7. Beryl Markham was a female pioneer aviator who began her flying career in Kenya in the early 1930s and went on to break a number of solo long-distance records.
8. Elizabeth 'Betty' Woodville was a direct descendant of Elizabeth Woodville, widow of King Henry IV.

Chapter 4

1. In 1934 G.P. 'GPO' Olley formed Olley Air Services and wrote in the same year his book entitled *A Million Miles in the Air* (Hodder & Stoughton Ltd, 1934).
2. *TD* was soon sold on, doing a stint in Cairo with a Captain E.H. Tinker, and was later impressed into the RAF for war service in 1941.
3. The Avro 618 X *G-AASP Achilles* subsequently crashed as it was taking off from Almaza Airport, Cairo, in 1940. Both members of the BOAC crew were injured but survived.
4. From an interview recorded by R.A.'s son in 1991.
5. *Beyond the Blue Horizon*, Alexander Frater (William Heinemann, 1986).

6. Captain Wilcockson was appointed Manager of the Atlantic Division of Imperial Airways Ltd in 1938.

7. According to Alexander Frater, Mollard 'having been forced down beside a deserted, roofless fort one evening, sent his charges out to collect dried camel dung in their hats. Doused with petrol, the stuff burned well enough to warm them through the night. Months later they met for a reunion dinner at the Trocadero and sent Mollard a signed menu "From the Camel Dung-Burners Club". Mollard commented: "Passengers took the whole thing in a spirit of adventure".' (*Beyond the Blue Horizon*, Alexander Frater, William Heinemann, 1986).

8. *Beyond the Blue Horizon*, Alexander Frater (William Heinemann, 1986).

9. *Beyond the Blue Horizon*, Alexander Frater (William Heinemann, 1986).

10. Captain Egglesfield was appointed Deputy Director of Civil Aviation in India in 1939; Captain Prendergast was killed on 15 November 1934, in Queensland while on a delivery flight from London to Brisbane in a DH.86 Express.

11. *Beyond the Blue Horizon*, Alexander Frater (William Heinemann, 1986).

12. Major H.C. Brackley – known fondly as 'Brackles' – was Imperial Airways' Air Superintendent, with overall responsibility for pilot selection, training and supervision. He was described by one of Imperial's senior captains as 'calm, immaculate and extremely proper in all his conduct'. In his role as Air Superintendent, it was his responsibility to test new aircraft before they joined the fleet. Brackley piloted the very first Empire boat built by Shorts, *G-ADHL Canopus*, on its initial flight on behalf of Imperial on 17 September 1936.

13. 'BA100 Imperial to Bangkok: Orient Express', P.Harris, *Aeroplane Magazine*, July 2019 (www.aeroplanemonthly.com).

14. Mr Flynn evidently never found out the lady's full name.

15. From an interview recorded by R.A.'s son in 1991.

16. The full story of this remarkable rescue is told in *West with the Night*, Beryl Markham (1942).

17. The *Messenger*, Beryl Markham's Percival Vega Gull, crash-landed when its Gipsy engine suffered fuel starvation due to icing of the fuel tank vents.

18. Only two Avro 642s were ever built. The four-engine second aircraft registered *VT-AFM* was handed over on 12 December 1934 and christened *The Star of India*. By arrangement with the Indian government the aircraft was operated and maintained by Indian National Airways when not required by the Viceroy.

Chapter 5

1. This particular Calcutta, *G-EBVG*, was the first delivered to Imperial Airways, in August 1928. A week prior to delivery, *VG* was landed on the Thames in the centre of London and was moored off the embankment for three days of inspection by Members of Parliament - including the then Chancellor of the Exchequer, Winston Churchill – and Members of the House of Lords, as well as a number of other worthies. She was destroyed at Mirabello Bay, Crete, during a storm on 28 December 1936, just six months after Alderson's flying boat conversion course.
2. This boat, *Centaurus G-ADUT* was sunk by Japanese Zero fighters on 3 March 1942 in Roebuck Bay, Broome, Australia.
3. Imperial Airways opened their new flying boat base at Hythe, Southampton on 5 March 1937. Imperial Airways continued to use Southampton for their passenger flying boat operations until the Second World War when their base was transferred to Poole (by which time BOAC had been formed).
4. There were just three Short Kent S.17 Scipio Class boats built for Imperial, entering service in May 1931. These were basically four-engine versions of the Calcutta Class flying boats, with a longer range and able to carry fifteen passengers in great comfort. *G-ABFC Satyrus* was the last of the three to be built, the other two being *Scipio G-ABFA* and *Sylvanus G-ABFB*. *Satyrus* was the only boat to survive service, being scrapped in 1938: *Sylvanus* was destroyed by fire in Brindisi in November 1935, while *Scipio* sank after a heavy landing off Crete in August 1936, with the loss of two lives.
5. *Cygnus* was lost on 5 December. The official report stated: 'Shortly after take-off from the harbour of Brindisi, the seaplane stalled and

crashed into the sea. Six people were injured while two others (a crew member and a passenger) were killed.[*]

6. Sir John Salmond later headed up the Committee of Enquiry into the loss of RMA *Cavalier* in January 1939. As one of the survivors of the *Cygnus* accident, he had first-hand experience of being involved in such an event.

7. **The *Southern Daily Echo***, quoted in *Imperial Airways' Flying Boat Services 1936 to 1939*, Peter Wingent (Winchester, 1997).

8. **The *Southern Daily Echo***, quoted in *Imperial Airways' Flying Boat Services 1936 to 1939*, Peter Wingent (Winchester, 1997).

Chapter 6

1. Captain Cumming later became Group Captain Cumming, DFC, OBE and Master of the Guild of Air Pilots and Air Navigators of the British Empire (of which R.A. was also a member).

2. Letter from R.A. to Allan Finch, *BA Touchdown*, 17 April 1987.

3. Captain Griffith James 'Taffy' Powell was one of the earliest Master Pilots – No.17 – who later became Air Commodore Powell CBE. He was the very first pilot to be endorsed for land and sea aircraft, and he had been with Imperial since 1930. In February 1937 he had become the first airman to fly the 1,300 miles around Britain non-stop, aboard the Empire boat *G-ADUV Cambria*.

4. 'RMA' denotes that *Cavalier* was a Royal Mail Aeroplane.

5. During the 'Golden Years' of flying boat travel, one of the favourite haunts of the crews visiting New York was the famous speakeasy bar, known as the '21 Club' at 21 West 52 Street in downtown Manhattan, which was opened in 1930. In fact, the very first 'corporate toy' to be hung from the ceiling of the club was a model of an Imperial Airways flying boat. Since then, hundreds of toys have been hung, including a model PT109 donated by John F. Kennedy and a smashed tennis racquet by John McEnroe. Humphrey Bogart and Lauren Bacall got engaged there, at table 30, in 1944. It is quite possible that R.A. attended a Christmas singalong hosted by the Salvation Army band especially for '21 Club' patrons in December 1938: he was certainly a regular and revered visitor, and as such was

presented with a silver cigarette box by the proprietors as a wedding gift in June 1942.

6. Letter from R.A. to Allan Finch, *BA Touchdown*, 17 April 1987.

7. 'S.I.' refers to the starboard inner engine.

8. From a conversation between Paul Bewshea and R.A.'s son, on a visit to New York in 1979.

9. POB – Persons on Board.

10. In accordance with regulations, the commander of the aircraft was in charge of all outgoing radio communication.

11. This refers to winding in the trailing aerial. Without this aerial, the R/T (Radio Telegraphy, i.e., voice radio) range was only 80–100 miles; even with the 280ft trailing aerial – which was manually deployed and recovered using a hand winch – the maximum range was only 250–300 miles. The *Cavalier* was therefore at, or very close to, its extreme range for R/T. Once out of R/T range, communication was only possible via W/T, i.e., Wireless Telegraphy, using Morse Code. On this occasion it also became necessary to earth the fixed aerial due to the severity of the static. The transmission 'May have to earth' was incorrectly quoted in the press as 'May have to land' – a complete misinterpretation of the original signal.

12. The hulls of these flying boats were required to conform with the strength requirements of the Airworthiness Handbook for Civil Aircraft (Air Publication 1208). However, they were designed to operate from protected waterways – and certainly not for alighting on the open ocean. Following the loss of the *Cavalier*, a complex hull strengthening procedure was carried out by Shorts to the remaining in-service Empire boats.

13. The known survivability in 40–50°F is from one to three hours, and in 50–60°F, one to six hours. In 60–70°F, it increases dramatically to between two and forty hours.

14. A memorial plaque dedicated to the memory of Robert Spence in The Warrior's Chapel in Bermuda Cathedral reads: 'In Memory of Robert "Bobby" Spence who perished in the disaster of the Air-Liner *Cavalier* after he had exhausted his strength in saving others 21st January 1939.'

15. The Cable & Wireless Company's Bermuda station had been operational since 1928. In 1936, the world's first short-wave direction-finding facility – the Adcock RDF – had been installed at

Town Hill, Bermuda's highest point. This was followed in 1937 by an air-to-ground station in anticipation of the new Bermuda-New York flying boat services.

16. Letter from R.A. to Allan Finch, *BA Touchdown*, 17 April 1987.

Chapter 7

1. Edna Watson was 43 at the time of the *Cavalier* incident, and one of three Bermuda passengers on the flight. She was hailed a heroine for saving the life of Captain Alderson, helping to keep him afloat after he lost consciousness. She also buoyed up the group's flagging spirits in the long hours prior to rescue. Asked whether she was concerned about sharks, Watson told *The New York Times*: 'No, nobody said anything about sharks. But all felt that with three dead, they might be attracted.' She was subsequently awarded the Royal Humane Society Silver Medal.

   During the Second World War Watson served as a physiotherapist with the Canadian armed forces. (Family folklore relates that she lied about her age in order to be allowed to serve – too old – as she had also done in the First World War – too young!) In 1943, the ship she was travelling on, part of an Allied convoy, was torpedoed in the Mediterranean by a German U-Boat. Once again, Watson defied the odds and was pulled from the sea. Her nephew Michael Hayes testifies that 'after the war a number of the soldiers and officers, whom she had treated as a physiotherapist on the front lines during War, became Ambassadors and Consul Generals. Edna was often royally treated by those same soldiers and officers at embassies and consulates in the countries she visited.'

   Meredith Ebbin, Editor of *Bermuda Biographies* records that 'Edna Watson was one of the first two women elected to Bermuda's House of Assembly in 1948. She served until 1953 and was the first woman to speak in the House as well as the first woman to chair a government board. Six months after her election victory, she was appointed Chairman of two Government Boards, Transport Control and the newly created Board of Social Welfare, a hefty responsibility for a newcomer to the workings of parliament. While she won respect for her abilities, she became frustrated with government's reluctance to fund much-needed social programmes. It resulted in her decision in 1951 to found the 'Committee of 25 for Handicapped Children', and in 1953, a hospital in Dockyard for children with disabilities. Her memory is honoured by a portrait hanging in Bermuda's House of Assembly.'

Michael Hayes adds: 'Asia and Africa featured very heavily in Edna's world travels. Her world travels were extensive, varied, interesting and very adventurous for a single lady.' He continues: 'She was a great lady and enjoyed being treated as the "Grande Dame". When you, as host, had her out for dinner she would tell you what she wanted to eat but expected you to place the order with the waiter!'

Captain Alderson never forgot Watson's act of heroism. In February 1976, one month before her death, he visited her in hospital in Bermuda. This turned out to be Alderson's final visit to the colony.

2. The Air Accidents Investigation Branch (AAIB) started life on 28 June 1922 when the UK government formalised the 'The Air Navigation (Investigation of Accidents) Regulations 1922' under Section 12 of the 1920 Air Navigation Act.

3. *Clare* was subsequently lost off Bathurst, British Gambia, on 24 September 1942, killing all nineteen on board.

4. Leslie Runciman, Viscount Runciman of Doxford, was the first Director-General of BOAC, from 1940 until 1943.

5. This Patek Phillipe watch remains in the Alderson family.

6. On 30 January 1942, *Corio* was attacked by a flight of seven Japanese fighters in West Timor. The commander of *Corio*, Captain Koch – in spite of serious injury – managed to shake off the enemy in an extraordinary show of flying skill, finally ditching the badly damaged boat. Koch and four of the passengers survived, but thirteen others perished.

7. It was later confirmed that this convoy reached its destination without mishap.

8. The 1981 film *Das Boot* was based on the exploits of *U-96* and her skipper Captain Heinrich Lehmann-Willenbrock. Lehmann-Willenbrock survived the war and died in April 1986 at the age of 74. The emblem of *U-96* was a green 'Laughing Sawfish'.

9. Group Captain Sir Douglas Bader, CBE, DSO and Bar, DFC and Bar, DL, FRAeS was one of the most successful RAF fighter

pilots of the Second World War. Bader lost both legs in a flying accident at Woodley Airfield in December 1931. After several failed applications, he was finally readmitted to the RAF, becoming one of the highest-scoring fighter pilots of all time. He and Roly Alderson became friends through their flying connections, and he was a regular visitor to the Alderson's home after the war. Bader was immortalised in the 1956 biographical film *Reach for the Sky*.

10. This Longines pilot's watch was designed to be worn over a heavy flying jacket – hence the large size and wide wrist strap: it was used by R.A. throughout the Second World War while piloting the Boeing 314As. It remains in the family.

11. BOAC's flying-boat base was shifted from Southampton to Poole, but many flights used Foynes on the Shannon, on the west coast of Ireland; this was reached by shuttle flights from Whitchurch, near Bristol. The use of Foynes reduced the chance of enemy interception or 'friendly fire' incidents over the English Channel. Many of those using Foynes during this period would have savoured the now world-famous 'Irish Coffee', which was invented in 1943 at Brendan O'Regan's terminal restaurant by his chef Joe Sheridan as a warmer for chilled passengers arriving off the flying boats.

12. Churchill's 1942 Flying Bermuda Visit, International Churchill Society (Bulletin #47 - May 2012).

13. RAF Castle Archdale was used by the flying boats of 209 Squadron, whose Consolidated Catalinas and Short Sunderlands patrolled the North Atlantic for German U-boats. A secret agreement with the government of Ireland allowed aircraft to fly from Lough Erne to the Atlantic along the Donegal Corridor.

14. Quote from original hand-written letter R.A to J.B., retained by the latter and discovered after her death in 2017.

15. These vital talks culminated in Operation Torch, the invasion of French North Africa later that year.

16. *A Different World*, Dulcie Blair (Tulloh Books, 1983).

17. The 'PNR' (Point of No Return) is the point during a flight at which an aircraft is no longer capable of returning to the airfield from which it took off due to fuel considerations.

18. Barnes Wallis – later Sir Barnes Wallis – made a huge contribution to the war effort, not only being responsible for the dam-busting

Bouncing Bombs, but also the 12,000-lb Tallboy and the monumental 22,000-lb Grand Slam.

19. The actions of 617 Squadron during the bombing raid in the Ruhr valley on the night of 16/17 May 1943 were immortalised in the 1955 film *The Dam Busters*.

20. The York was a powerful general-purpose machine, equipped with four Rolls-Royce Merlin engines of 1600hp each – the same engines that were fitted to the illustrious Spitfire fighter.

Chapter 8

1. George Errington was an eminent test pilot whose career spanned three decades. He tragically lost his life when the HS Trident he was piloting, *G-ARPY*, entered a superstall and crashed in June 1966, just weeks before both he and Roly Alderson – close friends for decades – were due to retire. The full story of Errington's life as a pioneer aviator can be found in *George Errington: A Test Pilot's Story* by Mike Phipp (Amberley Publishing, 2020).

2. Airspeed was founded in 1931 by Nevil Shute Norway and the aircraft designer Hessell Tiltman. Norway later gained fame as the novelist Nevil Shute. The company was particularly noted for its contribution to the war effort in the form of the A.10 Oxford (of which 8,500 were built) and the famed Horsa glider (3,800 built). It was also involved in the production of various de Havilland types such as the Mosquito, the Sea Vixen and the Vampire. After the war, Airspeed Ltd went on to manufacture the elegant pressurised twin-engine AS.57 Ambassador airliner. The company was subsumed by de Havilland in 1948, although the name Airspeed continued in use until 1951.

3. *Star Ariel* was lost two years later – on Monday, 17 January 1949 – some 250 miles southwest of Bermuda en route to Jamaica, almost exactly ten years after the *Cavalier* went down in the same area. All twenty passengers and crew were lost; no wreckage was ever found, but fuselage depressurisation was theorised as the cause.

4. It may well have been the Hermes IV that was ultimately responsible for BOAC's unfortunate acronym 'Better On A Camel'. On 26 May 1952 – just a week after the Comet jetliner had made its

groundbreaking first scheduled landing at Singapore – a Hermes IV *G-ALDN Horus* made a crash-landing in the Sahara due to a navigational error en route from Libya to Nigeria. Camels were used as part of the process to successfully extract the eighteen passengers and crew from the desert.

Chapter 9

1. Group Captain Cunningham, CBE, DSO and two Bars, DFC and Bar, AE, DL was already a household name post-war, having been the highest-scoring night fighter pilot of the Second World War – hence the nickname 'Cat's Eyes'.
2. On 1 February 1952 the BOAC Argonaut Atalanta, *G-ALHK*, transported Princess Elizabeth and the Duke of Edinburgh to Kenya to begin a Commonwealth tour. Five days later, it was again *G-ALHK* which returned the newly acceded Queen Elizabeth II to England upon the death of her father, King George V.
3. From the eulogy delivered by Sir Ross Stainton at R.A.'s funeral.
4. *Meet the Man who manages the Comet Fleet*, Wings, March 1953.

Chapter 10

1. The Guild of Air Pilots and Air Navigators was established in 1929 and was granted the status of a Livery Company in 1956. The Guild's motto is 'Per Cælum Via Nostra', Latin for 'Our Way Is By The Heavens'. It was granted 'Honourable' status by Queen Elizabeth II in 2014 and is now known as The Honourable Company of Air Pilots.
2. This cross-channel service began in 1948. It was operated by Silver City Airways, which had been started in 1946 by R.A.'s old friend from the *Cavalier* days, Air Commodore Taffy Powell.
3. Bill Deedes – Baron Deedes, KBE, MC, PC – was married to Joan Alderson's sister, Hilary. Deedes was a Tory MP and former government minister and was editor of *The Daily Telegraph* from 1974 to 1986. At the time he was dubbed 'Britain's most celebrated journalist'. He was the subject of the *Private Eye*'s 'Dear Bill Letters', and the main character in Evelyn Waugh's book *Boot* was also allegedly based on him. Lord Deedes died in 2007 at the age of 94.

Chapter 11

1. 'LBJs' – aka Little Brown Jobs, or in other words any small, swift members of the avifauna group of winged mammals.

2. Bruce Tulloh started his trans-American running attempt in April 1969, and broke the existing record by ten days, covering an average of 45 miles a day for nine weeks. He died in 2018 at the age of 82, just two years after running from his home in Marlborough to Westminster to celebrate his eightieth birthday. The story of the record-breaking feat is told in *Four Million Footsteps* by Bruce Tulloh (Pelham Books, 1970) (50th Anniversary edition available from thewindinthetrees.com).

3. The 'Green Flash' is a momentary meteorological optical phenomenon which sometimes occurs at sunset (or sunrise). It is more often sighted at sea, due to the unobstructed horizon. It is nevertheless relatively uncommon and has become part of mariners' folklore over the centuries.

4. R.A. and Ross Stainton were lifelong friends and colleagues, joining Imperial Airways together as trainees in 1933, recruited by the Managing Director, John Woods Humphrey. Ten years later Ross Stainton was in Baltimore, Maryland, managing the Boeing 314As while Roly Alderson flew them. In the early 1970s he was appointed Managing Director of BOAC, and then Chairman and Chief Executive; in 1977 he became Chief Executive of British Airways, and two years later was appointed Chairman. He was awarded the CBE in 1971 and was knighted in 1981. Sir John Ross Stainton died in 2011, at the age of 97.

Bibliography

Websites

Air-Britain (www.air-britain.com)
Aviastar (www.aviastar.org)
Aviation Safety Network (www.aviation-safety.net)
Bermuda Biographies (www.bermudabiographies.bm)
Blue Star Line (www.bluestarline.org)
Britannica (www.britannica.com)
British Aviation Projects to Production (www.britishaviation.ptp.com)
Bureau of Aircraft Accident Archives (www.baaa-acro.com)
Civil Aviation Authority (www.caa.co.uk)
De Havilland (www.dehavilland.com)
Douglas Bader Foundation (www.douglasbaderfoundation.com)
Hansard – UK Parliament (www.hansard.parliament.uk)
Historic UK (www.historic-uk.com)
Historic Wings (www.historicwings.com)
History Collection (www.historycollection.com)
History Press (www.thehistorypress.co.uk)
Imperial War Museum (www.iwm.org.uk)
International Churchill Society (www.winstonchurchill.org)
International Historic Films (www.ihffilm.com)
Museum of Berkshire Aviation (www.museumofberkshireaviation.co.uk)
National Air and Space Museum (www.airandspace.si.edu)
National Archives (www.nationalarchives.gov.uk)
National Geographic (www.nationalgeographic.co.uk)
Pan Am Clipper Flying Boats (www.clipperflyingboats.com)
Pan Am Historical Foundation (www.panam.org)
Plane & Pilot Magazine (www.planeandpilot.com)

Researching The Lives and Records of WW2 Soldiers (www. researchingww2.com)

Royal Air Force Museum (www.rafmuseum.org.uk)

San Diego Air & Space Museum (www.sandiegoairandspace.org)

Science Museum Group (www.sciencemuseumgroup.org.uk)

Simple Flying (www.simpleflying.com)

Smithsonian National Air and Space Museum (www.airandspace.si.edu)

This Day in Aviation (www.thisdayinaviation.com)

Uboat.net (www.uboat.net)

UK Airfield Guide (www.ukairfieldguide.net)

Warfare History Network (www.warfarehistorynetwork.com)

Wikipedia (www.en.wikipedia.org)

Wonders of World Aviation (www.wondersofworldaviation.com)

Publications

Aeroplane, The (1952): London: Temple Press Ltd

Royal Gazette, The (1967/1968): Hamilton, Bermuda

Blair, D. (1983) *A Different World*: Marlborough: Tulloh

Cassidy, B. (1996) *Flying Empires: Short 'C' Class Empire flying boats*: Bath: Queens Parade Press

Chief Inspector of Accidents (1939) *Air Ministry Report by the Chief Inspector of Accidents on the loss of the Aircraft G-ADUU 'Cavalier' between New York and Bermuda on 21st January 1939 C.A.92 Feb 28 1939*: London: His Majesty's Stationery Office

Dawson, L. (2013) *Fabulous Flying Boats – A History of the World's Passenger Flying Boats*: Barnsley: Pen & Sword Books

Frater, A. (1986) *Beyond The Blue Horizon*: London: Heinemann Ltd

Hensser, H. (1953) *Comet Highway*: London: John Murray

Johnson, G. (2014) *The Last British Dambuster*: London: Ebury Press

Killen, J. (1969) *A History of Marine Aviation*: London: Frederick Muller Ltd

Markham, B. (1942/1984) *West with the Night*: London: Virago Press

Olley, G.P. (1934) *A Million Miles in the Air*: London: Hodder & Stoughton Ltd

Phipp, M. (2020) *George Errington, A Test Pilot's Story*: Stroud: Amberley

Pomeroy, C.A. (2000) *The Flying Boats of Bermuda*: Dorchester: Pomeroy

Robertson, Major F.A. de V., *Cambridge University Air Squadron: Annual Attachment at Old Sarum, 'Flight'* magazine (Royal Aero Club) 28 June 1928

Sims, P.E. (2000) *Adventurous Empires – The Story of the Short Empire Flying-Boats*: Shrewsbury: Airlife Publishing

Southern Daily Echo (1937/1938): Southampton

Wingent, P. (1997) *Imperial Airways' Empire Flying Boat Services 1936 to 1939*: Winchester: Wingent

About the Author

Throughout his life, Mark Alderson has worn many coats of different colours. He began his working life as a land agent, morphed into an antiques dealer, became a sailor and yacht chandler, and finally trained as a palliative care health professional. In his spare time he has been a pilot, a lifeboatman, a long-distance yachtie and a horseman. Now without aeroplane or boat, he lives in the depths of Devon with two horses, a dog and his wife – not necessarily in that order.

Abbreviations

APOC – Anglo-Persian Oil Company
A&EAA – The Aircraft and Experimental Armaments Establishment
BAT – Blind Approach Training
BOAC – British Overseas Aircraft Corporation
CUAS – Cambridge University Air Squadron
DF – Development Flight
GAPAN – The Guild of Air Pilots and Navigators of the United Kingdom
HMS – His Majesty's Ship
IAL – Imperial Airways Limited
NASA – National Aeronautics and Space Administration
OD – Overseas Division
P.1 – Pilot In Command
RAE – Royal Aircraft Establishment
RAF – Royal Air Force
RFC – Royal Flying Corps
RMA – Royal Mail Aeroplane
RNAS – Royal Naval Air Station
RNVR – Royal Naval Voluntary Reserve
SOE – Special Operations Executive
SS – Steamship
USAF – United States Air Force
USCG – United States Coast Guard
USS – United States Ship

Index

Aircraft (By Registration)

INDEX

INDEX